SEX, MIND, AND EMOTION

SEX, MIND, AND EMOTION

Innovation in Psychological Theory and Practice

Edited by

Janice Hiller, Heather Wood, and Winifred Bolton

KARNAC
LONDON   NEW YORK

First published in 2006 by
Karnac Books Ltd
118 Finchley Road
London NW3 5HT

British Library Cataloguing in Publication Data

A C.I.P. for this book is available from the British Library

ISBN-13: 978-1-85575-349-5

Edited, designed and produced by The Studio Publishing Services Ltd,
www.publishingservicesuk.co.uk
e-mail: studio@publishingservicesuk.co.uk

Printed in Great Britain

10 9 8 7 6 5 4 3 2 1

www.karnacbooks.com

CONTENTS

Naomi Adams is a clinical psychologist specializing in psychosexual and sexual health difficulties in the NHS. She works mainly from a systemic perspective and provides supervision, training, and consultation to other professional groups from within this model.

Winifred Bolton is a consultant clinical psychologist currently specializing in the treatment of personality disorder in the NHS and heading a service in Camden and Islington, London. She previously worked in forensic and adult mental health settings.

Anne-Marie Doyle is a clinical psychologist working in adult mental health and physical health. Special interests include reproductive health, trauma, chronic physical health problems, and health and exercise. She works in the NHS at Chelsea and Westminster Hospital and in private practice.

Brigid Hekster is a clinical psychologist working in the South London and Maudsley NHS Trust. She is based in an HIV mental health team and specializes in child and family work.

Janice Hiller is a consultant psychologist specializing in psychosexual and relationship problems in the NHS. She publishes and teaches on these topics, and also has a private practice in London for individuals and couples.

Diane Melvin is a consultant clinical psychologist who works as part of a multi-disciplinary family HIV service. Throughout her professional career she has worked primarily with children and young people managing chronic illness or disability, trauma, or other adversity.

Bernard Ratigan is a psychoanalytic psychotherapist in private practice in Leicester who also works as a consultant psychotherapist in the NHS Gender Identity Clinics in Nottingham and Leeds. His interests lie in the area between sexuality, gender, psychoanalysis, and religious belief.

Simon Thomas is a consultant clinical psychologist specializing in HIV & sexual health, and a UKCP registered psychoanalytic psychotherapist. He works for the NHS within a GUM setting, as well as in a specialist psychotherapy service.

Deirdre Williams is a clinical psychologist working in an NHS personality disorders service in Camden and Islington. She is a trained CAT practitioner. Her main interests are in severe mental disorders and in maternal mental health, and she has previously worked for an assertive outreach team and for Surestart.

Heather Wood is a clinical psychologist, a psychoanalytic psychotherapist and member of the BAP, and a practitioner and supervisor of Cognitive Analytic Therapy. She works in the NHS in London in a specialist psychotherapy service and in private practice.

Sarah Zetler is a South African trained clinical psychologist who currently leads the Psychology Service at the Department of Sexual Health, Homerton University Hospital Foundation Trust. The majority of her clients come from diverse communities and many of them are seeking leave to remain in the UK. Her research interests include sexual and relationship issues, sexual dysfunction, and the development of culturally sensitive sexual health services for ethnic minority users.

Introduction: sex, mind, and emotion

Sex is the subject matter of this book: sexual relationships, sexual development, sexual trauma, sexual and gender identity, and sexual practices that are potentially problematic for the individual or for others. Recent decades have seen a decline in the emphasis on sexuality in psychoanalytic theory, while clinical psychology has witnessed the growth of a new specialism of sexual health psychology, a development partly fuelled by concern about, and the availability of funds for, services for people with HIV and AIDS. Whatever the intellectual fashion, sexuality remains at the core of human experience. This book includes chapters written by specialists working in the field of sexual health, but others are informed by work in adult mental health, psychological therapies, forensic services, and specialist psychotherapy services. Sexuality does not respect service boundaries. Where there are psychological and psychotherapeutic treatments, there will be sexual issues to be addressed.

Sex, Mind, and Emotion is a collection of predominantly clinical papers describing innovative work in the psychological treatment of people with sexual problems and related disorders. This is a developing field: existing models of psychotherapy are being applied to new client groups, novel treatment methods are being applied to long-recognized problems, and conditions such as HIV demand new thinking about the psychological impact of sexually transmitted diseases. *Sex, Mind, and Emotion* explores the range of psychological and psychotherapeutic work being undertaken at the frontiers of this area.

A central tenet of this book is that sexual behaviour cannot be divorced from the emotional context in which it occurs and the emotional significance of that behaviour to the individual; equally, we are not merely biological organisms seeking to reproduce, but in possession of complex minds which assign meaning to events, hold information about anticipated consequences of actions, and enable us to override impulses or drive us to act compulsively and self-destructively. An appreciation of conscious thought processes and unconscious processes may be vital to an understanding of the complexity of the sexual response. In parallel with this assumption of the interrelatedness of sexuality, affect, and cognition, treatments may address affect, thoughts, and behaviour. Hence, no chapter is about sex without also addressing "mind" and "emotion".

In this volume nine out of twelve chapters address manifestations of sexuality that might be seen to be problematic. The issue of defining a problematic sexual behaviour is, of course, fraught with difficulty. In the past, moral, ethical, and legal objections to specific sexual practices have been used to persecute those with minority sexual interests. At the level of the law, some sexual behaviours are proscribed: at present, this would include bestiality, sex with minors, and non-consensual coercive sexual contact. But even legal definitions are culturally relative and potentially fluid; changes in the state's definition of those behaviours that are lawful influences, and is influenced by, the degree to which they are, or become, socially acceptable.

One chapter in this book, Winifred Bolton's chapter on work with convicted sex offenders with Asperger's Syndrome (Chapter Two), addresses a group whose behaviour has been deemed to be problematic by the law. In Chapter One, Janice Hiller, surveying biological and psychological models of sexual functioning and development, opts for a biostatistical definition of normality and abnormality. Other chapters all take as their starting point the admission of subjective distress by the patient, or, in the case of adolescents with HIV, concern in others about the potential distress to the young person of embarking on adult life while carrying this infection.

Adults usually seek help because they are troubled about their own or others' behaviour or fantasies. The risk of failing to intervene and offer assistance may be a permanent sense of damage to the sexual self (as in the case of sexual assault—Chapter Eight) the transmission of life-threatening infections (in the case of unsafe sexual practices—Chapter Five), impairment or loss of an intimate relationship (Chapters Nine and Twelve), or the broader psychological consequences of living with behaviours that are felt to be conflictual, ego-dystonic, or compulsive and suffused with a potential for guilt or unhappiness (as in the case of paraphilic-type behaviours or addiction to internet pornography—Chapters Three and Eleven). Psychologists and psychotherapists are often able to sidestep the hazardous issue of diagnosis of "normality" and "abnormality", and seek instead to treat those who experience their own predicament, thoughts, feelings, and behaviour as unsatisfactory.

A number of organizing assumptions are present, implicitly or explicitly, in every chapter of *Sex, Mind, and Emotion*. These are the value of empirical science, the importance of theory in informing clinical treatments, and an emphasis on clinical practice in a public sector context.

Scientific investigation is the touchstone against which practising psychologists evaluate theories and therapies. At the very least we ask the questions, "Are the theories consistent with the evidence and the evidence consistent with the theories?" and "Do the therapies deliver the predicted gains?" Historically, clinical and counselling psychology have demonstrated an investment in the methods of science to establish the truth of their theories and the effectiveness of their practices. This commitment underpins the work discussed in this volume, and research evidence is presented wherever appropriate to support propositions. It is, nevertheless, the case that much evidence remains to be sought and the new "evidence" presented here is often flimsy by standards of scientific proof. Clinical vignettes are used to illustrate theoretical points, but these have been heavily disguised to protect confidentiality (see below), and so do not even represent strict individual case studies. Nevertheless, we hope that the volume demonstrates a reliance on research evidence and literature, a constant process of comparing clinical evidence with theoretical models, and the refinement of both practice and theory in accordance with observations.

The second organizing assumption is the value of theory in informing clinical practice and ensuring rigorous and coherent thought. Theory informs the process of clinical formulation; it informs the development of models of psychological processes and functioning; and it challenges us to reconsider data and observations from different perspectives. It is striking that, throughout this volume, the theoretical model to which practitioners return, time and again, is a psychoanalytic one. Despite the difficulties in its empirical base and its lack of widespread availability in the NHS as a treatment, psychoanalysis has a richness and breadth of explanation of psychological functioning, and specifically of sexual functioning and development, that is still unrivalled. In this book we are attempting to put theories—psychoanalytic, systemic, and cognitive—to work in a manner that is compatible with practice in a public service setting.

In Britain, psychoanalytic psychotherapy has developed largely in relation to private practice, and this is reflected in the literature in an emphasis on intensive and long-term work. In contrast, clinical psychology has traditionally provided treatments within the NHS. Because the NHS has an obligation to respond to all health needs, practitioners in the NHS have been required to respond quickly to the emergence of new types of problem (the compulsive use of internet pornography, sexual risk-taking) and newly-identified client groups (transsexuals, refugees, adolescents with HIV, sex offenders with Asperger's Syndrome) with the creative adaptation of old methods and the innovative development of new ones. The clinical work described in this book is marked by a pragmatic search for effective treatments in complex or new areas. The majority of treatments described, practised by psychologists and psychotherapists alike, are time-limited and focused. Many treatments, nevertheless, draw on the insights derived from longer-term and more intensive therapies.

While science, theory, and the NHS are important background influences on the therapeutic work described in the volume, several common themes can also be drawn from the content of the chapters.

The first of these is the inextricable interrelatedness of biology and psychology. Although it is a truism to say that "nature" cannot exist except in the presence of "nurture", and that their polarity is in many ways a false one, the attribution of physical or psychological characteristics to one cause or another continues to provoke controversy. In Chapter One, Janice Hiller sets the scene by describing a biopsychosocial perspective on sexual development that illustrates the interrelatedness between biology and psychology in the domain of sexuality. In particular, she shows how the neurobiological systems regulating sexual behaviour, emotion, and attachment are closely connected. Throughout the lifespan, healthy sexual development and sexual expression require a synchrony between sexual impulse, emotion regulation, and security in relationship. The absence of synchrony in these areas can give rise to sexual difficulties. The way anxiety affects sexual responsiveness, and the use of sex to manage anxiety are also discussed in other chapters.

Chapters Two and Seven examine two conditions, Asperger's syndrome and gender dysphoria, which come with a history of dissent about their causation. The overly simple question of whether biology or environment is the more powerful determinant has got in the way of understanding the phenotypic development of these disorders, and how their presence early in life, in whatever seed-like form, shapes the growth of the personality. Winifred Bolton discusses theories about the core deficit in Asperger's Syndrome from a developmental perspective, and argues that difficulties in sexual experience, sexual expression, and relationship are inevitable, with corresponding increased likelihood of legal transgression in adulthood. She believes that treatment strategies need to take account of this. Bernard Ratigan argues that gender dysphoria can usefully be conceptualized as the catalyst to a developmental trauma, which can similarly exert a distorting effect on personality. He is concerned that assessment and treatment services for this client group need to be sufficiently robust to contain the powerful emotions evoked by this most profoundly disturbing disorder.

This brings us to the second theme running through the chapters, which is the importance of a developmental perspective. The form of adult sexual behaviour is undoubtedly influenced by childhood experience in complex ways. But, just as it is foolhardy to expect to establish one-to-one correspondences between genes and complex phenotypic characteristics, so the same applies to early experience and adult behaviour. Many mediating variables, still poorly understood, intervene to moderate or potentiate the impact of childhood.

It may be useful to conceptualize the developmental perspective in terms of the embeddedness of sexuality in the whole personality. Whatever biological or environmental factors impinge on personality development, so these will affect sexual development and adult sexual expression. Patterns of emotion regulation and relationship functioning will be especially important in this regard. In Chapter Eleven, Heather Wood discusses the treatment of problems associated with types of sexual relating and sexual expression that psychoanalysts have designated "perverse". These problems usually involve extreme and unusual sexual behaviours employed for defensive purposes. Her application of Cognitive Analytic Therapy (CAT) to this type of problem offers a pragmatic yet searching initial treatment. In a similar vein, Deirdre Williams in Chapter Ten describes the use of CAT to treat the sexual problems encountered in people, usually women, assigned the diagnosis of borderline personality disorder. Childhood sexual trauma is a common precursor of this type of disorder, and the presence of adult sexual difficulties is, therefore, a frequent occurrence.

Continuing with this theme of the connectedness of developmental experience and sexuality, Chapters Six and Eight contain a discussion of the treatment of problems arising from trauma experienced in adulthood: cultural displacement and rape and sexual assault. In Chapter Six Sarah Zetler argues for the importance of a culturally sensitive approach to working with refugees who present with sexual difficulties, often in the context of recent exposure to extreme threats to survival. She believes that the diagnosis of post-traumatic stress disorder (PTSD), often conferred by clinicians to support a request for Exceptional Leave to Remain, frequently leads to a distortion of the refugee experience. In Chapter Eight, Anne-Marie Doyle presents an integrative approach to the treatment of survivors of rape and sexual assault, employing a combination of cognitive behavioural and psychoanalytic methods. She considers that the former have utility in equipping the client to cope with symptomatic responses to trauma in the form of fear and avoidance, while psychoanalytic methods, particularly the elucidation of unconscious factors in the context of a therapeutic relationship, permit a restructuring of the meaning of the event.

A further group of chapters may be seen to address the manner in which some individuals respond to contemporary challenges in the social environment. In Chapter Three, Heather Wood advances an argument, influenced by psychoanalytic theory, that the compulsive use of internet pornography may be thought of in terms of the opportunity it affords for the re-enactment of primitive manic and narcissistic defences in individuals who may be vulnerable as a result of early experiences. Simon Thomas and Bernard Ratigan also explain the compulsion to engage in unsafe sexual activities in terms of the operation of primitive defence mechanisms. They argue for the need to adopt psychotherapeutic, as well as psycho-educational methods, in treating individuals for whom unsafe sex is a manifestation of personality rather than informational deficits.

While some environmental challenges such as internet pornography or sexually transmitted diseases are inherently sexual, other challenges are not specifically sexual but impact on sexual functioning. In Chapter Twelve, Janice Hiller describes a therapeutic practice combining behavioural methods and analytic understanding for the treatment of individuals and couples in whom a distressing loss of sexual interest has occurred in one partner. She conceptualizes this as a response to negative feelings that originate sometimes in current life stress and sometimes in early experience.

In Chapter Four, Brigid Hekster and Diane Melvin explore the impact on adolescents of learning that they are HIV positive through vertical transmission. Given that adolescence is a critical time for the consolidation of identity, especially sexual identity, and for developmental achievements such as separation from family and emotion regulation, the knowledge of HIV status could seriously compromise healthy adjustment. Hekster and Melvin describe a multi-faceted approach to care that seeks to minimize the negative consequences.

Much of the work presented in this book focuses on the individual. Naomi Adams' and Janice Hiller's chapters (Chapters Nine and Twelve) are an important reminder of the relational context in which problems may occur. Naomi Adams approaches the issue of sexual difficulties from the point of view of contemporary systemic theory. She is concerned with the manner in which problems, including sexual problems, are constructed within language as belonging to an individual, when they may more helpfully be construed as a system which has become fixed or "stuck". This system might include the relationship and the wider contexts of the relationship such as gender, ethnicity, and sexuality. In systemic therapy, shifts in the conceptualization of the problem and/or in the pattern of interaction in the relationship open new possibilities for meaning and action, help to free the system and may thus lead to resolution of the problem.

Confidentiality

We have been concerned throughout the preparation of this book with the confidentiality of clinical material. It is the unique stories of each of our patients, and each person's unique way of expressing their own story, that is at the core of the "art" of our profession. Very often it is what inspires, moves, and engages us as clinicians. These unique narratives are also the basis of the "science"—the empirical foundation upon which theory, or at least, theorizing, rests. It is on the basis of these narratives that we learn and that our discipline—as an art and a science—progresses. Yet each story is deeply personal, intimate, and disclosed within the bounds of trust of the consulting room. Sensitivity about confidentiality is heightened when the content of that material is people's sexual lives, which are often felt to be private and, in some respects, may be secret even from intimate partners.

A book about psychological therapies and psychological theories of sexual behaviour that included no clinical material would be very dry. Yet any clinical illustrations or clinical evidence offered in support of theory risk breaching the trust of the relationship within which they were disclosed.

We have therefore asked all contributors to respect the following guidelines:

1. Where written consent is sought from the patient for the use of clinical material, ensure that consent is freely given and that it would not influence any other clinical decision (e.g., whether treatment is offered, or with whom or when). Even when

consent has been obtained, some disguise of the material will probably still be necessary.

2. In all cases ensure that a minimum of personal details is given, and disguise those details wherever possible without jeopardizing the accuracy of the illustration.

3. Opt for a number of brief illustrations of a particular point, rather than a single, in-depth case study wherever possible.

4 Use composite cases where appropriate to maintain some scientific validity while masking the identity of individuals.

As a test of these procedures, we have specified that while a patient might recognize themselves in a vignette, the material should be such that not even their closest friends or family should be able to recognize them from the text.

As a result of these measures, the cases presented here may serve more as illustrations than scientific evidence for our propositions. This is a compromise that is necessary to preserve the anonymity of our patients.

If any person who has been a patient of one of the authors thinks that they recognize themselves in one of the illustrations in the following chapters, we hope that they will appreciate the role that they have played in contributing to the development of their clinician's understanding, and in disseminating that understanding to others in the field. We are deeply grateful to all those patients whose experiences inform and develop our knowledge of this complex and sensitive area, and we hope that they feel that their most personal thoughts and communications have been received and treated with respect.

Janice Hiller
Heather Wood
Winifred Bolton
August 2005

PART I

DEVELOPMENTS IN THEORY

CHAPTER ONE

Sex, mind, and emotion through the life course: a biopsychosocial perspective

Janice Hiller

Introduction

Humans seek social and sexual bonds for security and nurturance, as well as for pleasure and procreation. Nevertheless, social warmth, a sense of belonging and rewarding sex do not always co-exist in intimate relationships, and the inability to achieve a balance between these drives can lead to powerful feelings of despair. Fulfilling sex, in contrast, can create emotional closeness and shared joy that contributes to the sense of attachment in ongoing relationships. Sexual expression in humans then, is multidetermined, and serves several functions. For interpersonal sexual behaviour, what people feel and think about each other sexually and non-sexually is as important as the physiological responses to erotic stimuli. This means that sexual activity between people is part of a repertoire of communications signifying what is wanted and needed from the other, and must therefore be conceptualized within an interpersonal framework (Friedman & Downey, 2002).

As a clinical psychologist specializing in sexual and relationship therapy, I have always been aware that a purely psychological model is inadequate to describe the complexities of sexual functioning. Sexual behaviour is an interpersonal, affective, and biological phenomenon; people's sense of gender, responsiveness, and attractiveness is founded in their mind's appraisal of their bodies. Moreover, many people present for help when mind and body fail to synchronize: despite feeling love and desire the body does not respond; someone can experience anxiety about being wanted even when others express desire; it is possible to feel like a woman when the body is anatomically male. Sometimes, psychological intervention is sufficient to effect a change at a biological level: a decrease in anxiety that facilitates arousal, or a reduction in hostility that enables responsiveness between people. Often it is not, and the work of therapy is to understand the relationship between mind and body and their respective developmental paths in the hope of fostering greater integration.

Psychological approaches can, I think, only be enriched by recognizing the extensive research on the neuroanatomical and neurophysiological substrates of gender identity, the sexual response, bonding and attachment. Rigid distinctions between "nature" and "nurture" are no longer upheld in other areas of scientific enquiry, and cannot be sustained in psychological therapies. During individual development, our genetically programmed neurobiological systems will interact with, and be modified by, the psychological and social environment. A multitude of overt and covert messages will be transmitted from environmental cues, to gradually build an internal world, unique to each individual, that imbues the external world with particular meanings. Despite a considerable amount of literature in each area, there is still much to learn about how the inner and outer world interact in sexual expression.

While sexual desire and reproductive urges are not essential for the survival of any one individual, they are, along with many mating patterns and subtle brain and bodily mechanisms, vital for survival on a population level. Central to sexual function is the emotional limbic brain, an evolutionarily primitive neural system that is regulated by hormones, from which sexual urges emanate. Research into brain differentiation and hormonal release in the womb has shown that human sexual and gender potentials are laid down during foetal development (Friedman & Downey, 2002; Panksepp, 1998). These potentials continue to develop and to influence behaviour patterns throughout our lives. Investigations into the brain substrates of sexuality indicate that female and male sexual urges derive from different neuroanatomical and neurochemical pathways, and are therefore subservient to different brain controls (Panksepp, 1998). This results in frequent dissimilarities between women and men in the expression of emotional and sexual needs. Although many neural systems are shared, differences between the genders are significant and are one of the factors contributing to relational and psychosexual issues that can lead to considerable distress in adult life.

In another area of neuroscience, recent theories differentiate between emotions (visceral states) and feelings that are the private, mental experiences of emotions represented in the mind, whereas emotional states are collections of responses that can be partly observed by others. Feelings arise from neural activity in the evolutionarily modern part of the human brain, the neocortex, which is in constant interaction with the (subcortical) emotional limbic system. A specific part of the neocortex, the prefrontal cortices, has direct connections to every motor and chemical response occurring in the brain and has been identified by Damasio (1994) as the area dedicated to categorizing the unique features of individual experiences and personal identity. Neural activity in the prefrontal cortices gives rise to conscious processes, which add the capacities of reasoning, reflection, and decision-making to our more primitive emotional states. What differentiates humans from other mammals is the availability of a mind with consciousness, which allows us to plan and reflect, and to use reason to control "the pervasive tyranny of emotion" (Damasio, 1999, p. 56). Our ability to control these primitive responses is, however, far from complete. This is because there is an interaction between the subcortical systems in the brain registering emotions (bodily states) and the neocortical circuits that are involved in reasoning; emotions can impact on reasoning as well as reasoning exerting some influence over emotions. In the area of sexual behaviour it is apparent that conscious thought impacts on biological urges to varying degrees in people, at different life stages. This chapter represents a selective review of recent research, in an attempt to describe a truly biopsychosocial model of human sexual development that interweaves sex with mind and emotion throughout the life-course.

Foetal development and sexual brain differentiation

Although the view taken in this paper is that sexuality acquires meaning through the interpersonal context (real or fantasized) and the cultural setting within which the response occurs, abundant evidence on neurobiological factors in brain organization indicates how prenatal sex steroid hormones influence male and female brain differentiation, sexual tendencies, and gender role behaviour. Whether an embryo is genetically female (two X chromosomes) or genetically male (XY chromosomes) it will develop initially along female lines, sometimes called the "default" plan. Sexual differentiation is determined by the presence of a Y chromosome in an XY embryo due to the sex-determining gene region of the Y chromosome (the SRY), which is responsible for male differentiation (Haqq & Donahoe, 1998). Influenced by the SRY a testis will develop rather than an ovary. This produces testosterone to stimulate male reproductive organs and an inhibitory factor to suppress parts of the embryo which would otherwise develop into internal female organs (Bancroft, 2002).

The emergence of maleness in an XY embryo starts when testosterone manufactured in the male gonadal system is converted, in separate biochemical reactions, into dihydrotestosterone (DHT), which mediates body masculinization, and into oestrogen which mediates brain masculinization. For a brain to be masculinized (from the female template) means many things, but the most widely studied brain differences are found in subcortical areas that contain high levels of sex-steroid receptors. In particular, the hypothalamus, situated at the base of the brain, has anatomically distinct areas that govern complex patterns of sexual responses (Friedman & Downey, 2002; Panksepp, 1998). In males it is the medial preoptic area (POA) of the hypothalamus that regulates sexual behaviour, whereas the ventromedial hypothalamus (VMH) has a central role in female sexual responses. These hypothalamic brain areas are the sites where the peptide hormones oxytocin and vasopressin are synthesized, after pubertal changes, for release into the bloodstream during sexual activity. Oxytocin and vasopressin (manufactured from oestrogen and testosterone respectively) have been the focus of much laboratory research into mammalian attachment behaviours and are now viewed as essential components of the neurochemical underpinnings of sexual and social bonding and love (Carter, 1998). Their manufacture in the VMH and POA brain areas provides a neural substrate for the balance between anxiety and attachment in human sexual behaviour, a balance that is central to both sexual function and to emotional bonds, and will be discussed more fully in later sections of this chapter.

During a sensitive period of prenatal life (between 18 and 24 weeks), testosterone secreted from the foetal testis is converted into oestrogen, which changes the structure of the hypothalamus and masculinizes the brain as described above. This eliminates the female hormonal reproductive cycle, decreases female-typical sexual behaviours and increases behaviour more typical of males, including the choice of a female as a sexual partner (Friedman & Downey, 2002). In a female embryo, the absence of testosterone secretion results in female brain development. It is possible, though, for circulating maternal oestrogen to masculinize the female embryo, unless the embryo manufactures steroid-binding proteins that prevent this happening. When these proteins are below a certain level, or maternal oestrogen levels are high, male pattern development of the brain or the body can occur in a female foetus. Thus, the manner in which female and male brain and body development proceeds in the womb is determined by two distinct hormonal signals based on the timing and intensity of testosterone, oestrogen, and DHT release (Panksepp, 1998). Foetal brain differentiation in terms of sexual circuitry is complex, and psychoendocrine evidence for the determining effects of brain structures and hormones on erotic desire and sexual object choice appears to be strong. Researchers working in the sensitive area of gender differences in brain chemistry and sexual expression are careful to explain that describing behaviours as male- or female-typical refers to behaviours that are more common to one gender than another. Such terminology does not imply in any way that atypical behaviours are either pathological or undesirable, merely less usual (Le Vay, 1991). Throughout this chapter, a similar biostatistical concept is used when describing female and male behaviour patterns and brain structures.

Of relevance to understanding the link between biological factors and sexuality is evidence concerning the gender identity and sexual orientation of people with the genetically determined disorder AIS (androgen insensitivity syndrome). Infants with this unusual condition have XY chromosomes (genetically male), but the developing embryo has lacked androgen receptors to enable testosterone, secreted by the testes, to influence target tissues in the brain or body (Meyer-Bahlberg, 1999). Such infants therefore have female external genitals and female brain organization and appear in every way to be normal girls. Without ovaries and internal female reproductive organs (due to genetic maleness) they are unable to menstruate at puberty and seek medical help, when the condition is often diagnosed. Despite a male chromosomal configuration, the brain structures, gender identity, and sexual orientation of such individuals remains typically female and their romantic and sexual interests are directed towards men, thereby demonstrating the centrality of foetal hormones in the shaping of gender identity and sexual orientation (Friedman & Downey, 2002).

Conceptualizing the organization of body and brain development along two distinct biochemical pathways allows for the existence of female-like circuitry in a male body and male-like circuitry in a female body. Panksepp (1998) describes the brain differentiation possibilities on a gradient from female to male sexuality, thereby creating a range of sexual potentials from same sex to opposite sex object choice that eventually become fully manifest at puberty. This model takes into account the extensive neurobiological findings of recent years to offer a way of thinking about the varieties of sexual preferences and orientations found in all societies. Writing from the perspective of psychiatrist-psychoanalysts interested in sexual orientation, Friedman and Downey (2002) point out that many aspects of Freudian theory, including instinct and libido theory, as well as the role of the Oedipus complex in sexuality, have not withstood the test of time. They urge psychoanalytically-orientated therapists to consider empirical research on gender identity formation and the role of sex steroids in utero, in order to revise clinical theory and practice, especially with respect to same-sex attraction. Separate hormonal triggers for brain and body differentiation can also explain why intrinsic gender identity and body morphology do not always match up. Zhou, Hofman, Gooren, and Swaab (1995) found that a part of the brain that is larger in men than women (the bed nucleus of the stria terminalis) was female-sized in the six male-to-female transsexuals they investigated. It is conceivable that brain organizations of this type give rise to the sense of mind and anatomy not "matching" that is encountered in gender dysphoric states, outlined in Chapter Seven. In Panksepp's (1998) view, both gender identity and sexual object choice are firmly rooted in the biochemistry of foetal development.

A wider understanding of the naturally occurring variations in sexual brain differentiation, and their implications for gender and sexual potentials would, hopefully, increase tolerance and enhance therapeutic approaches for those who are troubled by feelings that occur less commonly in the population. How brain organization results in later sexual expression will, of course, be determined by ongoing psychosocial influences throughout the life span, which can encourage and promote, hinder or suppress particular aspects of an individual's sexual behaviour.

Infancy and genital integration

As well as different neural circuitry and potentials, the girl and boy baby have different sets of genital anatomy to assimilate psychologically. Exploration of genital organs is similar to play with other bodily parts at this stage, and is important for the formation of mental representations or schemas of the body, which require integration with other aspects of psychological maturation. For healthy, integrated psychosexual functioning, the child's body schematizations will eventually create a link between physical and sensory processes to form a psychosomatic whole.

Initially the infant is entirely dependent for physical and emotional care on the primary caregiver, usually the mother, in what Winnicott (1960) described as the "maternal holding environment". He suggested that primitive sensory exchanges in this phase create a "psycho-somatic partnership", which enables the growth of symbolic functioning and the organization of a personal psychic content as a basis for future relationships. Attachment theory research into the quality of the early bond indicates that caregiver sensitivity—the parent's capacity to think about the feelings, thoughts and desires of the infant—is related to secure attachment and fosters the child's self-development (Fonagy, 2001). Intimate skin contact and sensitivity to psychological needs is central to successful mother–infant attachments. Scharff and Scharff (1991) have linked this early psychosomatic partnership to the adult sexual relationship, which can re-evoke the experiences between caregiver and baby in complex ways. It is suggested that these interactions form part of a couple's sexual bond, which is also referred to in object relations couple therapy as a psycho-somatic partnership (Scharff and Scharff, 1991). Although this concept has theoretical appeal, Fonagy (2001) points out that evidence for object relations theory assumptions that later adaptation is shaped by early attachments is inconsistent and unreliable at this stage. Most studies do not show developmental continuity, which is thought to depend on mediating aspects of family life that were not measured by the research. Rather than a straightforward process whereby early relationship patterns form the basis for adult relationships, the current view is that the quality of caregiver sensitivity enables the infant to form mental processing systems or psychological templates. These mental mechanisms will then generate relationship representations that influence actual relationships in adult life (Fonagy, 2001).

Cowan and Cowan's (2001) longitudinal study on the transmission of attachment patterns was encouraging and found that some individuals with insecure working models were able to establish a relationship that buffered their newly-formed family from the repetition of destructive patterns in the next generation. Results from this research suggested that there was a definite tendency for patterns to be repeated, but that mental templates were not fixed by early attachment patterns. Although predictions from early attachments to later relationships cannot be made reliably, attachment theory research has clearly demonstrated that a secure base, in attachment terms, is significant for exploratory behaviour and a range of social and cognitive competencies (Fonagy, 2001). These skills, which include naming, role-labelling and identification with parents, contribute to a core gender identity as a girl or boy by about two years of age (Stoller, 1976).

At the same time as basic cognitive, affective, and interpersonal learning takes place, the discovery of the body through physical exploration is essential for body image formation. Research has shown that the infant girl can experience genital excitement in the form of clitoral sensations (Kestenberg, 1968) and male infants are capable of erections (Masters, Johnson, & Kolodny, 1982). Early genital play, which has no erotic aim, functions to integrate genital awareness and sensations with evolving psychic structures. For the boy, with his external organs, the process is relatively uncomplicated as he can see and touch the penis, which has focused sensations and a perceived shape. In addition, the holding of his penis during urination, in imitation of his father or other men, brings an early source of identification with a man in association with urethral eroticism, which is the pleasure and satisfaction in urinating (Tyson, 1982). The little girl has a more difficult task in comprehending her concealed, internal, and more complex genital anatomy (Bernstein, 1990). There is no similar desexualized reason for her to hold her genitals and she may be reprimanded for doing so. Taboos surrounding genital awareness have been linked to confused or absent naming of girls' genital parts, particularly the vulva and clitoris, which parents often avoid mentioning (Lerner, 1976). Gender identity studies show that the girl's sensory sensations are only given full meaning in the psychosocial context of responses from parents and significant others in her life (Stoller, 1976).

Although the girl is disadvantaged in achieving mental representations of bodily parts that are less accessible, female external genitals do include a vulva with a parting between the labia, suggesting an opening with a potential inside space. Child development literature shows that the ability to mentally represent "in" and "inside" is present by the end of the first year, which is important for the girl's early acquisition of a mental image of genital femaleness (Mayer, 1985). In the absence of a sense of voluntary control of the vaginal opening, but with recognition that boys have shaped external organs and that babies come from inside the mother's body, girls may become aware from a young age of the possibility of vaginal penetration. These learning experiences will occur at the same time as parent–child interactions over urinary control, feeding, and general bodily maturation that are central to the caregiving environment. In Bernstein's (1990) view, the assimilation and reflection of genital anatomy is inherent in female development, but relies on a sensitive parental approach to the girl's body. As the girl has specific developmental tasks in forming a mental representation of her unseen, open genital, that moreover is connected with possible penetration anxieties, she will be particularly dependent on her mother for support (Bernstein, 1990). Boys and girls are, of course, both dependent on the primary caregiver to provide the context for bodily experiences that contribute to later sexual empowerment. Caregiver management of the child's body (e.g., during bathing, and learning bladder and bowel control) will become internalized to form part of the individual's sense of ownership, control, and value of genital experiences.

I have suggested elsewhere that an over-intrusive mothering approach, lacking clear boundaries and helpful messages, may create confusion and impede the girl's successful integration of her genitals into psychic structures, especially as a potential source of pleasure, to be valued along with other sensual experiences. A parental style that denigrates, forbids touching, and is generally negative about the female genitals, or one that over-values or exposes the child's body before she can make choices, is potentially damaging. The risk for the girl is perpetuation of dependence, inhibition in securing her own sexual identity, and the unconscious splitting of her genital experiences from other areas of psychosomatic functioning (Hiller, 1996). Boys' assimilation processes are different as they become aware of changes in genital shape as part of daily experiences and can readily comprehend the source of physiological sensations. This may help boys during later years in the developmental task involved in the change from experiencing the penis as an anatomical structure to an organ with sexual significance. Despite having external organs that are more easily understood, boys are equally vulnerable to negative and intrusive management of the developing body by parental figures. Ogden (1991) suggests that the boy's intense dependence on his opposite-sex parent means that prior to encountering the father as a separate object he will first encounter the father in his mother's mind. Thus, his mother's mental representation of his father, or available father figure, is significant for male identification before he identifies with his actual father, as owner of a phallus with sexual meaning. Lack of separation or difficulties with the mothering bond, and problems with the availability of adequate objects for sexual identification, can therefore pose a threat to the boy's acquisition of sexual empowerment in adult life (Hiller, 1993).

Psychoanalytic ideas that refer to this developmental phase include a concept of the oedipal situation as the child's recognition

of a psychic world that excludes her/him from the parental relationship, and the creation of what Britton (1989) has called a "triangular space". This refers to a concept of the links between the
parents and the child forming a hypothetical triangle that acts as a
uniting inner space in which potential relationships between three
people can exist. Here Britton (1989) is describing the beginning of
the capacity for "seeing ourselves in interaction with others and for
entertaining another point of view whilst retaining our own, for
reflecting on ourselves whilst being ourselves" (p. 87). He also
seems to suggest that a secure triangular space and benign parental
links can facilitate individuation and the capacity to form attachments with others, eventually, outside the original triangle.
Through experiences with the parental unit the child will internalize a perception of their relationship, in combination with the
parents' views of themselves as a couple, to form an "internal coital
couple" (Feldman, 1989). This internalization is considered significant for the development of a capacity to create links between
thoughts and feelings, and to tolerate the anxiety that results from
such links. Feldman (1989) observed that the nature of the internalized coital couple could give rise to high anxiety levels, such as
when a child feels deprived of proper attention or love, experiences
destructive, uncontrolled, parental behaviour, or when the parents
avoid intimacy with each other or their child. If anxiety associated
with the internal parental couple is too great, there could be a
corresponding interference with the capacity for making healthy
connections in the individual's mind, which will influence later
relationships and, it is postulated, the capacity to think about
affective responses.

How does the quality of environmental care impinge on an individual's biological development? Whilst genetic make-up helps to
set the structure of those parts of the brain that are concerned with
regulating the basic homeostatic mechanisms that are essential for
survival (endocrine and immune systems, viscera, etc.), the genome
does not specify the entire structure of the brain. In particular, the
human neocortex, where conscious feeling, planning, and reasoning takes place, has been described by Damasio (1994) as a "to-be-
determined structure" (p. 112). Some circuits in the neocortex are
repeatedly modifiable and therefore evolve throughout the life
span. Modifications occur when the innate (subcortical) circuits

respond to changes in the internal milieu, caused by experiences in the environment: neocortical circuits then appraise the effect of experiences on the individual's biological state. Different experiences shape the design of circuits by altering synaptic strengths within and across neural systems. This neural plasticity is ongoing, but childhood is a particularly sensitive phase. In children's brains, synapses (neural connections) increase rapidly to reach adult levels by the age of two, and from four to ten years of age, synaptic numbers are greater than adult levels; they then drop to adult levels by the age of eighteen (Ehrhardt, 2000).

It is possible at this stage to speculate further on the psychophysiological effects of the quality of caregiver sensitivity on later sexual expression. Extensive research into the neurophysiology of social and sexual attachments and love has focused on the operation of transmitter molecules in the brain. Many studies have linked the release of the two neuropeptides mentioned previously, oxytocin and vasopressin, with the decrease of anxiety and the facilitation of reproductive behaviours, including parenting and sexual behaviour (Carter, 1998; Insel, 1997). Developmental research on prairie voles, whose subcortical system are very similar to those of humans and who also form monogamous pair bonds for reproduction, has demonstrated the effects on neural systems of stressful experiences that stimulate the release of glucocorticoids (cortisol and corticosterone). These stress hormones can influence the synthesis of receptors for oxytocin and vasopressin, which are manufactured and secreted in different amounts in the female and male brain. Thus, an individual's developmental history, in as much as it influences security, early attachment, and the management of anxiety, and hence the potential for managing stress, will influence neural systems that release the peptide hormones crucial for the expression of intimacy, aggression, and sexuality in adult life.

Is there a developmental model that can link neuroendocrine release with later sexual expression? Within a range of caregiver experiences that create a homeostatic balance for anxiety levels, neural systems (hypothalamic structures and receptor sites for neurotransmitters and peptide hormones) will develop that enable the individual to secrete the chemicals underpinning the formation of bonds in connection with positive social attachments. Eventually, if development proceeds without intrusion, these interpersonal bonds will have the capacity to include the psychological and physical stimulation that facilitates pleasurable sexual intimacy as part of adult relationships. Individuals in this category may nevertheless be vulnerable to disruptions such as life events, communication difficulties, and negative states of mind that have the potential to impair sexual response mechanisms and give rise to the psychosexual problems mentioned later in this chapter (see also Chapters Nine and Twelve for treatment approaches).

By contrast, if an infant experiences anxiety levels that are significant or prolonged, development of the systems for oxytocin and vasopressin in particular may be linked to anxiety reduction rather than to the formation of positive bonds. The individual is then at risk of using sexual activity to decrease stress and tension, or to express aggression, to an extent that seriously undermines fulfilling intimate attachments. Chapters Three and Ten on compulsive and borderline sexuality respectively, address these clinical issues. From this perspective, major intrusions, such as child sexual abuse or severe neglect that generate high anxiety, could interfere with neuropeptide manufacture and thereby impair the integration of feelings, sensations, and genital functions. At the same time, serious developmental intrusions will create negative emotional and cognitive links between genital sensations and intimate contact, so that sexuality becomes imbued with frightening and destructive meanings. At the extremes this could produce fear reactions such as freezing or immobilization, which are physiological states in which positive emotional bonds and sexual activity are not possible. How much neural plasticity remains for each individual, for which functions and at which point in the life cycle, is not known. As clinicians we are still exploring the extent to which therapeutic endeavours can alter feelings, thoughts, and behaviours, so that a different sense of self and physiological responsiveness can emerge in a clinical population presenting with emotional and sexual difficulties.

Thinking about the design of human brain circuits and neurochemical systems as continually dependent upon environmental input as well as innate bioregulatory feedback, helps to explain how unique mental processing systems are formed in the infant's mind and how they continue to unfold and change. It also highlights the inadequacy of framing an account of mind, brain, and behaviours as either genetic or environmental, and points to the need for a biopsychosocial concept of development and responsiveness, as more representative of the complexities of the human condition.

Childhood and gender-valued self regard

Childhood play with peers is the predominant psychosocial influence beyond the family in the years before puberty, and is considered crucial for the development of gender-valued self regard (Friedman & Downey, 2002), although its relevance for psychosexual development and function has been insufficiently addressed in the literature to date. As well as rehearsing adult roles in pretend settings, natural curiosity about the bodies of other children and adults can arise, and children sometimes compare genitals with friends of both sexes (Goldman & Goldman, 1982). This form of sexual play seems to have little impact on sexual adjustment in late teens (Okami, Olmstead, and Abrahamson, 1997). The most consistent finding across cultures concerning childhood play is that same gender social groupings are far more common than those of mixed gender and are, moreover, thought to be highly relevant for later sexual interactions (Maccoby, 1998). Typically, gender differences in play behaviour, which peak between the ages of eight and eleven, are for girls to show a propensity for nurturant or parenting rehearsal play in child or infant care games, whereas boys engage in physically energetic behaviours (rough-and-tumble play), and use more physical threats and arrange their groups in a dominance hierarchy. Differences in play patterns are stable, although statistical plotting of indices of play generates overlapping curves between boys and girls, which indicates some individual differences. Ehrhardt (2000) proposes a psychobiological predisposition to learn certain behaviour patterns more readily, and cites support for this hypothesis from a series of studies with girls and boys who were exposed to prenatal hormonal anomalies, showing that gender-related behaviour cannot be explained solely by the various social and environmental factors assessed in the research.

Specifically, there are many reports of girls with a metabolic disorder of the adrenal glands, congenital adrenal hyperplasia

(CAH), in which high levels of prenatal androgens have altered brain structures and masculinized the genitals. Medical and surgical intervention in early infancy can correct physical abnormalities, and enable girls with CAH to have normal, if delayed, pubertal development. Despite some prenatal androgenization of the brain they are able to menstruate but, compared to control groups, the CAH group showed less interest in stereotypically female play (dolls and self-adornment) and a greater propensity for boy playmates and rough-and-tumble play (Hines & Kauffman, 1994). This effect on childhood games and fantasy occurs irrespective of parents' attitudes about appropriate female activities. Berenbaum (1999) found that teenagers with CAH who have had more socialization experiences with same-gender role behaviour continued to prefer male-typical activities. Most girls with CAH do develop opposite-sex attraction, but a sufficient increase in same-sex fantasies is shown in this group to support the prenatal androgen hypothesis of effects on brain systems (Friedman & Downey, 2002). In another set of studies, different masculinizing effects of prenatal androgens were shown through observation of girls born to women who were given a synthetic oestrogen, diethylstilbestrol (DES) to prevent miscarriage. Outcome research on the behavioural effects of foetal DES exposure showed that in these girls same-sex orientation was greater (Ehrhardt *et al.*, 1985), but childhood play was not masculinized compared to controls (Ehrhardt *et al.*, 1989). The specific masculinizing effects of prenatal androgenization appear to depend on whether the excess hormones occurred through natural causes, as with CAH, or by medical intervention, in the case of DES administration, but the reasons for this are not clear.

While gender-segregated play has an impact on development from mid to late childhood, it is experiences within the family that are believed to give rise to the mental encoding of caregiver representations, both consciously and unconsciously, during the first five to six years. Following this phase, girls and boys will be on different developmental pathways, arising from their innate temperamental differences in play styles, activity preferences, and patterns of peer relations (Friedman & Downey, 2002). Research on childhood play themes is based on observations in natural settings of same-gender groups that highlight their distinctive features. For boys, issues of dominance, competition, and control are more prevalent, while girls seem averse to these forms of play and prefer conversation and persuasion, with attempts to maintain group cohesion. Evidence strongly indicates that gender-segregated play occurs regardless of the values of parents and teachers, or adult directives for play styles; rather, it is initiated by children themselves (Fagot, 1994). These differences in narrative themes are reflected in children's stories and art from all over the world (Friedman & Downey, 2002). Boys' narratives usually involve heroic combat with powerful adversaries, while girls express themes of parenting, families, and relationships, so that by late childhood their inner representational worlds will be quite different.

Such asymmetry in developmental pathways represents a divergence in psychological functioning that becomes more pronounced with time. Despite this fundamental divergence though, the first remembered experience of sexual attraction for both genders is around nine to ten years of age, shown by retrospective studies of heterosexual and homosexual young adults (McClintock & Herdt, 1996). As this is before gonadarche (hormones released from the gonads at puberty) it has been argued that the secretion of androgens from the adrenal glands (adrenarche) at about six to eight years is responsible for the effects seen in sexual attractions (Herdt, 2000). Levels of circulating androgens climb steadily and are within activational range by about ten. In Herdt's (2000) view, the concept of puberty should be enlarged to include two separate maturational processes: adrenarche and gonadarche. Other researchers remain unconvinced that a hormonal cause of first sexual attraction should be assumed (Meyer-Bahlberg, 2000), and in the absence of further evidence, the adrenarche theory remains speculative.

Children on a developmental path of same-sex orientation, who are drawn frequently towards gender non-conformity, may experience considerable discomfort in this phase, which is so important for gendered self-esteem. Boys, in particular, may struggle as male groups tend to condemn those boys who show an interest in more "feminine" activities. Girls, in contrast, are generally much more tolerant of atypical gender-role patterns. Such sexist values are maintained even when parents and teachers approve of cross-gender role behaviour. As boys' groups react negatively to behaviour that does not conform, powerful feelings of shame at being different from peers (as well as from the heterosexual majority) are often reported, although this feeling is not restricted to those on a homosexual developmental path (Friedman & Downey, 2002). Indeed, children whose play styles and interests do not fit in with parental aspirations could experience conflictual family relationships, even when their innate tendencies conform to peer-group norms. For example, a parent who aspires to academic achievement might be distressed by a child who is strongly drawn to sports and physical activities, while one that values rivalry and ambition could show disapproval of dressing-up and domestic pursuits, whether shown by a daughter or a son.

How could the experience of non-conformity in this phase, either with peers, in the home environment, or both, be hypothesized to influence psychosexual development and eventual sexual function? Within a biopsychosocial framework the feelings engendered in children by being different and not belonging could mobilize a strong sense of insecurity and isolation from others, which in turn could lead to the physiological response associated with anxiety and fear. These stress responses inhibit not only cognitive development and identification processes, but also put at risk the integration of a sense of femaleness or maleness with bodily responses and sexual attraction, which, as mentioned above, is present for many children long before puberty. In these circumstances, feelings of shame about thoughts and behaviour that are not considered acceptable might drive a child to withdraw socially and, at the same time, to unconsciously split off painful areas from psychological functioning, thereby impeding psychosexual development. In another scenario, children with aggressive reactions to feeling excluded might demonstrate hostile, antisocial, or exhibitionistic behaviours, and perhaps precocious sexuality, thereby compounding the impact of non-conformity.

Maccoby (1998) views such same-gender play themes as the social precursors of gender -specific styles in sexual interactions, such as men's emphasis on sexual performance and women's greater need for intimacy. Additionally, from the perspective elaborated in this chapter, it is also the interaction between family and peer group expectations and the child's innate predispositions for certain behaviour patterns, including play and sexual orientation, that will ultimately influence psychosexual development. Underlying physiological states associated with feeling secure through a sense of belonging, or feeling anxious from a sense of exclusion, are suggested as the intervening variables that can aid or disrupt the integration of a gendered sense of self with positive interpersonal interactions and an emerging awareness of romantic attraction.

Adolescence and sexual activation

With the onset of puberty, psychoendocrine changes take place in multi-layered social contexts that shape and define sexual potentials. Gender differences in play themes, the nurturant–expressive compared with the competitive–active dimension, show general continuity into teenage years: adolescent girls, on the whole, have belief systems that tie romance, sex, and faithfulness together, while for boys the mechanics of sexual achievements and conquests tend to be more preoccupying. While for each individual there may be various ideologies of sexuality available in the culture, gaining peer-group acceptance remains important for the construction of a personal sexual identity (Breakwell, 1997). Research into views on appropriate sexual behaviour conducted on sixteen to twenty-one-year-olds showed agreement between the genders on the female role, which was seen as sensitive, faithful, and passive, with less willingness to engage in sex. Interestingly, Breakwell (1994) found disagreement on the representations of male sexuality: girls described male sexuality as exploitative and focused on sexual experimentation, but boys viewed it more positively, as seductive and controlling of the pace and nature of sexual interactions. However named, the trend in perception, in post-feminist times, is for men to initiate and women to set boundaries.

Underpinning these well-observed patterns are the neurochemical changes of puberty, triggered initially in the brain by the release of gonadotrophic hormones from the hypothalamus that control sex steroid manufacture in the gonads. A chain of reactions occurs, resulting in oestrogen secretion from the ovaries and testosterone secretion from the testes, thereby activating the dormant female and male potentials that are present to different degrees in the neural circuitry. Central to this partially understood process are the roles of the two neuropeptides that are dependent on oestrogen and testosterone for their manufacture: oxytocin, which is present in both female and male brains but more abundant in the female brain, and vasopressin, more of which is present in the male brain (Panksepp, 1998).

For most, but not all, young people, the first sign that brain–body sexual systems have been mobilized, prior to sexual experience with others, is usually masturbation, defined as self-stimulation accompanied by fantasy. Sexual fantasies tell a more or less elaborated story of people and situations and are associated with erotic physiological arousal throughout the body. Adolescents begin with strong sexual yearning, which leads to imagining a first meeting, then the seduction scene and further details of the encounter (Breakwell, 1997). Fantasies provide the stimulation for masturbation and also imbue the actual sexual situation with meaning. In adolescent development, masturbation is seen as an important self-gratifying activity that weakens early mother–infant bonds and connects the inner object world with mature forms of relatedness (Scharff, 1982). Imagined sexual encounters can be elaborated over several years to form the basis of adult sexual fantasies and in that way serve as a rehearsal of wished-for sexual routines. Alternatively, they could be a way of inhibiting sexual behaviour and restricting sexuality to the imagination. Breakwell (1997) found no difference between more and less sexually active adolescents in terms of the vividness and frequency of their sexual fantasies, but suggests that there are differences between the genders concerning the nature of their preoccupations: girls are far more likely to imagine sexuality as part of a romantic relationship, whereas boys tend to focus on sexual mechanics and acts for their own sake.

Additionally, there is some evidence that sexual fantasy programming in males tends to be more rigid than in females, so that early erotic imagery associated with sexual arousal, occurring at a critical period of brain–mind sensitivity in late childhood, determines subsequent stimuli for sexual arousal for most males. Girls' erotic experiences tend to be more variable and contextual. For girls, nuances of meanings and feelings ascribed to certain situations will mobilize conscious arousal, whereas female genital changes per se are not generally experienced as sexual without meaningful attribution. This enhanced response to context is related to greater female sexual plasticity, enabling fluidity in sexual object choice, but it is also recognized that there are subgroups of men whose sexual plasticity is similar to that found in women. For these men, images outside the initial erotic frame can change from neutral to arousing with later life experiences (Friedman & Downey, 2002). This area of research supersedes Laufer's (1976) notion of a "central masturbation fantasy" that becomes integrated during adolescent development to form an irreversible sexual identity.

Adolescents engage in sexual intercourse at an increasingly young age. Heaven (2001) summarizes retrospective studies from various countries showing that greater numbers of young people report having had sex before the age of sixteen, and patterns of first sexual intercourse vary by ethnic group, with men engaging in intercourse at younger ages than women. This trend has been explained by the substantial lengthening of the gap between biological maturation and readiness, and the decision to make a permanent commitment (DeLamater & Friedrich, 2002). Alternatively, Breakwell (1997) suggests these changing patterns could reflect a revision of dominant codes of sexual behaviour leading to greater willingness to admit to sexual intercourse before the age of sixteen, rather than a change in actual behaviour.

Experiences of sexual intercourse tend to follow a predictable and discrete sequence of events: holding hands and kissing progressing to more intimate mutual touching and caressing, followed by manual stimulation before penetrative sex. Through reflection on their ability to meet the demands of the sexual situation, young people are thought to develop a sense of sexual self-efficacy, which is linked with greater assertiveness and a perception of decision-making in the relationship concerning when and where sex takes place (Breakwell, 1997). At every stage at which comparisons have been made, young men as a group appear to be more erotically motivated than women. They masturbate earlier and more frequently, begin sexual intercourse at a younger age and have more sexual partners (Day, 1992; Oliver & Hyde, 1993). Such gender differences reflect the preoccupation with sexual acts found more commonly in boys, and the focus on meaningful attachments as the foundation for interpersonal sex shown by girls. Associated with these behaviour patterns are the effects of increased levels of sex steroids on the hypothalamic areas that differentiate between female and male brain systems. Puberty is recognized as impacting more markedly on emerging sexuality in boys than girls, mediated by raised testosterone. Male sexual interest and arousability remain dependent on a necessary (but in itself not sufficient) level of circulating testosterone throughout the life span (Bancroft, 2002). Testosterone stimulates the manufacture of vasopressin in the medial preoptic area of the hypothalamus, and visual stimuli become significant for adolescent boys as secondary sexual characteristics develop. Vasopressin is also the neuropeptide associated with aggression circuits and therefore contributes to the sense of urgency, persistence, and also rivalry often manifest in adolescent boys (Panksepp, 1998). For adolescent girls, raised oestrogen levels stimulate brain oxytocin release, the peptide involved in social bonding, empathy, and feelings of emotional closeness.

Male stimulation by visual cues and female arousability to romantic themes in books and films, show continuity to adult sexual behaviour (Ellis & Symons, 1990), and may partially account for the larger number of men who become compulsive users of internet pornography (see Chapter Three). Another factor may be the release of oxytocin at ejaculation, and the high level of conditionability of the oxytocin molecule.

Clearly though, environmental factors interact significantly with endocrine systems, as demonstrated by research on teenagers' transition into sexual activity following a disruption in the primary family. Surveys show that both boys and girls are twice as likely to be sexually active under sixteen when families split up and they remain with single mothers, while for girls the move into a reconstituted family appears to be the major risk factor for early sexual intercourse (Heaven, 2001). Father absence has received considerable attention in the research literature, which has demonstrated that girls whose parents have separated are younger at menarche (Surbey, 1990) and begin earlier sexual activity involving more partners (Walsh, 2000). While Rossi (1997) has suggested that social stress in the home may increase gonadal and adrenal hormone release, thereby speeding up sexual maturation and early sexual activity, Hrdy (2000) points out that this would not be predictable on the basis of animal research or evolutionary theory, as scarce resources and stress should have the opposite effect and delay ovulation to suppress reproduction. Walsh's (2000) life history theory uses the concept of attachment by proposing that children who experience interpersonal relationships as undependable are less likely to expect commitment from a partner and are more likely to engage in unrestricted sexual behaviour, with weaker attachments. Theories so far have not incorporated the evidence that unfamiliar males entering the environment can alter the social situation and facilitate the manufacture and processing of sex steroids, so that young females may become sexually mature more rapidly (Panksepp, 1998).

From the perspective developed in this chapter, how can we understand this cultural influence on teenagers' sexual behaviour, and the effect on girls in particular? As discussed above, psychoanalytic theory postulates that the young child internalizes a mental representation of the parents' sexual union, which becomes the internal coital couple thought to influence later behaviour. This representation is modifiable by changes in external reality, and especially by a split in the parental relationship. A young person can become aware (unconsciously if not consciously) of one or both parent's sexual activity outside the "triangular space" of the primary family unit. Indeed, the introduction of another partner for one parent is a common cause of family disruption. Thinking of a parent being sexually active with a new partner at a time when the adolescent is occupied with elaborating their own sexual identity not only provides a different object for identification concerning sexual expression, but also collapses generational boundaries. In this situation the same-sex parent may be experienced as more like a peer group member than a parental object, especially if the parent confides in the teenager about new relationships or introduces a new partner into the home. As well as an identification with the parent, there may be feelings of loss and anxiety about family changes and a powerful sense of abandonment by the parent. Separation from significant attachment figures involves the secretion of stress hormones such as cortisol and corticosterone and tends to mobilize a search for social bonds and connections that will reduce anxiety and provide a sense of security, as part of the individual's drive for emotional homeostasis (Carter, 1998). For teenagers from split families, early sexual activity can represent an emotional and physical connection with another that reduces isolation fears and conforms with their social norms, both cultural and familial. Such an early move into sexual activity is, though, unlikely to represent psychological maturity or to be based on the ability to fully enjoy sexual experiences. Rather, it may indicate a need for emotional and physical closeness that has been lost, and which then becomes eroticized by the upheaval due to hormonal and cultural influences in the teenage years.

A fascinating example of the opposite process, whereby the neural substrates of gender differentiation overwhelm social factors, is shown by a small number of children from the Dominican Republic who are genetic males. During foetal development they lacked the enzyme to convert testosterone to DHT, which is essential for body masculinization, so they were born with female-like genitalia and reared as girls. Imperato-McGinley, Peterson, Gautier, and Sturla (1979) carried out detailed fieldwork in the rural villages where these children were born. Of the eighteen subjects raised unambiguously as girls, seventeen changed successfully to a male gender-identity, and sixteen to a male gender role. Changes occurred during puberty when circulating testosterone stimulated body masculinization, including penis growth and descent of the testes. Despite certain insecurities, these young people were able to re-orientate their lives, and showed typical male sexual interests following puberty. This unusual occurrence is thought to be due, in this group of children, to the initial organization of brain structures along male lines, so that testosterone could also reach receptors in differentiated areas of the brain, enabling a sense of maleness to predominate.

As sexual experimentation in adolescence continues, young people tend to alternate between group allegiances and pair formation. Peer groups provide valuable support when relationships end, while reinforcing the generational boundary during the young adult's move towards independence. Parent and child sexual development can interlock at this stage, especially if the adolescent's burgeoning sexuality stirs up conflictual aspects of the parent's own teenage development (Scharff, 1982). Youth culture presents many sexually explicit images through music, fashion, popular films, and magazines that can encourage very different modes of socializing compared with those of a previous generation. Parents' reactions will depend, to an extent, on their own adolescent experiences, but if a more liberated or experimental approach is threatening, parents may react enviously by criticizing or attempting to suppress sexual behaviour. Alternatively, inhibition of their own sexual wishes may lead to compensatory encouragement of sexual expression before the young person is ready through projection of feelings of sexual need on to the adolescent. For many teenagers the move into a sexual relationship is a sign of personal growth, but for others who experience parental absence (emotional or physical) or intrusion from the parents' own preoccupations, there may be interference with developmental needs that put at risk the drive to integrate bodily pleasure with rewarding intimate attachments.

Love, adult sexual bonding and pair formation

Many people have sexual experiences with various partners as part of a search for a specific person with whom to form an intimate, and hopefully, lasting attachment. There are some people, especially those with strong religious beliefs, for whom sexual experimentation is not an option before a committed relationship is formed, and learning takes place after marriage. Generally though, falling in love is an intrinsic feature of choosing a mate, although cultural differences abound in the debate on marriage as either a private choice or public commitment that is essential for traditional societal values (Clulow, 1993). Whether a legal ceremony takes place or not, how does sexuality interact with falling in love, and with changes inherent to relationships over time?

At the start of a new relationship the intense excitement and exhilaration experienced by the partners is characterized by a shared longing to be together, increased energy, focused attention, and constant thoughts about the love object. Being in love is a passionate, visceral, often longed-for state, and as one of the prime motivators of human behaviour it is a frequent theme for musicians and creative writers. In the domain of social anthropology and psychology, passionate love has been viewed rather differently, and has been studied as a primary emotion-motivation system for mutual attraction that evolved to underpin the search for a preferred, genetically-suitable mating partner (Fisher, Aran, Mashek, & Brown, 2002). A brain state that mediates heightened arousal, attention to novelty, and goal-directed behaviour is the neurotransmitter balance of increased central dopamine (DA) and noradrenaline (NA) and lowered central serotonin, and this has been associated with the affective state of being in love (Fisher, 1998). This constellation of neural correlates is central to the powerful emotions that occur early in a relationship, and for the intensity of sexual pleasure, as will be discussed in more detail below. It is not a brain response that can be maintained indefinitely, however. Familiarity gradually and inevitably overtakes novelty, and as idealization subsides, early high levels of passion tend to diminish, or to become less frequent. Faced with the reality of the relationship rather than the fantasy of unconscious projections, partners may need to assess whether their attachment can continue, with love, or whether the sense of being in love has been replaced by diminished interest and the partnership can no longer be sustained.

Partner choice, or unconscious attraction, and the psychophysiology of sexuality, are inextricably interwoven at this stage of the life course, as the sexual bond reflects the need for both attachment and separateness that is inherent in the emotional fit, as well as the link between feeling and bodily (genital) response that defines the quality of the sexual fit. The psychoanalytic concept of unconscious partner choice provides an understanding of how couples choose to form a long-term commitment, and has been described as a mutual transference relationship that is an unconscious contract for both development and defence (Ruszczynski, 1993). "Developmental" attraction allows for repudiated parts of the self to be externalized and located in the other, whereby regular contact can enable re-introjection of that part of the personality in a more tolerable form. In "defensive" attraction there is a collusion to retain splits and projections in a way that provides a shared defence against anxiety. When partners cling rigidly to illusions and defences (about themselves or others), this may become a limiting feature of the relationship. The nature of the shared unconscious contract will be reflected in a couple's sexual interactions, which can provide a unique forum for self-expression, growth, and personal development, but may also, through what remains unexpressed or avoided, represent individual or shared fears of being overwhelmed or trapped by an intimate physical relationship. Object relations theorists use the concept of a good-enough sexual relationship (from Winnicott's (1960) concept of good-enough mothering) to describe one that enables partners to renew their physical bond and thereby helps them to tolerate phases of distance and stress. Shared sexual pleasure that allows each person to feel loved by giving love, in the context of coping with the threat of closeness and anxiety about managing distance, can then symbolize a form of reparation to damaged internal objects (Scharff, 1982).

A lasting relationship requires continuing effort to recognize and accept the reality of each partner. For a harmonious relationship partners also need the capacity to forgive each other for not turning out to be all that was originally projected (Lyons, 1993). To the extent that this is achieved and the vicissitudes of life are prevented from intruding too deeply on the nature of the couple fit, elements of the initial romantic passion can be sustained as a healing and integrative force. Some couples struggle with feelings of disappointment, envy, and resentment as early idealization falls away. Others may experience life events that lead to depressive reactions or emotional pain. Such negative reactions often alter couple communications and sexual activity, with the potential to further undermine the relationship.

Anxiety and stress arising from any source (family, intrapsychic, or work issues) can impair the underlying physiology of the sexual response cycle in women and men. Conscious and unconscious anxiety can inhibit arousal and cause a range of erectile difficulties, which are the most commonly presenting male problem. The equivalent and less common sexual disorder in women is impaired genital responsiveness, which prevents vaginal expansion and thereby causes coital pain (dyspareunia), or a muscle spasm that completely prevents penetration (vaginismus). Women's difficulties in subjectively experiencing arousal, despite genital changes that allow penetration, have recently been recognized as clinically significant. Basson (2003) emphasized that women can choose to engage in sex for reasons other than desire, but that a lack of subjective arousability is reflected in women's greater tendency to lose interest in sex in a committed relationship. Difficulties with desire for sex, ranging from low interest and pleasure to complete avoidance of sexual contact, are often associated with resentment and anger, and are the most frequent issue for which women request help in sexual problem clinics. Men can, of course, also lose interest in sex with their partners, although this is less common, and a difference in sexual need between people is a frequent source of friction that brings couples to psychological therapy. Unconscious and conscious anger, linked with loss of sexual interest, and the therapeutic approaches that are employed to address them, are elaborated in Chapter Twelve.

What is known about the psychophysiology of negative emotional states and sexual responding? Sexual desire, arousal, and orgasmic responses are discrete but related neurobiological and physiological systems that depend on complex, and only partially understood, interactions between hormones, blood flow, and muscular contractions. Blood flow to the genitals (vasocongestion) is essential, and results from increased outflow in the parasympathetic branch of the autonomic nervous system. Genital vasocongestion causes erections in men and lubrication with inner expansion of the vaginal passage in women, allowing penile containment. Negative emotions such as anxiety, tension, and hostility, which involve the sympathetic autonomic nervous system, therefore have the potential to inhibit the physiological concommitants of blood flow to the genitals (parasympathetic outflow) and impair arousal responses. Oxytocin manufactured in the hypothalamus is secreted into the pituitary gland and is suggested to have a pivotal integrative role in sexual responding (Murphy, 1998). Laboratory studies show that during sexual arousal and orgasm, oxytocin increases in the plasma blood samples of both sexes, with women having significantly higher levels than men. Men secrete vasopressin only during arousal, with a drop in vasopressin at the point of ejaculation, when oxytocin rises sharply (Carmichael, Warburton, Dixen, & Davidson, 1994; Murphy, Seckel, Burton, Checkley, & Lightman, 1987). Circulating oxytocin is thought to influence arousal by facilitating vasocongestion, and acting on smooth and striated muscle activity in the pelvic area that triggers the involuntary neuromuscular events of female and male orgasm. Moreover, oxytocin and vasopressin are proposed as the neuropeptides that are linked to erotic mood changes, with oxytocin promoting sexual pleasure and vasopressin secretion leading to a sense of urgency and persistency in male sexual expression (Panksepp, 1998). In the Carmichael, Warburton, Dixen, and Davidson (1994) study, the temporal pattern of oxytocin secretion was related to subjective feelings of sexual pleasure, but there is evidence that concurrent brain opiate release is also required for pleasure to be experienced (Murphy, Checkley, Seckel, & Lightman,

1990). Sexual activity that leads to high brain oxytocin and opioid secretion at the point of climax appears to provide a shared neuroendocrine substrate for attachment, love, and sexual enjoyment in women and men.

Although there is generally a similar level of sexual interest between partners when a relationship begins, the trend is for male sexual drive to be more easily sustained, while women's patterns of sexual need are more likely to fluctuate over the life cycle. Feeling disrespected, devalued, or belittled can intrude on female sexual functioning, and for some women increased domestic chores and life events, especially childbirth and child rearing, can alter stress levels, decrease self esteem, and create disharmony (Leiblum, 2002).

Both men and women need a normal level of circulating testosterone, and men have ten to twenty times more than women. Although testosterone has a clear role in male central arousal mechanisms, much less is known about testosterone and various aspects of sexuality in women, and studies present conflicting results to date (Bancroft, 2002). Despite this, speculations can be made concerning the psychobehavioural and neurochemical events that are linked to a gradual decline in women's sexual interest, in contrast with male drive, which tends to be more consistent. Research shows that DA and NA can regulate the effects of oxytocin and vasopressin in the central nervous system (Carter, 1998) suggesting that increased levels of these neurotransmitters during early romantic attraction would enhance oxytocin and vasopressin secretion, thereby facilitating sexual arousal in women and desire for sex in men. In the context of a committed relationship, women who lose interest in sex report a range of experiences, from the absence of warmth and emotional closeness to resentment and anger related to conflictual aspects of the relationship and daily family life. Without the raised DA and NA associated with romantic passion, and with the intrusion of hostility towards a partner, women may struggle to maintain arousability, and may eventually withdraw from sexual contact that has become unrewarding. Male drive would also be susceptible to changes when passion fades, but the effects of vasopressin release on the urge for sex could be the basis for men's greater consistency of sexual need. There are, of course, couples in considerable distress because the man has lost interest while the woman yearns for sexual contact. These patterns may be linked to differences in the meaning of sex for each person, which reflects individual developmental experiences of attachment, connectedness, and sexual expression. An individual's ability to maintain a homeostatic balance in response to high emotion or stress will partly depend on these aspects of their developmental history. On a neurochemical level, this will impact on the manufacture and secretion of oxytocin and vasopressin in response to specific stimuli. As these peptide hormones are released rapidly in the brain, current thinking on the neurochemistry of psychological function suggests that oxytocin and vasopressin could provide a link between biology and the demands of the social environment. Many complex aspects of the interaction between biological and psychological factors are still far from understood. Withdrawal of sexual interest for a particular partner may have an adaptive protective function on an individual level, but for the couple this issue has potentially detrimental consequences and needs thorough assessment in each case.

Absence of sexual activity or incompatibility of sexual needs, as well as emotional distance, is often a basis for seeking sexual expression outside the committed relationship, where psychosexual development continues in a different way with a new partner. Social surveys have indicated that 60–70% of married men, and over half of married women, have had an affair at some time (Lawson, 1990). As fidelity is a defining characteristic of most opposite sex partnerships, another partner has the potential, if revealed, to cause enormous upset. Same sex couples tend to view other sexual partners more tolerantly. Research on gay men has shown that casual sexual encounters are far more accepted, and while there can be discrepancies between partners concerning the extent to which the relationship is open or closed, this aspect can be addressed frankly in therapy (Cove & Boyle, 2002). Sexual activity with a different person may be a highly exciting and sexually fulfilling experience. As women have greater sexual plasticity, more women than men tend to change to a same-sex partner at this stage. A new partner may enable some individuals to remain in a committed partnership for other reasons, including love, security, and family responsibilities, despite the absence of rewarding sex. Others would find it impossible to remain with someone who is involved in a sexual or emotional bond elsewhere, and such an event frequently causes a split in the primary couple relationship.

Women and men are able to make choices about how to combine sexual urges with security and attachment, and also procreation, if desired. These aspects of human bonding and love are regularly linked but can also operate independently. Individuals can feel desire and attraction for a person they do not love, and can be deeply attached to someone without sexual desire or attraction. Fisher, Aran, Mashek, and Brown (2002) have hypothesized that the possibility of this diversity of human behaviour is due to three primary neural systems that are discrete but interrelated, for mating (the sex drive), reproduction (romantic attraction), and parenting (attachment). Lust, or sexual drive, is dependent on oestrogens and androgens; romantic attraction is correlated with elevated central DA and NA and lowered central serotonin. The attachment system facilitates close proximity with a mating partner, social comfort and emotional union, and is associated with a neural system that is believed to have evolved for the purposes of specific parental duties, namely oxytocin and vasopressin. Contemporary relationship patterns and difficulties, including infidelity, sexual jealousy, and emotional pain due to partner rejection, are postulated to be based on the neural independence of these three primary emotion-motivation systems. Individuals vary considerably in their propensity for connections between a sense of attraction for a partner, attachment feelings, and a drive for sex, with implications for the nature of intimate relationships. Whether the sexual and relational issues that bring people to psychological therapy are anxiety-, hostility- or rejection-based, powerful feelings are often expressed in a clinical setting. Management of these feelings is essential to engender trust and safety as a basis for therapeutic work. Careful assessment, formulation, and reformulation in the light of new material should form the basis for integrating a range of psychological approaches for individually tailored treatment and management of relationship issues (Hiller & Cooke, 2002).

Continuing sexuality in middle to later years

Pleasurable sexual activity can be ongoing throughout the life span, and there is much diversity in the enjoyment, quality and amount of sexual behaviour for people beyond mid-life. Moreover, rewarding sex is a major contributor to emotional well-being and self-esteem (Weeks, 2002). Physical health also benefits from sexual activity at this stage: a prospective heart-disease study found that the mortality risk for men who had orgasms twice a week or more was 50% lower than those with a frequency of less than once a month (Davey-Smith, Frankel, & Yarnell, 1997). Positive effects arising from sensual touch, sexual arousal, and orgasm may be linked with the central release of oxytocin, which acts as a natural antistress hormone as well as a neural substrate for emotional attachment and sexual bonding (Carter, 1998). Far from sexual satisfaction declining, many women become more physically sensitive in terms of orgasmic response, and are able to perceive differences between orgasms achieved by different means (Davidson & Darling, 1988). As with earlier life stages, a combination of interpersonal, biological, and cultural components will determine the expression of sexuality, but the interactions between these still remain poorly understood. What does emerge from the literature is that partner-related factors have a greater influence on the quality of sexual activity than those associated with ageing or hormonal changes (Weeks, 2002). Emotional intimacy, tenderness, and sensitive bodily contact remain central to rewarding sexual expression. Mature partners who have been in longer relationships may actually reach their sexual potential through deeper emotional and sexual intimacy in mid-life. At the same time there are increasing numbers of couples separating in later years, providing the opportunity for new relationships to form. With the passion and intensity that initial excitement can bring to a romantic encounter, psychosexual development with a new partner can be rewarding in a different way.

Enjoyment and frequency of sexual activity in older people is significantly correlated with their past interest in sex (Weeks, 2002). Nevertheless, if an individual feels physically unattractive due to their perception of age-related bodily changes, this can potentially inhibit further sexual encounters, despite previous levels of sexual behaviour. For those people who have not experienced sexual contact for some time, due to either partner loss or separation, attempting penetrative sex once more can be problematic, and may create anxiety that compounds physical changes. The majority of men will experience erectile difficulties to some degree by middle age (Feldman, Goldstein, Hatzichriston, Krone, & McKinley, 1994) and may subsequently withdraw from sexual contact to avoid experiencing distress or disappointing a partner. Prior to the introduction of Viagra, the first oral medication for male arousal problems, the most significant variable affecting sexuality in women over sixty was the partner's sexual difficulties (Loehr, Verna, & Seguin, 1997). When such couples seek help for their relationship issues it often emerges that whereas the man misses penetrative sex, the woman tends to express greater sadness at the loss of physical closeness and intimacy, rather than intercourse. If an older man is unable to take Viagra or Cialis (a newer similar preparation) for health reasons, the focus of couple psychotherapy is frequently to enable the male partner to adjust to pleasure from sensual touch, without the aim of penetration. In the same vein, Malatester, Chambless, & Pollack (1988) found that the absence of social activities and sensual contact in general is more important for older women without a partner, rather than explicitly sexual experiences. For couples who can benefit from oral medication use, the woman especially may need a gradual re-introduction to penetrative sex after a period of abstinence, if the man is keen to resume intercourse with the return of erectile capacity (Kingsberg, 2002).

How significant are hormonal changes to sexuality in women and men at this life stage? Many men beyond fifty have reduced testosterone levels, but in contrast to younger men, for whom testosterone replacement therapy results in a return of sexual interest, there is no clear evidence that this can occur in older men when testosterone is increased (Bancroft, 2002). This may be due to a decline in responsiveness to testosterone with age. Women also have less free testosterone in later years, and a clinical syndrome of "female androgen insufficiency" has been described, despite the difficulty of determining normal levels (Kingsberg, 2002). Testosterone replacement for women has unpleasant side-effects; moreover, not all women with this insufficiency actually have the symptoms, which include impaired sexual function, mood changes, and low energy. In addition, studies on the correlation between sexual behaviour and testosterone levels in women have contradictory results (Bancroft, 2002). There is agreement that declining oestrogen levels impact on sexual function, due to vaginal discomfort, although this does not appear to influence women's perception of sexual satisfaction.

Another area of confusion in the literature concerns the relevance of the menopause: some evidence indicates that decreased desire is due to ageing rather than menopausal status (Bancroft, 2002; Kingsberg, 2002) while other studies suggest that menopausal changes are more significant for women's declining sexuality than their age (Dennerstein, 1996). Research in this area is compounded by cultural differences in the meaning of the menopause, its physical manifestations and its significance for women's status in society as well as the possibility of genetic determinants that vary between races (Bancroft, 2002).

Notwithstanding issues of appropriate methodology in comparisons across cultures, sexual interest involves far more than sufficient oestrogen, and the testosterone-based drive component of desire. Both psychological and interpersonal motivation, as well as beliefs and expectations about sexuality, play a significant part in determining the willingness to be sexually active with a given partner (Levine, 1992). This may be particularly true for people in their later years, for whom societal values can be an undermining influence. There appears to be no fixed biological limit to pleasure from sexual activity in whatever form. On the contrary, evidence shows that positive sexual experiences, especially within a loving relationship, can promote an active and healthy life span.

Concluding comments

Throughout the life course innate predispositions and hormonal changes will provide the biological bedrock for psychosocial influences that ultimately determine sexual behaviour. As clinicians we work with psychological functioning to mobilize change, both within and between people, drawing on the capacity to alter feelings, thoughts, and behaviour patterns in response to life experiences, including psychotherapy, and to reflect on those changes. Our inability to make an impact on wider familial and cultural contexts is all too apparent, but therapy can nevertheless try to affect the way these are construed. A recognition of that which lies beyond our scope seems essential for a rational perspective and realistic therapeutic aims. This chapter has attempted to highlight some of the biopsychosocial elements in sexual development, in an attempt to broaden conceptual thinking and facilitate appropriate goals in the treatment of troubled sexuality.

References

Bancroft, J. (2002). Biological factors in human sexuality. *The Journal of Sex Research, 39*(1): 15–21.

Basson, R. (2003). Biopsychosocial models of women's sexual response: applications to management of "desire disorders". *Sexual and Relationship Therapy, 18*(1): 107–115.

Berenbaum, S. A. (1999). Effects of early androgens on sex-typed activities and interests in adolescents with congenital adrenal hyperplasia. *Hormonal Behaviour, 35*: 102–110.

Bernstein, D. (1990). Female genital anxieties, conflicts and typical mastery modes. *International Journal of Psychoanalysis, 71*: 151–165.

Breakwell, G. M. (1994). The echo of power. *The Psychologist*, February: 65–72.

Breakwell, G. (1997). Adolescents and emerging sexuality. In: L. Sherr (Ed.), *AIDS and Adolescence* (pp. 133–143). Amsterdam: Harwood Academic.

Britton, R. (1989). The missing link: parental sexuality in the Oedipus Complex. In: J. Steiner (Ed.), *The Oedipus Complex Today*. London: Karnac.

Carter, S. C. (1998). Neuroendocrine perspectives on social attachment and love. *Psychoneuroendocrinology, 23*(8): 779–818.

Carmichael, M. S., Warburton, V. L., Dixen, J., Davidson, J. M. (1994). Relationships among cardiovascular, muscular and oxytocin responses during human sexual activity. *Archives of Sexual Behaviour, 23*: 59–79.

Clulow, C. (1993). Rethinking marriage. In: C. Clulow (Ed.), *Rethinking Marriage: Public and Private Perspectives*. London: Karnac.

Cove, J., & Boyle, M. (2002). Gay men's self-defined sexual problems, perceived cause and factors in remission. *Sexual and Relationship Theory, 17*: 2.

Cowan, P., & Cowan, C. P. (2001). A couple perspective on the transmission of attachment patterns. In: C. Clulow (Ed.), *Adult Attachment and Couple Psychotherapy*. London: Brunner-Routledge.

Damasio, A. (1994). *Descartes' Error: Emotion, Reason and the Human Brain*. New York: Putnam.

Damasio, A. (1999). *The Feeling of What Happens*. London: William Heinemann.

Davey-Smith, G., Frankel, S., & Yarnell, J. (1997). Sex and death: are they related? Findings from the Caerphilly cohort study. *British Medical Journal, 315*: 1641–1644.

Davidson, J. K., & Darling, C. A. (1988). The sexually experienced woman : multiple sex partners and sexual satisfaction. *Journal of Sex Research, 24*: 141–154.

Day, R. (1992). The transition to first intercourse among racially and culturally diverse youth. *Journal of Marriage and the Family, 54*: 749–762.

DeLamater, J., & Friedrich, W. N. (2002). Human sexual development. *The Journal of Sex Research, 39*(1): 10–14.

Dennerstein, L. (1996). Well-being, symptoms and the menopausal transition. *Maturitas, 23*: 147–157.

Ehrhardt, A. A. (2000). Gender, sexuality and human development. In: J. Bancroft (Ed.), *The Role of Theory in Sex Research*. The Kinsey Institute, Volume 6, Indiana University Press.

Ehrhardt, A. A., Meyer-Bahlberg, H. F. L., Rosen, L. R., Feldman, J. F., Veridiano, N. P., Zimmerman, I., & McEwan, B. S. (1985). Sexual orientation after prenatal exposure to exogenerous estrogen. *Archives of Sexual Behaviour, 14*: 57–77.

Ehrhardt, A. A., Meyer-Bahlberg, H. F. L., Rosen, L. R., Feldman, J. F., Veridiano, N. P., Elkin, E. J., & McEwen, B. S. (1989). The development of gender-related behaviour in females following prenatal exposure to diethylstilbestrol (DES). *Hormones and Behaviour, 23*: 526–541.

Ellis, B. J., & Symons, D. (1990). Sex differences in sexual fantasy: an evolutionary psychological approach. *Journal of Sex Research, 27*: 527–555.

Fagot, B. I. (1994). Peer relations and the development of competence in boys and girls. In: C. Leaper (Ed.), *Childhood Segregation, Causes and Consequences* (pp. 53–65). San Francisco: Jossey-Bass.

Feldman, H. A., Goldstein, I., Hatzichriston, D. G., Krone, R. J., & McKinley, J. B. (1994). Impotence and its medical and psychosocial correlates: results of the Massachusets Male Ageing Study. *Journal of Urology, 151*: 54–61.

Feldman, M. (1989). The Oedipus complex: manifestation in the inner world and the therapeutic relationship. In: J. Steiner (Ed.), *The Oedipus Complex Today*. London: Karnac.

Fisher, H. E. (1998). Lust, attraction and attachment in mammalian reproduction. *Human Nature, 9*(1): 23–52.

Fisher, H. E., Aran, A., Mashek, D., & Brown, L. L. (2002). Defining the brain systems of lust, romantic attraction and attachment. *Archives of Sexual Behaviour, 31*(5): 413–419.

Fonagy, P. (2001). *Attachment Theory and Psychoanalysis.* New York: Other Press.

Friedman, R. C., & Downey, J. I. (2002). *Sexual Orientation and Psychoanalysis.* New York: Columbia University Press.

Goldman, R. J., & Goldman, J. D. G. (1982). *Children's Sexual Thinking.* London: Routledge and Kegan Paul.

Haqq, C. M., & Donahoe, P. K. (1998). Regulation of sexual dimorphism in mammals. *Physiological Reviews, 78,* 1–33.

Heaven, P. C. L. (2001). *The Social Psychology of Adolescence.* Basingstoke: Palgrave Macmillan.

Herdt, G. (2000). Why the Sambia initiate boys from age 10. In: J. Bancroft (Ed.), *The Role of Theory in Sex Research.* The Kinsey Institute Series, Volume 6, Indiana University Press.

Hiller, J. (1993). Psychoanalytic concepts and psychosexual therapy: a suggested integration. *Sexual and Marital Therapy, 8:* 9–26.

Hiller, J. (1996). Female sexual arousal and its impairment: the psychodynamics of non-organic coital pain. *Sexual and Marital Therapy, 11*(1): 55–76.

Hiller, J., & Cooke, L. (2002). Issues and principles in the assessment and management of psychosexual disorders in sexual health settings. In: D. Miller & J. Green (Eds.), *The Psychology of Sexual Health.* Oxford: Blackwell Science.

Hines, M., & Kaufman, F. R. (1994). Androgen and the development of human sex-typical behaviour: rough and tumble play and sex of preferred playmates in children with Congenital Adrenal Hyperplasia (CAH). *Child Development, 65:* 1042–1053.

Hrdy, S. B. (2000). Discussion paper. In: J. Bancroft (Ed.), *The Role of Theory in Sex Research.* The Kinsey Institute series Volume 6, Indiana University Press.

Imperato-McGinley, J., Peterson, R. E., Gautier, T., & Sturla, E. (1979). Androgen and the evolution of male-gender identity among male pseudohermaphrodites with 5-alpha-reductase deficiency. *New England Journal of Medicine, 300:* 1233–1237.

Insel, T. R. (1997). A neurobiological basis of social attachment. *American Journal of Psychiatry, 154:* 726–735.

Kestenberg, J. (1968). Outside and inside, male and female. *Journal of the American Psychoanalytical Association*, 4: 453–476.

Kingsberg, S. A. (2002). The impact of ageing on sexual function in women and their partners. *Archives of Sexual Behaviour, 31*(5): 431–437.

Laufer, M. (1976). The central masturbation fantasy, the final sexual organisation and adolescence. *Psychoanalytic Study of the Child, 31*, 297–316.

Lawson, A. (1990). *Adultery*. Oxford: Oxford University Press.

Leiblum, S. R. (2002). Reconsidering gender differences in sexual desire: an update. *Sexual and Relationship Therapy, 17*(1): 58–67.

Lerner, H. (1976). Parental mislabelling of female genitals as a determinant of penis envy and learning inhibition in women. *Journal of the American Psychoanalytical Association*, 24: 269–284.

Le Vay, S. (1991). A difference in hypothalamic structure between heterosexual and homosexual men. *Science*, 253: 1034–1037.

Levine, S. B. (1992). *Sexual Life*. New York: Plenum.

Loehr, J., Verma, S., & Seguin, R. (1997). Issues of sexuality in older women. *Journal of Women's Health*, 6: 451–457.

Lyons, A. (1993). Husbands and wives: the mysterious choice. In: S Ruszczynski (Ed.), *Psychotherapy with Couples*. London: Karnac.

Maccoby, E. E. (1998). *The Two Sexes: Growing Apart, Coming Together*. Cambridge, MA: Harvard University Press.

Malatester, V., Chambless, D., & Pollack, M. (1988). Widowhood, sexuality and ageing : a lifespan analysis. *Journal of Sex and Marital Therapy, 14*: 49–62.

Masters, W. H., Johnson, V. E., & Kolodny, R. C. (1982). *Human Sexuality*. Boston: Little, Brown.

Mayer, E. L. (1985). Everybody must be just like me: observations in female castration anxiety. *International Journal of Psychoanalysis, 66*: 331–348.

McClintock, M., & Herdt, G. (1996). Rethinking puberty. The development of sexual attraction. *Current Directions in Psychological Science*, 5: 178–183.

Meyer-Bahlberg, H. F. L. (1999). Variants of gender differentiation. In: H. C. Steinhausen & F. C. Verhulst (Eds.), *Risks and Outcomes in Developmental Psychopathology* (pp. 298–313). New York: Oxford University Press.

Meyer-Bahlberg, H. F. L. (2000). Discussion paper, sexual orientation. In: J. Bancroft, (Ed.), *The Role of Theory in Sex Research*, The Kinsey Institute Series, Volume 6, Indiana University Press.

Murphy, M. R., Seckel, J. R., Burton, S., Checkley, S. A., & Lightman, S. L. (1987). Changes in oxytocin and vasopressin secretion during sexual activity in men. *Journal of Clinical Endocrinology and Metabolism, 65*: 738–741.

Murphy, M. R., Checkley, S. A., Seckel, J. R., & Lightman, S. L. (1990). Naloxone inhibits oxytocin release at orgasm in man. *Journal of Clinical Endocrinology and Metabolism, 71*(4): 1056–1058.

Murphy, M. (1998). The neuroendocrine basis of sexuality and organic dysfunction. In: H. Freeman, I. Pullen, G. Stein, & G. Wilkinson (Eds.), *Seminars in Psychosexual Disorders*. London: Gaskell.

Ogden, T. (1991). *The Primitive Edge of Experience*. London: Jason Aronson.

Okami, P., Olmstead, R., & Abrahamson, P. (1997). Sexual experiences in early childhood: 18 year longitudinal data from the UCLA Family Lifestyles Project. *The Journal of Sex Research, 34*: 339–347.

Oliver, M. B., & Hyde, J. S. (1993). Gender differences in sexuality: a meta-analysis. *Psychological Bulletin, 14*: 29–51.

Panksepp, J. (1998). *Affective Neuroscience: the Foundation of Human and Animal Emotions*. New York: Oxford University Press.

Rossi, A. (1997). The impact of family structure and social change on adolescent sexual behaviour. *Child and Youth Services Review, 19*, 369–400.

Ruszczynski, S. (1993). Thinking about and working with couples. In: S. Ruszczynski (Ed.), *Psychotherapy with Couples*. London: Karnac.

Scharff, D., & Scharff, J. S. (1991). *Object Relations Couple Therapy*. London: Jason Aronson.

Stoller, R. J. (1976). Primary femininity. *Journal of the American Psychoanalytical Association, 24*(Suppl): 59–78.

Tyson, P. (1982). A development line of gender identity, gender role and choice of love object. *Journal of the American Psychoanalytical Association, 30*: 61–86.

Walsh, A. (2000). Human reproductive strategies and life history theory. In: J. Bancroft (Ed.), *The Role of Theory in Sex Research*. The Kinsey Institute series Volume 6, Indiana University Press.

Weeks, D. J. (2002). Sex for the mature adult: health, self-esteem and countering ageist stereotypes. *Sexual and Relationship Therapy, 17*(3): 231–240.

Winnicott, D. W. (1960). *The Maturational Process and The Facilitating Environment*. London: Karnac.

Zhou, J. N., Hofman, M. A., Gooren, L. J. G., & Swaab, D. F. (1995). A sex difference in the human brain and its relation to transsexuality. *Nature, 378*: 68–70.

CHAPTER TWO

Developmental theory and developmental deficits: the treatment of sex offenders with Asperger's Syndrome

Winifred Bolton

Introduction

T he development of social policy with respect to sex offenders has been turbo-charged in recent years by public horror, and the resulting political pressure, arising from a number of high profile cases involving offences against both children and adult women. The Sex Offender Register now allows closer monitoring of convicted offenders who, after detention, are released back into the community. In addition, the Home Office has supported the development of a Sex Offender Treatment Programme, a cognitive-behaviourally based psychoeducational intervention, which has shown demonstrable benefits to those sex offenders who meet specified criteria (Friendship, Mann, & Beech, 2003). The aim has been to make this as widely available as possible in prison and hospital settings. Unfortunately, the two demands, to reduce the level of sexual crime and to identify those interventions that contribute to its reduction, have given rise to a tendency to regard sex offenders as a homogenous group and, therefore, to apply the same change programme to them all. But sex offending is not a diagnosis, and will be underpinned by a range of psychopathologies. I argue in this chapter that "one size fits all" packages obscure important differences among sex offenders. In particular, I am concerned about a subset of the group whose sexual offences were committed against adult women. I believe that they are suffering from undiagnosed Asperger's Syndrome and that treatment approaches for this subset need to be reviewed.

In this chapter, I describe my observations and experiences in individual and group therapy with a small group of six young men that led me to theorize that the core deficit in Asperger's Syndrome is a failure in non-verbal communication, specifically the interpretation of facial expression, and that this deficit gives rise developmentally to the abnormalities in social interaction, cognition, speech, and use of language, which are the defining features of the syndrome. I argue that an appreciation of the central importance of non-verbal communication to the development of symbolic thinking, the capacity to reflect on the content of one's own mind, to "read" others' minds and thereby to connect with them, capacities that are absent in Asperger's, significantly extends our understanding of normal social and emotional development. I also wish to suggest that our understanding of Asperger's syndrome has been strongly affected by the fact that both theory and diagnosis have developed on the basis of observations of children. This has led to a failure to account for some features, specifically poor emotion regulation, because in the normal individual the capacity to regulate emotion is acquired in the course of development. Its absence, therefore, may not be apparent until adulthood. I would argue that poor emotion regulation is a core feature of Asperger's syndrome, and is clearly apparent in the adult. I believe that this difficulty is also evidenced in poor management of sexual arousal, which, together with the currently recognized difficulties in social interaction, make problems of sexuality and sexual relationship inevitable. A truly developmental theory then is required to understand sex offending in adult men with Asperger's syndrome.

The context

In the medium secure unit for mentally disordered offenders with a learning disability in which I worked as a clinical psychologist, the group of men with convictions for sexual offences included both those whose victims had been children, male or female, and those whose victims were adult women. I am concerned with the latter category. Of the six men thought to have Asperger's syndrome, two had convictions in both categories but were primarily sexually motivated towards adult women.[1]

According to the provisions of the 1983 Mental Health Act, currently undergoing review and revision, a judge can assign a convicted offender to a secure or medium secure hospital if s/he is persuaded by psychiatric recommendation that the offence was committed under the influence of a mental disorder. Within the definition of the Act, mental disorder encompasses mental illness, treatable personality disorder, and mental impairment (learning disability, defined as a low IQ accompanied by deficits in social and interpersonal functioning). Unlike a prison sentence, a hospital order under the Mental Health Act is for an indeterminate length of time, discharge occurs only when the responsible medical officer, in consultation with a multi-disciplinary team, deems the patient to be no longer a risk as a result of an improvement in his mental disorder brought about by "treatment". Obviously, in the case of mental impairment, there can be no improvement in the intellectual deficit, only a hope that psychosocial interventions will produce an improvement in social functioning, and a supportive environment can be provided on discharge that will minimize the likelihood of re-offending. Given these ambiguous conditions, the learning disabled offender can be detained for long periods of time for an offence that is relatively minor on a scale of severity from minor assault to rape or murder.

As previously stated, during detention the main psychosocial intervention provided to the sex offender is a cognitive-behaviourally derived group programme. Using a combination of structured learning tasks, skills training, role play, and cognitive modification, this aims to facilitate the development of a sense of personal responsibility for the sexual offending, a reduction in distorted thinking and perceptions of the offence, enhancement of empathy for one's victims leading to remorse, and a commitment to a relapse-prevention plan derived from functional analysis of the offending behaviour. For learning disabled offenders, this process is time-consuming and arduous, requiring continuous repetition and

rehearsal. Studies conducted on sex offenders in the prison population have demonstrated that this type of programme is effective
in reducing distorted thinking with respect to the motivation and
intentions of prospective victims, and in improving empathy
(Friendship, Mann, & Beech, 2003.). But those offenders with identified mental health difficulties are excluded from the programme.
It is not clear, therefore, whether the same gains can be expected to
occur with mentally disordered sex offenders. The situation is
further complicated for a sex offender with Asperger's Syndrome,
where mental health difficulties are likely to be present but
secondary to the neurodevelopmental condition. So far, in many
settings, the same cognitive–behavioural intervention is delivered
to all sex offenders, irrespective of the likely aetiology of the sexual
offending and with, as yet, unpredictable benefits.

I would like to contrast the more typical sex offender, in my
experience, with the type with Asperger's Syndrome. In the secure
setting within which I worked, the typical sex offender had an IQ in
the moderately disabled range (55–70), a diagnosis of mental illness,
usually schizophrenia, and an early history involving, in different
combinations, social deprivation, emotional neglect, and physical
and sexual abuse. Diagnostically, they would be considered to
present with co-morbid conditions of learning disability, mental
illness, personality disorder, and often substance misuse. The sexual
offence could be anywhere on the continuum from more to less
severe. Some had convictions for rape. In contrast, those patients
with Asperger's Syndrome were technically not learning disabled,
having IQs within the low average to borderline range. They were
more likely to have been brought up in a middle-class professional
family with emotional nurturance in the normal range, though
family relationships were inevitably disorganized in an attempt at
adaptation to the developmental disorder. Sexual and physical
abuse were never present except in one atypical case, and then in the
context of institutional, rather than family, care. Substance abuse
was rarely part of the picture. The sexual offence was less severe and
usually consisted of the touching of breast or buttocks of a strange
woman in a public place, carried out on a multitude of occasions,
with repeated conviction and imprisonment failing to act as a deter-
rent. In another, more unusual, case, the offence had the same perseverative quality, but consisted of repeated telephone calls to random

women in an attempt to engage them in conversations that were sexually arousing to him. Psychological dominance, though not physical coercion, appeared to be an element here. With the exception of this patient, none of the men showed patterns of deviant sexual arousal, either with respect to the object of their sexual choice, or the degree of violence or coercion they sought, in reality or fantasy. These differences suggest that the developmental pathway underlying the sexual offending is different in the two groups. Given the range of factors likely to be contributing to an outcome of sexual offending in the non-Asperger group, the aetiology must be complex. In the Asperger's group, it seems possible, if not likely, that the sexual offending is one more manifestation of the pervasive difficulty in social interaction that is definitional of the syndrome. On this basis, it was felt that the conventional cognitive–behavioural intervention for sex offenders, designed to remedy past learning deficits, might not be adequate for the Asperger's group, whose difficulties may include a failure to benefit from any experience, rather than learning on the basis of socially deviant experiences. I wanted to try to develop a form of therapeutic intervention that would more directly target the core deficit of Asperger's syndrome.

The diagnostic features of Asperger's Syndrome.

What we now call Asperger's syndrome was first described by Hans Asperger in 1944 as "autistic psychopathy", which he considered a form of personality disorder consisting of a pattern of poor social interaction, abnormality of communication, and restricted interests observed in a small group of young boys. More recently, several systems of diagnosis have been developed that vary in the strictness of their thresholds and, therefore, give rise to different prevalence rates.

The *Diagnostic and Statistical Manual of Mental Disorders* (*DSM IV*) (American Psychiatric Association, 2000) describes two main criteria for diagnosis, which are applied with high thresholds: severe and sustained impairments in social interaction and the development of restricted, repetitive patterns of behaviour, interest, and activities. The Gillberg criteria (Gillberg & Gillberg, 1989) include social impairment, narrow range of interests, repetitive routines, speech and language peculiarities, problems in non-verbal communication, and motor clumsiness. These are more loosely applied and give rise to prevalence rates of one in 300 children in Sweden (Ehlers & Gillberg, 1993).

These criteria have only recently been developed and are still not widely known, with the result that many adults in mental health, learning disability, or forensic settings remain undiagnosed or continue to carry an inappropriate diagnosis that has not been revised in the light of new knowledge. Describing my patients as "deserving" a diagnosis reflects the fact that those over the age of thirty are unlikely to have received the diagnosis in childhood, and in adulthood may be misdiagnosed with schizophrenia or personality disorder. Scragg and Shah (1994) investigated the prevalence of the disorder in a secure hospital and found a 2.3% prevalence using the Gillberg and Gillberg criteria, a rate six times higher than the base rate inferred in the general population by Ehlers and Gillberg using the same criteria. Not all neurodevelopmental disorders are over-represented in forensic settings to this degree. This suggests that the quality of the deficits in Asperger's increases the likelihood of offending and subsequent hospitalization.

Even at a superficial level, it is not difficult to see how this may be so. In the area of social and sexual relationships the Asperger's man is severely disadvantaged by his lack of empathy, extremely literal appreciation of language, stiff gait, absent facial expression and body language, and limited capacity to interpret the non-verbal communications of others. A composite clinical example may illustrate this further.

> A. was thirty two. He had many convictions for the type of offence described earlier. Living alone in the community, and with little daytime occupation, he longed for a relationship within which to satisfy his strong sexual impulses. He developed the habit of hanging around a busy shopping centre. When he saw an attractive woman, possibly in revealing clothes, he would go up to her and touch her on the breasts or buttocks. He saw this as a means of expressing his interest and hoped that it might invite reciprocated interest. Unfortunately, it did occasionally lead to consensual sexual contact, although more frequently it led to him being arrested. More often than not, however, he was ignored. For him, it was impossible to distinguish between a sexual encounter that led to arrest, dismissal, or gratification. In

appearance, he was tall and good looking. His gait was stiff, and when walking his arms and hands were held rigidly down. In conversation, his face and head were motionless and his voice had none of the usual variation in tone, but was flat and monotonous. He had been born to a loving, stable, middle-class, professional family, who were strongly established in a local religious community and carried high expectations for the academic and occupational success, and social functioning, of their offspring. He had an older sister who was highly intelligent, achieved well academically, graduating from university and settling into a valued profession. His father was of Asian origin, a successful businessman, and he had views about desirable gender roles which were a little out of kilter with those current in Britain. A. was of low average intelligence but, as a child, could not be maintained in mainstream schooling because of his poor social relations and unusual behaviour. He displayed narrow and rigid attitudes to food, willing to eat only certain types. He lost weight and had several admissions for "eating disorder". As an adult, through family connections, he gained low level work in a small business but was dismissed because of his misunderstanding of the requirements. His father became increasingly angry and frustrated with his apparently inexplicable behaviour and eventually distanced himself, subsequently disowning him completely because of his sexual behaviour. His mother, though equally puzzled and frustrated, was protective and gave him money to visit prostitutes in an attempt to divert him from sexually offensive behaviour.

A. would say "I've brought shame on my family". He was well-known in his local area on account of his sexual behaviour and the many prison sentences he served before being detained under the Mental Health Act. In discussion, he repeatedly stated that he would "never do it again". He had developed verbal and behavioural rituals that appeared to be an attempt to control his emotions and sexual arousal. "I'll never do it again" had acquired the status of just such a ritual. For him, the verbal statement, as a description of his psychic reality, was the equivalent of an objective reality. Saying he would not do it again was the same as not doing it again. He could, therefore, see no point in "working" towards this end even when it was pointed out to him that he had indeed "done it again", many times, having made the verbal commitment not to do so. Some staff saw this as "lying", evidence of further anti-social aspects of his personality. But a lie is an attempt to persuade another that something is the case when it is not the case and, therefore, to distinguish between personal psychic reality, objective reality and another's psychic reality. A. was not capable of this. I shall return to this later.

Apart from the small Scragg and Shah (1994) survey cited earlier, which was confined to one institution, there are no other data to indicate the prevalence of Asperger's Syndrome in individuals convicted of sexual offences, although there have been several case studies of Asperger's patients with a history of violence and/or sexual assault (Baron-Cohen, 1988; Kohn, Fahum, Ratzoni, & Apter, 1998; Murrie, Warren, Kristiansson, & Dietz, 2002). The extent of the problem is, therefore, unknown. In the setting in which I worked, at one point six patients out of thirty had convictions for sexual offences against adult women and met criteria for Asperger's, though this may have been due to the fact that interested clinicians attract such referrals.

It may be appropriate at this point to include a brief discussion of the differentiation of Asperger's Syndrome from autism. Though autism has acquired greater prominence in public awareness, perhaps due to the recent controversy regarding its putative association with the MMR vaccine, it is less common than Asperger's (21 cases per 10,000 population for autism, Wing & Gould, 1979). There is some disagreement about the criteria for differentiating the two conditions (see Happé, 1994 for a discussion) but most clinicians agree that while the two conditions are related in that they share the triad of impairments in social interaction, non-verbal communication, and imagination (as evidenced in repetitive behaviour and restricted interests), Asperger's individuals show, in addition, motor clumsiness, normal language development, and higher intellectual ability. These distinguishing features become more marked during the life course, so are more readily apparent in the adult than the child. Asperger's Syndrome is currently regarded as a disorder on the autistic spectrum, and Asperger's patients a subset of the autistic group, notwithstanding the fact that it is more common than autism. In terms of attempts at theoretical understanding, much of the effort has been directed at autism, with Asperger's being included by implication.

Theories of autism and Asperger's

Most researchers and clinicians now accept that autism has an organic aetiology (Steffenburg & Gillberg, 1989), though, in spite of increasingly sophisticated investigative technology such as magnetic resonance imaging, it has not been possible to establish agreement about a specific area of the brain or chemical pathway that is consistently involved. It is likely that a number of different biological causes may result in autism (Gillberg & Coleman, 1992), each of these giving rise to the characteristic constellation of impairments described. Nevertheless, without a theory to explain how and why these particular impairments should occur together, it remains difficult to establish what this common pathway might be.

In the absence to date of definitive evidence at a biological level, psychologists have continued to investigate what the pathway might be at a psychological level. Theories about autism have tended to be derived from, and evaluated against, observation of autistic children. The disorder may, of course, manifest itself differently in adults, as I have suggested. So far the most influential psychological theory to attempt to account for the triad of impairments found in autism has been Baron-Cohen, Leslie, and Frith's (1985) proposal of a "theory of mind" deficit. They argue that autistic children lack the capacity to represent psychologically the mental states (beliefs, desires, emotions, thoughts, intentions) of themselves and others and, therefore, to appreciate that it is mental states that determine behaviour rather than physical reality. They also fail to appreciate that it is mental states that mediate our experience of reality, rather than there being a direct correspondence between external reality and subjective experience.

Baron-Cohen, Leslie, and Frith conceptualize "theory of mind" as an innately given cognitive mechanism that emerges in the normal child according to a developmental timetable. In the normal infant, it is first in evidence between the age of nine and fifteen months in the form of "proto declarative pointing" (Charman et al., 1997). This is the utilization of the finger to point to an object in order to communicate interest to another and to draw the other's attention to the object. It reflects a capacity for "joint attention" and implies an awareness of the other's independent mental state in the form of the wish to induce a change of interest in the other.

Dennett (1978) has argued that conclusive evidence for the presence of "theory of mind" requires the understanding and prediction of another's behaviour based on false belief. Wimmer and Perner (1983) developed an operationalization of theory of mind based on the "Sally-Ann" task. Sally has a basket, Ann has a box. The child watches as Sally places a marble in her basket and leaves the room. While she is absent, Ann moves Sally's marble from the basket to the box. Ann then leaves the room. Sally returns and the child is asked the test question, "Where will Sally look for the marble?". When Baron-Cohen and colleagues (1985) tested twenty autistic children using this task, 80% answered in terms of their own knowledge rather than Sally's false belief. In contrast, 86% of children with Down's syndrome, who were less intelligent, succeeded on the task, as do normal children from about four years. This theory has spawned an enonomous research effort, applying the task to different groups, under different circumstances and at different ages. While there is far from universal agreement that a theory of mind (or mentalization as it is sometimes called) deficit, as operationalized above, is definitive of autism, or that it is a primary deficit, it is clear that individuals with autism do not acquire the capacity to mentalize to the same developmental timetable, to the same level of competence, and with the same degree of real-life flexibility as do non-autistic individuals.

The status of mentalization theories in relation to Asperger's syndrome is more complex. Notwithstanding a lack of agreement about the differential diagnosis between autism and Asperger's, it appears that Asperger's individuals perform relatively well on experimental mentalization tasks but have difficulty in applying their "theory of mind" in everyday life. Happé (1994) has suggested that Asperger's individuals may have delayed acquisition of mentalization, beyond the normal critical period, leading to a failure in activation of other developmental processes which are critical for normal social functioning.

We can imagine how disabling a poorly developed capacity for mentalization may be in circumstances where sexual encounters are being negotiated. Recall the form of sexual offence frequently undertaken by offenders with Asperger's. A man touches a woman sexually on the street and does not receive an aggressive or hostile response. A non-autistic observer may infer the woman's mental state to be fear or embarrassment. The Asperger's man makes inferences from the visible behaviour and concludes that the woman is expressing willingness. During a discussion about his sexual offending, an Asperger's patient described his confusion that he had seen men in night clubs touching women's buttocks with impunity. The same patient described his belief that the arresting policeman had condoned his sexual behaviour because he had bought him a hamburger while in custody. "He wouldn't have bought me a hamburger if he thought I'd done wrong."

Returning to autism, the most convincing challenge to the mentalization deficit hypothesis has emerged on the basis that mentalization is too sophisticated a process to underlie the very basic biological dysfunction that must be present in autism. Hobson (2002) believes that the cognitive account of autism, as represented by the theory of mind hypothesis, fails to consider the extent to which emotions are implicated in the development of the capacity to represent mental states. Hobson does not deny that a mentalization deficit occurs in autism, but he believes that it is not primary. He regards the mentalization deficit as one of the sequelae to another, more fundamental, deficit in the capacity to relate to another person, which he sees as rooted in the perception of, and responsiveness to, emotional expression in others. During infancy, the absence, in autism, of a capacity to read emotion in the face of the caregiver disrupts the achievement of emotional connectedness in relationship on which many social and cognitive developments depend.

> In my view, autism presents a kind of negative image of what social experiences contribute to intellectual life. What the person with autism lacks in the capacity for thinking, is what interpersonal relations provide for the rest of us. [Hobson, 2002, p. 184]

This is not to argue that autism is socially caused, but that the brain abnormality, currently not well understood, interrupts the establishment of processes of relationship and cognitive development. While there is as yet no definitive evidence one way or the other to confirm or disconfirm these competing theories, I have already stated that I find Hobson's more convincing. Interestingly, my clinical experience with Asperger's patients indicated that they were not disastrously poor at recognizing emotion in facial expression as depicted in Ekman and Friesen's (1976) photographs, and they were quite skilled at reading facial expression in videotaped film with the sound turned off. However, they did not use facial expression to communicate emotion themselves, nor could they use this as a cue to understanding social situations in everyday life. My guess was that, as intimated by Happé, they had acquired this skill relatively late in life and it was poorly integrated into their general social problem-solving strategies. Again, it is likely this would be a handicap in sexual encounters. One patient suggested that he believed that when a woman looked at him, this conveyed her sexual interest.

Staying with clinical experience for the moment, I observed that my Asperger's patients shared, in addition to the diagnostic features already described, a difficulty in regulating their emotions, a feature that is not usually mentioned in the literature. When they were anxious, angry, or excited, this appeared to be experienced as overwhelming and would be expressed in the form of extreme behaviours, usually without the verbal description that is indicative of some recognition of the emotion. For example, perseverative questioning and headbanging were observed frequently as manifestations of anxiety. Minor, and occasionally more serious, physical assaults and door slamming spoke of anger. This led me to speculate that sexual arousal may have been experienced by them in a similar manner to other emotions, as a raw, concrete, physical sensation without any secondary representation in the form of cognitive awareness or verbal description.

Berenbaum, Raghavan, Le, Vernon, and Gomez (2003) have attempted to create a taxonomy of emotional disturbance. They describe one category of disturbance as an "awareness disconnection". This occurs when awareness is disconnected from emotional expression or emotional experience. The deficit in mentalization of an Asperger's man may give rise to such an awareness disconnection with respect to sexual arousal. Sexual arousal may then be expressed in the form of the repetitive touching behaviour described. The awareness disconnection hypothesis also raises the possibility of a misperception of bodily sensation, so that anxiety or excitement may be experienced as sexual arousal, with the same result.

It is difficult to establish the degree of intensity of an individual's emotion, impulse, or arousal, independently of his verbal description of it. At the same time, we know from clinical experience that verbal self-report of an emotion, as well as aiding the expression of it, can also serve to reduce or to escalate it. It seemed to me that for these patients the relative weakness of mentalization reflected in the absence of verbal description of a mental state created not only difficulties in social interaction but difficulties in emotion and impulse regulation. This combination proved explosive, particularly in the sexual domain.

Pondering on the co-occurrence of poor emotion regulation and mentalization in my Asperger's patients prompted me to examine the psychoanalytic literature on this topic, which has been explored most recently by Fonagy, Gergely, Jurist, and Target (2004), partly in the context of an understanding of borderline personality disorder (BPD) (see Chapter Ten for a discussion of the manner in which sex itself can be used to regulate emotion in the borderline patient). Borderline personality disorder involves a chronic dysregulation of behaviour, relationship, emotion, and cognition. Although diagnostic criteria for the two conditions are quite different, their clinical presentation can share some of the same features, though in other respects they are different. As in autism, a deficit in mentalization has been posited as central to the unfolding of BPD. Unlike autism, however, which is assumed to have an organic cause, BPD is more likely to be explained, at least partially, by social factors, specifically childhood sexual abuse (Paris, Zweig-Frank, & Guzder, 1993). Fonagy and colleagues have proposed a theory to explain the development of the features of BPD. In their theory, a central role is assigned to an infant caretaker's failure to accurately "mirror" the infant's emotional experiences.

I want to examine Fonagy's theory in more detail. As an aside, however, this overlap in clinical presentation and theorizing about the two conditions suggests the possibility of a developmental pathway shared, to some extent, by the two conditions; one triggered by an organic abnormality, the other triggered by an environmental abnormality. This raises interesting questions about the neural substrate of emotionality, sexuality, and sociability, which are addressed in more detail in Chapter One of this volume. The radical implication, however, is that a given set of psychological outcomes, for example, those represented in the overlap between Asperger's syndrome and BPD, may be reached along a pathway that has either primarily organic precipitants, or primarily social precipitants. Hobson (2002) has presented a similar argument with respect to autism, that more often than not it has an organic aetiology, but cases have been identified where the aetiology appears likely to be more social, albeit in the most extreme social conditions. He cites in evidence Rutter *et al.*'s (1999) longitudinal research with Romanian orphans adopted by British families at the end of the Ceausescu regime. These children had experienced, prior to their adoption, almost inconceivably deprived conditions in orphanages where they had been placed in very early life. Clinical evaluation at the ages of four and six years indicated that a small, but higher than expected, proportion of them developed a presentation resembling childhood autism that could not be explained by pre-existing brain damage, as other organic conditions had been ruled out.

Fonagy and colleagues' theory of personality development.

In this context, then, my interest in Fonagy's theory about BPD is that, to the extent that it shares with Asperger's the feature of a deficit in mentalization, his account of its development may shed some light on the ontogenesis of Asperger's. The assumption of an organic aetiology can sometimes lead us to overlook crucial developmental processes that could otherwise be of assistance in designing therapeutic strategies. Fonagy's developmental theory is, of course, a theory about normal psychological development that, under certain circumstances, can be disrupted, with personality disorder as the outcome. I am suggesting that when the organic deficit underlying Asperger's syndrome is present in an infant, psychological development is necessarily disrupted, with a personality disorder-like syndrome being the outcome.

Fonagy and colleagues are concerned to account for the development of certain features of personality: the sense of the self as an agent, the capacity to regulate emotions and impulses, and the capacity to utilize representations of mental state in the self and in the other to interpret interpersonal events. Where this goes wrong, and there is instability of self, emotions, and relationships, the clinical presentation is one of personality disorder, though Asperger's syndrome can also look like this disruption of personality. These three features of personality are seen to emerge out of the emotional relationship between infant and primary caregiver. When an infant automatically expresses emotion, the normal caregiver responds by mirroring the emotion in her facial and vocal display. Through a "contingency detection mechanism" (Gergely & Watson, 1999) the infant "comes to associate the control they have over their parents' mirroring displays with the resulting improvement in their emotional state leading eventually to an experience of the self as a regulating agent" (Fonagy, Gergely, Jurist, & Target, 2004, p. 8). At the same time, internalization of the caretaker's mirrored display, while enhancing "sensitivity to self-states", constitutes a psychological representation of the emotion. The caregiver's empathic facial expression signifies the infant's emotion and, crucially, modifies it because it is separate and different from the primary experience. "The contingent responding of the attachment figure . . . is the principal means by which we acquire understanding of our own internal states, which is an intermediate step in the understanding of others as psychological entitities (*ibid.*, p. 127).

According to Fonagy and colleagues, normal psychological development requires, in addition to contingent and congruent mirroring of the infant's emotion by the caregiver, that the mirroring is "marked". This means that the caregiver conveys, by the quality of her display, that her reflected emotion is not real. Usually this is achieved through an exaggerated version of a realistic emotion. She conveys a sense that she is almost pretending to have the emotion. This internalized "marked" reflection of the infant's emotion leads to a "decoupling" of mental state from physical reality, a recognition that what exists in the mind need not exist in the external world. Prior to this decoupling of the internal and the external, the infant exists in a state of "psychic equivalence" in which an exact correspondence is experienced between an internal state and external reality. Where the affect mirroring is not marked as "pretend", the display may be felt to be the caregiver's own emotion, induced by the infant, with the implication that emotions are contagious or otherwise unmanageable. The effect is likely to be that the infant's own emotion escalates, leading to "traumatisation rather than containment" (*ibid.*, p. 9). This undermines both the creation of secondary representations of emotion and the sense of a boundary between self and other. On the other hand, the display may be marked but inaccurate, not reflecting the infant's felt experience. In this case, the representation created will be a distortion of a primary experience, leading to mislabelling of emotions and a feeling of emptiness.

Obviously the environmental failure described here is not a one-off occasion of incongruent or unmarked affect mirroring. Human beings must be adapted to accommodate to a considerable degree of incongruent or non-contingent affect mirroring. But when the dominate mode of response of the caregiver is unmarked or incongruent, then the outcomes described may emerge.

So, Fonagy and colleagues are proposing that three critical abilities for social cognition, the capacity to regulate emotion and impulses, the sense of the self as an intentional agent, and the capacity to represent emotional states at a psychological level, are dependent on the infant's perception and internalization of the mother's empathic affective display. We may wonder where this leaves the infant with Asperger's who, according to Hobson's theory, lacks this fundamental capacity to read and respond to emotional expression. He is severely handicapped by the absence of this building block to social and emotional development, irrespective of the degree of attunement of his caregivers.

Mapping the theory with the patient.

In this section, I attempt to use Fonagy's theory to make sense of the behaviours and modes of interaction observed in my patients with Asperger's. In no sense do these observations comprise evidence in support of the applicability of the theory to this group of patients. They are, rather, illustrations of the utility of the theory. The collection of evidence needs to come later. I shall discuss the composite case with respect to four implications of the theory.

Absence of secondary representation of emotion and its expression as action rather than verbal communication

On many occasions, my patient experienced unmanageable anxiety and anger. Sometimes his anxiety was so intense that he repeatedly banged his head against a wall in an attempt to discharge it. At these times, he pleaded with me to take the feeling away. The emotion seemed to be experienced as a concrete assault, with no secondary representation allowing for understanding and communication. On another occasion, he was in a very anxious state about a matter that could not be resolved. He wanted to know under which section of the Mental Health Act he would be discharged, even though his discharge was not at all imminent and had not been planned. He repeated this question to me without interruption for forty-five minutes, despite my attempts to answer to the best of my knowledge and without deceit. Sometimes, when he was overcome by anger, any person in his immediate environment was vulnerable to physical assault. In these examples, the emotion is expressed as an action rather than verbal communication.

Misattribution of source of emotion

Given the difficulties in cognitive (secondary) representation of emotion, the source of an emotion or impulse was frequently assumed to be external. If the patient was attracted to a woman, this suggested to him that the woman was responsible for the feeling; therefore, she reciprocated the desire. This led to considerable confusion when his advances were not welcomed. On one occasion, he was attempting to give up smoking but suffering frequent relapses. He overheard a member of staff informing another patient that it was National No Smoking Day. He immediately attacked the member of staff, subsequently saying that he felt that the staff member was criticizing him.

Psychic equivalence

Fonagy and colleagues refer to the conflation of internal experience and external reality as a state of psychic equivalence. "What exists in the mind must exist out there, and what exists out there must invariably also exist in the mind" (Fonagy, Gergely, Jurist, & Target, 2004, p. 9). I understood my patient to be demonstrating a kind of psychic equivalence when he repeatedly stated that he "would never do it again" (his offence). His verbal statement, expressing a wish and an intention at that moment, was for him equivalent to the attainment of an objective in reality. It did not correspond to an attempt to deceive the other. It meant that he could not understand the need to discuss past offences, or to work on controlling his impulses, because the intention, for him, was "realized".

Difficulties in deriving comfort from the words or availability of another person

This was perhaps the most painful aspect of the condition to witness. Given the absence of secondary representation of emotion, and the consequent need to discharge it through action, the presence or the words of another person could not function as containment or comfort. During the above described episode of perseverative questioning about his section after discharge, when my attempts to answer his question failed to assuage his anxiety, I pointed this out to him with the suggestion that we think about what would be helpful. He could only respond "But are you telling me the truth?" I do not think he literally suspected me of attempting to deceive him. It seemed that his anxiety was so intense about his discharge, he felt his fears must be valid, and therefore my words "untrue". He could not be comforted by the thought that they may be true.

Implications for treatment

I hope it is now clear that traditional cognitive–behavioural methods for sex offender treatment are unlikely to be effective with this client group, particularly the emphasis on recognising cognitive distortions and promoting empathy. In the first place, a very explicit form of sex education needs to be implemented. This is accepted practice within learning disabled populations but it may be that the higher intelligence of the Asperger's man has erroneously led to its neglect. The education needs to be as concrete and as literal as possible, with didactic instructions about the management of sexual arousal and a set of invariant rules taught about the management of sexual relationships.

Second, some aspects of the dialectical behaviour therapy skills training programme for borderline personality disorder (Linehan, 1993) could be adapted for use with these clients. The aim would be to improve emotion regulation, distress tolerance, and interpersonal effectiveness but with a strong emphasis on behavioural rather than cognitive interventions. It may be possible to improve aware-ness of emotion and sexual arousal by rehearsing the describing and naming of the associated physical sensations and action urges as opposed to the usual emphasis on cognitive representation. Behavioural skills such as breathing exercises, relaxation training, and yoga will be useful concrete strategies for the regulation of emotion. The clients will benefit from repeated coaching in the use of verbal communication to describe emotions, to substitute for acting on the emotion.

It may also be possible to improve *in vivo* recognition of another's facial expression as a cue to interpretation of their feelings by teaching this in the concrete, didactic manner described above.

The hope is that by more accurately targeting the deficits that are specific to Asperger's syndrome, treatment and prevention programmes can reduce the risk of sex offending in these men, and avert the tragedy of long periods in detention.

Note

1. A definitive diagnosis requires a detailed early history which was not available in every case.

References

American Psychiatric Association (2000). *Diagnostic and Statistical Manual of Mental Disorders*, 4th edn. Washington, DC: American Psychiatric Association.

Asperger, H. (1944). Die "Austistischen Psychopathen" Im Kindesalter. *Archiv für Psychiatry umd Nervenkrankheiten*, 117: 76–136.

Baron-Cohen, S. (1988). An assessment of violence in a young man with Asperger's. *British Journal of Psychiatry*, 29: 351–360.

Baron-Cohen, S., Leslie, A. M., & Frith, U. (1985). Does the autistic child have a "theory of mind"? *Cognition*, 21: 37–46.

Berenbaum, H., Raghavan, C., Le, H.-N., Vernon, L., & Gomez, J. (2003). *Clinical Psychology: Science and Practice*, 10(2): 206–226.

Charman, T., Swettenham, J., Baron-Cohen, S., Cox, A., Baird, G., & Drew, A. (1997). Infants with autism: an investigation of empathy, pretend play, joint attention and imitation. *Developmental Psychology, 33*: 781–789.

Dennett, D. C. (1978). Beliefs about beliefs. *Behavioural and Brain Sciences,* 4: 568–570.

Ehlers, S., & Gillberg, C. (1993). The epidemiology of Asperger's syndrome. A total population study. *Journal of Child Psychology and Psychiatry, 34*: 1327–1350.

Ekman, P., & Friesen, V. W (1976). Pictures of facial affect (available from Paul Ekman, University of California).

Fonagy, P., Gergely, G., Jurist, E., Target, M. (2004). *Affect Regulation, Mentalization, and the Development of the Self.* London: Karnac.

Friendship, C., Mann, R., & Beech, A. (2003). *The Prison-based Sex Offender Treatment Programme—and Evaluation.* Home Office Research, Development and Statistics Directorate Findings 205.

Gergely, G., & Watson, J. (1999). Early social-emotional development: contingency perception and the social biofeedback model. In: P. Rochat (Ed.), *Early Social Cognition: Understanding Others in the First Months of Life* (pp. 101–137). Hillsdale, NJ: Lawrence Erlbaum.

Gillberg, C., & Gillberg, I. C. (1989). Asperger's Syndrome—some epidemiological consideration: A research note. *Journal of Child Psychology and Psychiatry, 30*: 631–638.

Gillberg, C., & Coleman, M. (Eds.) (1992). *The Biology of the Autistic Syndromes,* 2nd edn. London: Mackeith.

Happé, F. (1994). *Autism: An Introduction to Psychological Theory.* London: University College Press.

Hobson, P. (2002). *The Cradle of Thought.* London: Macmillan.

Kohn, Y., Fahum, T., Ratzoni, G., & Apter, A. (1998). Aggression and sexual offence in Asperger's syndrome. *Israeli Journal of Psychiatry and Related Science,* 4: 293–299.

Linehan, M. M. (1993). *Cognitive–Behavioural Treatment of Borderline Personality Disorder.* New York: Guilford Press.

Murrie, D. C., Warrren, J. I., Kristiansson, M., & Dietz, P. (2002). Asperger's Syndrome in forensic settings. *International Journal of Forensic Mental Health,* 1: 59–70.

Paris, J., Zweig-Frank, H., & Guzder, H. (1993). The role of psychological risk factors in recovery from borderline personality disorder. *Comprehensive Psychiatry, 34*: 410–413.

Rutter, M., Andersen-Wood, L., Becke, H. C., Bredenkamp, D., Castle, J., Groothues, J., Keaveney, L., Lord, C., O'Connor, T. G., and the English and Romanian adoptees study team (1999). Quasi-autistic patterns following severe early global privation. *Journal of Child Psychology and Psychiatry*, 40: 537–549.

Scragg, P., & Shah, A. (1994). Prevalence of Asperger's syndrome in a secure hospital. *British Journal of Psychiatry*, 5: 679–682.

Steffenburg, S., & Gillberg, C. (1989). The aetiology of autism. In: C. Gillberg (Ed.), *Diagnosis and Treatment of Autism* (pp. 63–82). New York: Plenum.

Wimmer, H., & Perner, J. (1983). Beliefs about beliefs: representation and the constraining function of wrong beliefs in young children's understanding of deception. *Cognition, 13*: 103–128.

Wing, L., & Gould, J. (1979). Severe impairments of social interaction and associated abnormalities in children: epidemiology and classification. *Journal of Autism and Developmental Disorders, 9*: 11–29.

PART II

CLIENT GROUPS POSING
NEW CHALLENGES

CHAPTER THREE

Compulsive use of internet pornography

Heather Wood

Introduction

The compulsive use of internet pornography is a new phenomenon. Given how recently it has appeared, there is an impressive body of literature about the characteristics of users (e.g. Delmonico & Miller, 2003), compulsive activities (Schneider, 2000), attendant problems (e.g. Schneider, 2003), and treatment approaches (e.g. Delmonico, Griffin, & Carnes, 2002). Indeed, thorough reviews of the literature already exist, which obviate the need for further such reviews at present (see for example Griffin-Shelley, 2003). This literature is, however, marked by the scarcity of psychoanalytic perspectives. A psychoanalytic perspective may be useful in examining the phenomenon and its significance, in raising questions about the aetiology and psychodynamics of the condition and in considering whether psychoanalytic exploration offers an important dimension to treatment that would otherwise be lacking.

My perspective on these issues has two cornerstones: first, I share the excitement of many of the authors cited here for the internet, e-mail, this technology and its scope and complexity. I also think it is important to reflect on that excitement and its implications. Second, as a clinician in a specialist psychotherapy service, I work with people who are already in serious difficulty with the internet; some already have convictions, others risk conviction; some would be seen to have formal paraphilias, most feel that their compulsive use is damaging to them and their relationships. My perspective is shaped by working with people who are themselves very concerned about their behaviour and seek understanding that might enable them to surmount this problem, and not through experience with casual users.

In describing treatment strategies for individuals who become obsessed with sexuality on the internet, Delmonico, Griffin, and Carnes (2002) refer to such people as "sexually lost in cyberspace" (p. 148). "Lost in cyberspace" is also an expression used by Greenfield and Davis (2002) when discussing the use of the internet at work. The sense of being "lost" captures both the helplessness that some individuals feel in relation to this phenomenon, and the desire to "lose oneself", to escape into a fantasy world. The image of the patient who is "lost" is perhaps also intended to foster compassion and concern amongst clinicians. The sense of the individual in a vulnerable, powerless position is in keeping with much of the literature on compulsive users of internet pornography, which emphasizes a behavioural addiction to a potent, almost irresistible, sexual "drug". Greenfield and Orzak (2002) describe how the intoxicating mix of sexual stimulation and the "potent nature of the Internet medium", lead to a situation where a cycle of arousal and compulsion "almost . . . spontaneously ignites" (p. 135).

While individuals with such problems undoubtedly warrant compassion and concern, the risk of this model is that the patient is implicitly seen to be helpless in the face of an overwhelming stimulus and is thus disempowered. Some authors (e.g. Carnes, 2003; Laaser & Gregoire, 2003) question whether an addiction model or a model of obsessive–compulsive behaviour is more appropriate. From a broadly CBT perspective, Quayle, Vaughan, and Taylor (in press) challenge the validity of the addiction model and the failure to ascertain what exactly it is the individual is "addicted" to. They suggest that the terms "excessive, problematic or maladaptive" internet use may be more useful, and allow for the "unique role that the Internet may play in meeting other emotional needs". This is

is he afraid to go on the internet because of his compulsion to P.

not dissimilar to a psychoanalytic perspective, which would address the unconscious meaning that a particular image or inter-personal scenario has for an individual. A psychoanalytic perspective would ask what it is about the individual that determines whether a particular stimulus is experienced as boring, intoxicating, or aversive? What does the individual bring to this situation that leads to them "becoming lost" in the world of pornographic images, often for hours at a time? What enables some people to exercise self-control, while another loses all self-restraint? Although the exploration of such questions may involve facing painful truths about the self, in practice it may ultimately be more empowering to the patient.

A psychoanalytic perspective raises the question as to whether people who are addicted to internet pornography are "lost", or whether in fact they have found images or scenarios that have, for them, a profound and compelling unconscious resonance. Perhaps they have not arrived somewhere strange and unfamiliar, but have "come home" to a place in their minds that has a long history. To arrive at that place they appear to have opened doors in their minds that previously may have been closed. Imagery that they might once have considered shocking or unacceptable is now regarded as acceptable and, indeed, arousing. Carnes (2003) argues persuasively that the internet provides stimulation that accesses unresolved issues such as trauma, loss, or abuse in some individuals. He also poses the question of how it is that some individuals seem to become fixated on behaviours that they never knew existed prior to going on the computer (p. 311). To some extent these are empirical questions that warrant further investigation, but psychoanalytic insights, derived from theory and clinical work with patients, may cast some light on these issues.

The extent of the problem

What proportion of people who use online sexual activity may be in difficulty? Greenfield (1999) conducted a survey of 17,251 respondents and concluded that 6% were internet addicted, and of these 20% were sexually addicted, suggesting that a little over 1% of internet users may develop an addiction to online sexual activity.

Cooper, Delmonico, and Burg (2000) conducted an online survey of over 9000 people engaged in online sexual activity (chat rooms, viewing pornography, etc.). They found that 80% of respondents reported no significant repercussions from their online sexual activity, but the remaining 20% were deemed to be at risk of developing problems, or were out of control of their online sexual activity (Cooper, Delmonico, & Burg, 2000). Respondents who engaged in eleven hours or more per week of online sexual behaviours reported significantly more adverse consequences, and eleven hours per week has become a cut-off to discriminate recreational from compulsive users. Cooper, Delmonico, and Burg (2000) identified 1% of their sample as "cybersex addicts", based on eleven hours or more per week of online sexual activity and a score two standard deviations above the mean on Kalichman's Sexual Compulsivity Scale (Kalichman *et al.*, 1994). Given the number of internet users, the projected number of people likely to have serious difficulties with online sexual activity is very considerable.

Initial studies suggest that there may be gender differences in preferred online activities. Ferree (2003) offers a useful categorization of online sexual behaviours. She distinguishes between solitary activities (viewing and distributing pornography, reading written material) and interactive activity. Interactive activities include exchanging e-mail, participation in chat rooms, engagement in cybersex (communicating online while masturbating), and, at the more extreme end of the scale, "virtual locations" where the individual receives live video feedback and dictates the scenario to be enacted. Drawing on Cooper, Delmonico, and Burg's (2000) large survey, she concludes, "Simply put, women's online sexual behaviour mirrors their offline behaviour: Females most often favour relationally-oriented activity" (p. 388). However, it is important not to ignore the significant minority of women who access pornography, and the fact that women are disproportionately represented among those who progress beyond recreational use to compulsive or "addictive" use (Cooper, Delmonico, & Burg, 2000). Ferree also observes that women are much more likely than men to attempt to have real-life meetings with online sexual partners, with attendant risks.

In keeping with Ferree's observations, Schneider (2000), on the basis of an empirical study of forty-five men and ten women who identified themselves as "cybersex participants", concludes that, "Compared with men, the women clearly preferred chats to viewing pornography". In contrast to this view, Leiblum and Doring (2002) insist that any generalization about women's use of the internet is likely to be an oversimplification, as women use the internet in diverse and often contradictory ways. Early studies thus suggest trends, but there is no consensus about gender differences.

Characteristics of the literature

Much of the literature on internet usage and internet pornography is characterized by three phenomena: first, a sense of awe and excitement, second, novel research methodologies, and third, the use of new language and terminology.

The global scale of the internet seems to invite expressions of awe. Cooper and Griffin-Shelley (2002) assert that "A new sexual revolution has begun with the explosion of electronic technology, computers, and especially the recent, rapid expansion of the Internet" (p. 2). They refer to the "staggering growth" (*ibid.*) of the internet and its "exponential expansion" (*ibid.*, p. 4) and describe the power of the internet to "turbocharge, that is, accelerate and intensify" online sexual activity. Cooper (1997) coined the expression the "triple A engine" to describe the characteristics of (easy) access, affordability, and (apparent) anonymity that lend the internet particular appeal as a vehicle for sexual exploration and expression.

Delmonico, Griffin, and Carnes (2002), in likening "cybersex" to a drug, report that "Cybersex creates a virtual world in which participants can be whomever they wish, engage in erotic behaviours, and live out fantasies that could never before be realized" (p. 147). Corley and Corley (1994, cited in Griffin-Shelley, 2003) are credited with coining the notion that internet pornography is "the crack cocaine of pornography", and this equation is now prevalent in the literature (e.g., Schneider, 2000).

This rather excited representation of the power and range of the internet is not without basis in reality. Estimates from September 2002 suggest that 182.67 million people in the US and Canada had internet access, 190 million in Europe, and 605.60 million worldwide (nua.com). Cooper, Delmonico, and Burg (2000) estimated that 20% of internet users engaged in some form of online sexual activity, while Gabbard (2001) quotes from the *New York Times* that one third of adult internet visits are to sexually-orientated chat rooms, websites and news groups. Sexual pursuits apparently account for almost 70% of all dollars spent online (Sprenger, 1999, cited in Cooper & Griffin-Shelley, 2002). In a review of the use of "virtual sexuality in the workplace", Cooper, McLoughlin, and Campbell (2000) distill findings from a number of large-sample studies which suggest that 20% of respondents reported using the internet for sexual activities while at work. Carnes (2003) notes that 70% of internet pornography traffic occurs between nine and five.

Thus, internet usage, use for sexual means, and abuses of the internet at work are extensive. However, it may be this fusion of the rapid expansion of a technological phenomenon with sexuality that lends this field of study a particular air of excitement. Cooper and Griffin-Shelley (2002) consider that, "Since its inception, the Internet has been inextricably associated with sexuality in a synergystic dance, each fuelling and ultimately contributing to the transformation of the other" (p. 4). Young (1998) suggests that the intimacy and immediacy of the internet and e-mail communication make it inherently erotic "in the generic, early Freudian sense of serving the life force". Yet, it may be these very qualities that also render it an ideal target for exploitation by commercial sex industries and those with sexual interests that are socially marginalized or proscribed.

The second distinguishing characteristic of the literature is the huge sample sizes that can be obtained from posting questionnaires on websites. Cooper, Scherer, Boies, and Gordon (1999) report a sample size of 9,265 respondents. Greenfield (1999) obtained 17,251 responses to his "Virtual Addiction Survey". Young (1998) refers to an ongoing statistical survey of internet consumers that at that time, had had 25,623 respondents. The internet invites surveys using self-report questionnaires by self-selected subjects. While significant results generated from such studies may be seen to be very robust, the bias inherent in the sampling technique is evident. It is notable that those people who collect pornographic images from the internet often have vast collections. Those who are prosecuted are often reported to be in possession of tens of thousands of images. Sophisticated computer technology offers vast memory stores, easy access to thousands if not millions of people, and the potential to scan thousands of images in search of those that have the power to arouse or excite. There is a danger that the vast scale of such phenomena obscures the subtleties and differences between individual cases. Indeed, Quayle and Taylor's (2002) thought-provoking and detailed analysis of interviews with thirteen men convicted of downloading child pornography provides a refreshing counterbalance to this trend.

The third conspicuous phenomenon is the creation of a new language, the language of "cybersex", "cyberpsychology", "virtual sex addiction", "cyberstalking", "cyberspace" and "OSA (online sexual activity)". RL (real life) and f2f (face-to-face) also warrant abbreviations, as if they are just other domains to be visited in a virtual world. New technological phenomena may require new terms, but language may also be used to define "in-groups", to create a sense of belonging and to manipulate consumer perceptions of products. The language of cyberspace seems intended to define this phenomenon as futuristic, technological (clean, scientific), adventurous and on a vast scale. In "space" the person is weightless, free from the constraints of relationships. I would suggest that the language is also inherently concerned with power and a form of authority deriving from apparent mastery.

This sense of awe, excitement, and grandeur that characterizes the literature is in marked contrast to the reality for some people of masturbating compulsively to pornographic imagery, usually in social isolation and in secret.

Psychoanalytic characteristics of compulsive use of Internet pornography

A transitional space or narcissistic object-relating?

A distinct feature of the internet is the creation of a space that is both real and not real. Gabbard (2001), describing a patient who was able to express an erotic transference through e-mails to her analyst before being able to bring this into the consulting room, suggests that "Virtual space has a lot in common with transitional space, in the sense that it is not truly an internal realm, but lies somewhere between external reality and our internal world" (p. 734). He perceives this potential to play with self-expression and the sense of personal identity as a potentially constructive force. Young (1998) also briefly explores the idea that "cyberspace" may be seen as a Winnicottian "transitional space", "neither subjective nor objective but partaking of both".

Winnicott (1951) considers that, in earliest infancy, the mother's responsiveness and adaptation allows the infant the illusion that it has "created" the breast or the mother which is desired. In due course, the infant must face disillusionment, the realization that the mother is separate and beyond his or her omnipotent control. The transition from illusion to an accurate perception of external reality may be buffered if the infant is allowed "transitional objects", a thumb to suck, a piece of blanket to clutch or a bear, which represent in part the baby, in part the mother, but primarily the relationship between them. In Winnicott's terms "It comes from without from our point of view, but not so from the point of view of the baby. Neither does it come from within; it is not an hallucination" (*ibid.*, p. 233). This is an object that the infant can control, that can survive being loved and hated, until the distinction between internal and external reality is more comfortably established and the object can be allowed to diminish in significance.

It is a feature of transitional objects that they can bring great comfort and function as "soothers", symbolizing a relationship in which the individual feels held and contained. Some users of internet pornography appear to derive this type of comfort and relief from engaging with a medium in which there is some sense of an other, but an other who does not impose their own reality. The images that are viewed are not hallucinations, but neither do they have the autonomy and vitality of an other. The individual may explore fantasies of the perfect body, the idealized partner, or simply extend their sexual education in a world without apparent consequences. Shame about ignorance or inexperience may be lessened in this world where there is no other as witness, and the object may be loved or hated but no apparent harm is done. A significant proportion of people who use online sexual activity report doing so as a way of dealing with stress. Cooper, Griffin-Shelley, Delmonico, and Mathy (2001) found that 56% of individuals with online sexual problems reported using internet sexual activity as a way of dealing with stress, compared with 30% of internet users without problems of compulsive use. Quayle, Vaughan and Taylor (in press) develop a treatment model on the assumption that individuals use the internet to change or avoid negative mood states; this behaviour is then reinforced by the sexual response.

At the point at which the individual has developed a compulsive and problematic relationship to internet pornography, this transitional space appears to have lost the benign quality of a play space, and has become a forum for more pathological processes.[1] The "other" with whom the individual imagines they are engaged, whether it is a person in a static image or a respondent in a chat room, will only be tolerated while they comply with the scenario that is being sought. Thus, what is engaged with is not an other who embodies difference, nor a transitional space where an individual may safely play with the fantasy of an other, but an other who must have fixed characteristics that coincide exactly with the "script" that is sought. The "other" then has no independent existence, but becomes a vessel for the projection of fantasy. The relationship is not one of mutuality, but of narcissistic engagement with a projected internal object. Laaser and Gregoire (2003), in their discussion of pastors with cybersex addiction, acknowledge the role of pre-existing narcissistic traits. They note,

> For these pastors the attraction of the Internet lies in the sense of "control" gained from being in charge of turning it on and off, and selecting what they want to look at. They will gravitate towards the images of people who seem to be saying to them, "I find you incredibly attractive and I would do anything for you". [Laaser & Gregoire, 2003, pp. 398–399]

For some people this "real/not real" quality ceases to offer a pleasurable playground, but becomes an almost psychotic "riddle" by which they are tormented. If the character they view is "real", why can they not have him or her? The individual may worry that the barrier between fantasy and reality will be eroded, and that they will be drawn into enactment. Conversely, if the character is not real, why does he or she have such power to excite? People can recognize that the scenarios are staged and the actors are paid, and yet find them so convincing that they are disturbed that they could be duped or manipulated in this way. Thus, the "transitional space" can potentially become suffused with a feeling of being the object of seductive teasing or callous manipulation, and the individual may feel prey to primitive and disturbing anxieties.

Empowerment or manic defences?

The second key characteristic of the internet is that it can be empowering. Individuals can communicate with others across the world in an instant; staggering amounts of information are accessible within seconds; individuals can trace people who share the same name, the same academic interests, or the same sexual predilections or anxieties with ease. Tepper and Owens (2002) provide a moving case description of a thirty-seven-year-old quadraplegic man who, through the internet, not only began to be able to communicate about sexual thoughts and feelings, but subsequently met a partner with whom he developed a physical relationship. Adams, Oye, and Parker (2003) document the value of the internet for older adults in making contacts, experimenting and broadening their knowledge of sex, thereby challenging stereotypes about sexuality in later life. The potential for positive uses of empowerment is undeniable.

From a psychoanalytic point of view, those very qualities of the internet that bestow a potential for empowerment also bestow a potential for manic excitement. In psychoanalytic terms, the appeal of the internet for sexual activity may go beyond "access, affordability, and anonymity". Online sexual activity potentially feeds manic defences and omnipotence. The internet allows the individual to deny any reliance on another; the individual can control what happens, the part which they wish to play, and exactly when it should end. In pornography there is no unpredictable other who might accept or reject, cherish or criticize them. In chat rooms there is an other, but contact can be terminated in an instant. With both pornography and chat rooms the person can avoid the exposure entailed in intimacy with a partner: exposure of the physical body and aspects of themselves about which they feel ashamed or vulnerable. Young (1996) notes that this lack of physicality means that "the net is in important ways uncontained; it has no boundaries, no skin, no density" (p. 8). He quotes Turkle (1995), who questions the implications of "spinning off virtual personae that can run around with names and genders of our choosing, unhindered by the weight and physicality of embodiment?" (p. 249).

Segal (1975), summarizing Klein's views, notes that manic defences are organized against the whole experience of depending on, valuing, and being vulnerable in relation to the object, originally the maternal object. These experiences would be seen to characterize the "depressive position" in which the other is recognized to be separate, cannot be omnipotently controlled, may come and go at will, and may potentially be harmed by the aggressive and destructive feelings that emanate from within the self. Dependency is therefore inevitably accompanied by ambivalence, and potentially feelings of guilt, loss, and mourning. When manic defences are employed, feelings of dependency and vulnerability are replaced by "a triad of feelings— control, triumph and contempt" (Segal, 1975, p. 83). She suggests that "Control is a way of denying dependence yet compelling the object to fulfill the need for dependence since an object that is wholly controlled is, up to a point, one that can be depended upon". Triumph serves both to devalue the object (and so mitigate any potential feelings of envy), and to counter any feelings such as pining or longing. Contempt also devalues the object and an object that is of no value is not worthy of guilt— the object can be treated mercilessly because its fate is of no consequence.

While the "primary object" on whom our survival depends is usually seen to be the mother, the body is also a primary object on which the individual depends, which renders us vulnerable, whose imperfections we have to recognize and live with, and which may be ambivalently loved or attacked. Freud (1923b) recognized that the ego, the sense of self, is founded in the sense of the body.

In freeing individuals from all bodily constraints—in virtual reality the man can become a woman, a child, an Adonis, a fearless stud—the internet cuts the threads of physical embodiment that always tie us to an imperfect (and "depressive") reality.

A common theme in the literature is the disowning of responsibility for the images that are viewed. The distancing effects of scale, technology, and anonymity enable the individual to distance himself from guilt about the creation of images. Quayle and Taylor (2002) provide some stark evidence from their interview study that, for some, child pornography became "collectibles", likened by interviewees to baseball cards, stamps, or works of art to be collected, categorized, and traded. Respondents would emphasize the importance of collecting complete series, and sorting and categorizing pictures. This was invariably associated with an absence of any reference to the fact that what was being collected was child pornography. Indeed, "Depersonalising of the pictures was seen most strongly when reference was made to the pictures as trophies" (*ibid.*, p. 13). Manic defences are not simply allowed or endorsed, but seem to be actively fuelled by qualities of the internet.

Even when the internet is used to enact fantasies in which the individual is debased or made to suffer, that person is secretly in control, dictating the preferred scenario and terminating it when they have had enough. Thus, in the private world of the relationship with the computer, the individual may have the illusion that he or she is supremely powerful and invulnerable, or, if this is projected, that he or she is at the mercy of a supremely powerful other.

Self-expression or compelling regression?

Third, the quality of the sexual response is significant. For casual users of the internet, this may be a channel for sexual expression, experimentation, and the seeking of compatible partners. Some casual users may soon become satiated or bored. Goodson, McCormick, and Evans (2001), in a study of college students' responses to sexually explicit material on the internet, found that sexual arousal was the fourth most frequently cited response, less frequently acknowledged than entertainment, disgust, and general excitement. Many articles attest to the constructive potential of the internet for those who, as a result of disability, inhibition, or minority sexual interests, might otherwise have difficulty meeting potential sexual partners (e.g., Tepper & Owens, 2002).

There are a several groups for whom internet sexual activity may be less constructive or innocuous. Carnes, Delmonico, and Griffin (2001) suggest a typology for distinguishing between different types of users. They identify "appropriate recreational users", who report no adverse consequences, and "inappropriate recreational users", who are not compulsive users but use sexual information gathered from the internet at inappropriate times or share it with inappropriate people, as if they are unaware of or ignoring social norms. The "discovery group" reputedly have no prior inappropriate sexual fantasies or behaviours, but the internet serves as a trigger for problematic usage. The "predisposed" group already have indicators of problematic sexual behaviour, which seem to be fuelled by the internet. Finally, "lifelong sexual compulsives" have had longstanding problems and may use the internet as an extension of this behaviour as a way to avoid more risky forms of acting out, or to heighten arousal and add new risks to already problematic behaviours.

Empirical studies seem to bear out these distinctions. Schneider's (2000) survey of forty-five men and ten women who identified themselves as "cybersex participants", in difficulty with online sexual activity, has already been referred to. Subjects were contacted through therapists known to treat sex addicts. She concludes that "accessing sex on the Internet has the potential to escalate pre-existing sex addiction as well as to create new addictive disorders in previously at-risk users" (ibid., p. 18). Unfortunately, Schneider's data does not illuminate the risk factors in those without pre-existing "sexual addiction". Of her sample, 92% of the men and 90% of the women identified themselves as current and/or former sex addicts. However, the clinical group that is of particular theoretical interest is Carnes, Delmonico, and Griffin's "discovery group", the small minority in Schneider's study who have no apparent previous history.

Analysing in-depth interviews with thirteen men convicted of downloading paedophilic images from the internet, Quayle and Taylor (2002) see the internet, in most cases, as providing an embodiment and an escalation of pre-existing sexual fantasies. They suggest that the subjective response to pornography may depend on "how well the depicted content matches the individual's existing, preferred sexual script". However, they also acknowledge the existence of a small group in whom there was no apparent evidence of a prior interest in this material, and distinguish between the majority for whom excessive use of the internet for sexual purposes is symptomatic of pre-existing difficulties, and the small minority for whom the internet "may be functionally addictive" (ibid., p. 24).

Freud (1905d) championed the idea that adult sexuality is not a given, but is the end-product of a complex process of biological maturation and psycho-social development which commences in infancy. For the newborn, it is the mouth that is most charged with excitation and pleasure; experiences at this early stage combine with those of the anal, phallic, Oedipal, latency, and pubertal stages to shape adult sexual preferences. Adult sexual functioning does not replace these earlier stages, but bears the imprint of all of them, in the pleasure taken in the various erotic zones of the body, and varied sexual practices. Behaviour that was not directed to sexual intercourse with a heterosexual object was viewed as "perverse", but this perversity was so commonplace as to be normal (see Chapter Eleven). Freud therefore coined the term "polymorphously perverse" to describe the way adult sexuality adopted different forms.

Within this view, an adult who suddenly "discovers" that a particular sexual object, scenario, or behaviour is compelling and arousing will not be venturing into uncharted territory, but will be unearthing an image that has unconscious resonance, even from early childhood. In Freud's (with Breuer, 1895d) view, "symptoms" are often "overdetermined". In the course of analysis we discover that there is not a single cause, but multiple experiences that seem to have led to this point; one of these experiences alone would probably not have been sufficient to produce or sustain the symptom (see Laplanche & Pontalis, 1973). Thus, the person who develops a sexual fixation on being slapped may have been slapped at a pivotal moment in their sexual development by a character who was seen to be exciting or arousing; however, they may also have been subjected to repeated emotional humiliation (without any sexual component), and have witnessed physical brutality between the parents that at the time was terrifying. Sexualization of the humiliation and helplessness may enable the individual to convert pain to pleasure, powerlessness to empowerment, and "trauma to triumph" (Stoller, 1975). The slapping itself may have acquired additional meaning through a religious upbringing and association with the injunction to "turn the other cheek". Each of these childhood experiences may therefore have contributed to the eventual form of the symptom, but their significance may remain unconscious until exploration in therapy.

Laufer (1976) proposes that the child enters puberty with a "central masturbation fantasy", which may be largely unconscious, but which is an internalized scenario determined by their primary object relationships. In his view, the content of this fantasy "contains the various regressive satisfactions and the main sexual identifications" (*ibid.*, p. 300) Laufer considers that this fantasy is fixed by the resolution of the Oedipus complex, and although the fantasy may take on a new meaning in adolescence as the young person assimilates the significance of mature genitals, "*the content of this central masturbation fantasy does not normally alter during adolescence*" (*ibid.*, original italics). Thus, Laufer suggests that the core object relationships and erotic focus of an adult masturbation fantasy will have been established by pre-Oedipal and Oedipal experiences in the first years of life.

Psychoanalytic exploration often reveals that the particular pornographic scenario upon which an individual becomes fixated has multiple meanings in terms of the person's history, and may have been "overdetermined" in the way Freud describes. I would question Laufer's insistence that the central fantasy becomes fixed at such an early age, since latency and adolescent experiences seem highly influential, but the "compelling scenario" often seems to encapsulate pivotal experiences and object relationships from childhood and adolescence. What the internet appears to offer is a massive library that allows the person to trawl through vast numbers of images or scenarios at great speed, until they alight upon that particular configuration which is, for them, compelling. It is conceivable that, by this means, some people discover sexual preferences that they might never have discovered through ordinary experience. These images may seem "novel" because they are at odds with the sexual imagery or opportunities generally available in adult life. However, I would suggest that they are not "new" but are often very "old", referring back to adolescent, Oedipal or pre-Oedipal attachments to bodily functions, body parts, activities, or people. The internet also offers the possibility that when satiation renders the image less exciting, more extreme versions can be found to heighten arousal. A psychoanalytic perspective would dispute the view that it is the nature of the "addictive substance" or the pornography *per se* that fosters fixation and dependency. Rather, it is the invitation to regress to existing points of fixation (which may have remained unconscious were it not for this unusual stimulus) that renders this material so compelling. Carnes (2003), whose model is not psychoanalytic, arrives at a similar view when he suggests that "Core to this process [of therapy] is determining a 'governing scenario' or 'ideal fantasy' which has now become problematic" (p. 327). A challenging question for all in this field is whether those in Carnes, Delmonico, and Griffin's (2001) "discovery group" or Quayle and Taylor's (2002) subjects with a "functional addiction" actually develop a fixation on images that have no prior unconscious significance, or whether there is an unconscious significance that remains to be identified.

Powerful parent or corrupt superego?

The internet has many of the characteristics of a powerful parent: it knows "everything", it is immediately responsive, it can be summoned at will, and it relieves boredom and loneliness. Rather like a benign psychoanalyst, e-mail invites the person to "say whatever comes into their mind" and to express barely formed thoughts or ideas, free from the requirement that prevails in face-to-face interaction, to monitor the reaction of the other. Young (1996, 1998) describes the openness, co-operation and creativity which this can foster. Yet the internet is also a parent who never says "No". Indeed, elaborate systems exist to tempt the user to remain online, to visit additional websites, or to scan more extreme imagery.

Galbreath, Berlin, and Sawyer (2002), discussing paraphilias and the internet, draw on Berlin and Krout's (1986) typology of the ways people differ from each other sexually: the kinds of partners they are drawn to, the kinds of behaviours they find erotically stimulating, the intensity of their sexual desires, and their attitudes about whether or not they should resist doing so. It is this last area that is little discussed with reference to the internet, yet that seems central.

If people all have the capacity for "polymorphously perverse", regressive forms of sexuality, what is it that keeps the majority of adults pursuing relationships with other adults and employing sexual practices that do no harm to either? First, there are external controls: the law, which prohibits sex with minors or animals, and imposes restrictions on the materials that can be published and sold freely. Young (2003) suggests that these external controls have been eroded by the internet:

I submit that the internet is producing a large increase in deviant sexuality for the simple and obvious reason that one no longer needs to take the pornographic magazine to the cash till, enter a so-called "private shop" or receive an envelope or package in the post that might elicit curiosity from people in one's household. [Young, 2003]

Implicit in this account is the observation that others serve as witnesses and activate self-consciousness, which may act as a brake or restraint on behaviour. The world of internet pornography allows the illusion that there are no witnesses.

Second, there are internal controls, what Freud would have thought of as the superego, embracing the conscience and the ideals to which we aspire. In Freud's view, the superego forms when the child relinquishes longings for the opposite-sex parent at the Oedipal stage and recognizes that he or she is a child who could not be a partner for the parent. As Freud focused on development in the boy, it was the father who laid down the "law" of the social order, and represented the prohibition on an incestuous relationship between the boy and his mother. Contemporary psychoanalysts, following Klein and Bion (see Britton, Feldman, and O'Shaugh-nessey, 1989), believe that a primitive superego is in evidence from infancy onwards and bears the imprint, not only of Oedipal experiences at age four or five, but Oepdial and two-person relationships from the first year of life onwards. While the pivotal role that Freud attributed to the prohibition on incest in the development of the conscience may be in doubt, the comprehension of social taboos on specific sexual partners and extreme sexual behaviours remains an integral part of development and, ultimately, an integral part of the adult superego. A significant part of this capacity for self-control will be transmitted through the parents or carers and their sense of boundaries in relationships.

There are people in whom the superego is very firmly established, and who may exert their own controls, declining to view extreme pornographic imagery, quickly finding it unappealing, and preferring instead the challenges of an engagement with an adult partner. In some the superego appears fragile, and the influence of a persuasive, seductive, external "parent" such as the internet may be strong. There is anecdotal evidence that people with sexual addiction have commonly had early exposure to pornography, and it is striking how frequently patients with these difficulties refer to discovery of pornography belonging to the father or a male relative in early adolescence. From a psychoanalytic point of view it is as though the immature superego has been breached; the father no longer embodies prohibition, but is seen to be unable to contain his own polymorphous sexual interests and voyeurism (or exhibitionism if the pornographic materials were designed to be found by the son). From a social learning perspective, this might also be seen as a situation where the parental figure acts as a role model whom the child then imitates.

There may be other developmental factors contributing to this fragility or breaching of the superego that remain to be delineated. The impact of a mother who "turns a blind eye" and is seen to be complicit in the father's practices, may also be considerable. But in some vulnerable patients, the internet "parent" that communicates, "have more, don't stop, there are no rules" appears to function as a corrupt superego, seducing the individual into a universe where "anything goes".

Conclusions

While many authors attest to the constructive potential of online sexual activity, for some people the aim of such activity appears not to be to engage with others and to experience and express thoughts and feelings, but to avoid the anxiety of genuine engagement or the experience of emotions such as vulnerability, loneliness, or depression. Affects such as hostility, sadism, and triumph may be enacted in fantasy in the sexual domain. The sexual response, usually masturbating to orgasm, then becomes the "fix" that seals this behaviour as a source of visceral pleasure.

In psychoanalytic terms, use of internet pornography may be so compelling and addictive for some individuals because it allows the simultaneous enactment of manic defences, narcissistic difficulties in engagement, and regressive sexual fantasies. "Access, affordability, and anonymity" may play a part, but the allure of this mix of technology and sexuality may ultimately rest in its ability to allow enactment of unconscious conflicts and fantasies. In the presence of few external controls, restrictions, or prohibitions, some individuals are able to exert self-control; others, whose internal controls are more precarious, may find themselves caught in an unhappy spiral of increasingly compulsive behaviour. Treatment programmes that focus on regaining control may have an important role, but for some patients, unravelling the unconscious meaning of the compulsion and the compelling scenario seems to be essential.

Note

1. "Problematic usage" may be reflected in the amount of time spent accessing internet pornography, or it may be evident in the relationship to the images, irrespective of time spent.

References

Adams, M. S., Oye, J., & Parker, T. S. (2003). Sexuality of older adults and the Internet: from sex education to cybersex. *Sexual and Relationship Therapy*, *18*(3): 405–415.

Berlin, F. S., & Krout, E. K. (1986). Pedophilia: Diagnostic concepts, treatment and ethical considerations. *American Journal of Forensic Psychiatry*, *7*: 13–30.

Britton, R., Feldman, M., & O'Shaughnessey, E. (1989). *The Oedipus Complex Today*. London: Karnac.

Carnes, P. J. (2003). The anatomy of arousal: three Internet portals. *Sexual and Relationship Therapy*, *18*(3): 309–328.

Carnes, P. J., Delmonico, D. L. & Griffin, E. J. (2001). *In the Shadows of the Net; Breaking Free from Compulsive Online Sexual Behaviour*. Center City, MH: Hazledon Foundation Press.

Cooper, A. (1997). The Internet and sexuality: into the new millennium. *Journal of Sex Education and Therapy*, *22*: 5–6.

Cooper, A., & Griffin-Shelley, E. (2002). Introduction. The Internet: the next sexual revolution. In: A. Cooper (Ed.), *Sex and the Internet*. New York: Brunner Routledge.

Cooper, A., Delmonico, D., & Burg, R. (2000). Cybersex users and abusers: new findings and implications. *Sexual Addiction and Compulsivity: Journal of Treatment and Prevention*, *1–2*: 5–30

Cooper, A., Griffin-Shelley, E., Delmonico, D. L., & Mathy, R. (2001). Online sexual problems: assessment and predictive variables. *Sexual Addiction and Compulsivity: The Journal of Treatment and Prevention, 8*: 267–285.

Cooper, A., McLoughlin, I. P., & Campbell, K. M. (2000). Sexuality in cyberspace: update for the 21st century. *CyberPsychology and Behaviour, 3*(4): 521–536.

Cooper, A., Scherer, C., Boies, S. C., & Gordon, B. (1999). Sexuality on the Internet: from sexual exploration to pathological expression. *Professional Psychology: Research and Practice, 30*(2): 154–164.

Delmonico, D. L., & Miller, J. A. (2003). The Internet Sex Screening Test: a comparison of sexual compulsives versus non-sexual compulsives. *Sexual and Realtionship Therapy, 18*(3): 261–276.

Delmonico, D. L., Griffin, E., & Carnes, P. J. (2002). Treating online compulsive sexual behaviour: when cybersex is the drug of choice. In: A. Cooper (Ed.), *Sex and the Internet*. New York: Brunner Routledge.

Ferree, M. C. (2003). Women and the web: cybersex activity and implications. *Sexual and Relationship Therapy, 18*(3): 385–393.

Freud, S. (1905d). Three essays on the theory of sexuality. *S.E., 7.* London: Hogarth.

Freud, S, (1923b). The ego and the id. *S.E., 19.* London: Hogarth.

Freud, S., & Breuer, J. (1895d). Studies on hysteria. *S.E., 20.* London: Hogarth.

Gabbard, G. O. (2001). Cyberpassion: E-rotic transference on the Internet. *Psychoanalytic Quarterley, LXX:* 719–737.

Galbreath, N. W., Berlin, F. S., & Sawyer, D. (2002). Paraphilias and the Internet. In: A.Cooper (Ed.), *Sex and the Internet*. New York: Brunner Routledge.

Goodson, P., McCormick, D., & Evans, A. (2001). Sex on the Internet: College students' emotional arousal when viewing sexually explicit materials online. *Journal of Sex Education and Therapy, 25*(4): 252–260.

Greenfield, D. N. (1999). Psychological characteristics of compulsive Internet use: a preliminary analysis. *CyberPsychology and Behaviour, 2*(5): 403–412.

Greenfield, D. N., & Davis, R. A. (2002). Lost in cyberspace: the Web@ work. *CyberPsychology and Behaviour, 5*(4): 347–353.

Greenfield, D., & Orzak, M. (2002). The electronic bedroom: clinical assessment of online sexual problems and internet-enabled sexual behaviour. In: A.Cooper (Ed.), *Sex and the Internet*. New York: Brunner Routledge.

Griffin-Shelley, E. (2003). The Internet and sexuality: a literature review—1983–2002. *Sexual and Relationship Therapy, 18*(3): 355–370.

Kalichman, S. C., Johnson, R. R., Adair, V., Rompa, D., Multhauf, K., & Kelly, J. A. (1994). Sexual sensation seeking: scaled development and predicting AIDS-risk behaviour among homosexually active men. *Journal of Personality Assessment, 62*: 385–397.

Laaser, M. R., & Gregoire, L. J. (2003). Pastors and cybersex addiction. *Sexual and Relationship Therapy, 18*(3): 395–404.

Laplanche, J., & Pontalis, J. B. (1973). *The Language of Psychoanalysis.* London: Hogarth [reprinted London: Karnac, 1988].

Laufer, M. (1976). The central masturbation fantasy, the final sexual organization, and adolescence. *Psychoanalytic Study of the Child, 31,* 297–305.

Leiblum, S., & Doring, N. (2002). Internet sexuality: known risks and fresh chances for women. In: A. Cooper (Ed.), *Sex and the Internet.* New York: Brunner Routledge.

nua.com/surveys/how_many_online, visited 2.5.04.

Quayle, E., & Taylor, M. (2002). Child pornography and the Internet: Perpetuating a cycle of abuse. *Deviant Behaviour, 23*(4): 331–362.

Quayle, E., Vaughan, E., & Taylor, M. (in press). Sex offenders, Internet child abuse images and emotional avoidance: the importance of values. *Aggression and Violent Behaviour*

Schneider, J. P. (2000). A qualitative study of cybersex participants: gender differences, recovery issues and implications for therapists. *Sexual Addiction and Compulsivity, 7*: 249–278 (reprinted from the internet: www.jenniferschenider.com/articles/qualitative_cyber-sex.html, viewed 4.11.03).

Schneider, J. P. (2003). The impact of compulsive cybersex behaviours on the family. *Sexual and Relationship Therapy, 18*(3): 329–354.

Segal, H. (1975). *An Introduction the Work of Melanie Klein.* London: Hogarth.

Stoller, R. (1975). *Perversion: The Erotic Form of Hatred.* London: Quartet.

Tepper, M. S., Owens, A. F. (2002). Access to pleasure: onramp to specific information on disability, illness, and changes throughout the lifespan. In: A. Cooper (Ed.), *Sex and the Internet.* NewYork: Brunner Routledge.

Turkle, S. (1995). *Life on the Screen: Identity in the Age of the Internet.* New York: Simon & Schuster.

Winnicott, D. W. (1951). Transitional objects and transitional phenomena. Reprinted in *Through Paediatrics to Psycho-Analysis* (1958). London: Hogarth.

Young, R. M. (1996). Primitive processes on the Internet. Available on www.shef.ac.uk/uni.academic/N-Q/psych/staff/rmyoung.papers visited 7.3.04.

Young, R. M. (1998). Sexuality and the Internet. Available on http://human-nature.com/rmyoung/papers/pap108h.html visited 15.4.04.

Young, R. M. (2003). Boundaries of perversion. Available on http://human-nature.com/rmyoung/papers/pap143h.html visited 4.5.04.

CHAPTER FOUR

Psychosexual development in adolescents growing up with HIV infection in London

Brigid Hekster and Diane Melvin

"We are teenagers first—not infected people or HIV positive people. We may be living with a condition that threatens our existence but who we are inside is not defined by that . . ."[1]

Introduction

Worldwide human immunodeficiency virus (HIV) infection is spreading relentlessly, with over forty million people estimated to be infected. This poses a huge challenge to health services and to health education programmes (UNAIDS, 2002). When confronted with the statistics of this epidemic and the economic and social devastation it causes, it can be difficult to remember the individuals living with this condition and to understand the personal struggles they face or to celebrate the achievements that many are able to make in difficult circumstances.

This chapter focuses on the individual, and uses adolescence as the context in which to explore the ever present, and often unspoken, shadow that HIV casts, particularly on sexual development and identity. This theme will be explored through evidence, clinical experiences, and reflections on case material. The particular situation to be considered is that of vertically infected youngsters who acquired the virus from their mothers during pregnancy or around birth. These youngsters constitute a unique group within the HIV population, having grown up with the virus all of their lives. In the UK there are increasing numbers of such children entering adolescence, some of whom will be facing transition to adult services over the next years. It is timely to consider the influence HIV has on sexual and personal development.

Taking a biopsychosocial approach, the chapter will first consider the tasks facing any adolescent during transition into adulthood and then present research about the challenges chronic illness poses during this time. The influence that HIV may have on psychological and sexual development will then be considered, especially the potential impact such a stigmatizing and secretive condition has on the formation of a sense of self. Short narratives from youngsters who have had HIV all of their lives will be presented to highlight the issues and to give examples of some coping strategies that such young people use.

Background

Much has been learnt about the science of the HIV virus, the routes of its transmission between humans, and medicines that help manage, but not cure, the effects of the virus on the immune system (Mocroft et al., 1998). The main routes of transmission of the infection are sexual, vertical, or perinatal transmission (from mother to child), or by receiving contaminated blood products. Infections via these latter two routes have been significantly reduced in resourced countries. People with HIV in such countries are also now living longer and healthier lives, often involving a complex regime of daily antiretroviral medicines.

There is no debate about the vulnerability of young people to becoming HIV infected (see Table 1), nor that young people represent the future health and prosperity of societies and nations. Understanding the impact of HIV infection on young people and their lives not only helps in planning appropriate services for them

Table 1.   Worldwide figures: HIV and children and adolescents (UNAIDS, 2002).

11.8 million young people are living with HIV/AIDS: 7.3 million young women,   4.5 million young men   Half of all new infections (6000 daily) are occurring in young people between the ages of 15–24 yrs   An estimated 14 million children have lost one or both parents to AIDS

but, equally significantly, it helps to emphasize the importance and urgency of focusing on resources for HIV-preventative strategies.

The UK situation

In the UK the numbers of children and young people known to have HIV infection remains relatively small (less than 1000 children under sixteen years reported to be living with HIV) but these numbers are still increasing (Gibb *et al.*, 2003). This number comprises mainly children with perinatally acquired HIV infection who will have lived with HIV all of their lives.

The following summarizes the UK situation and what is known about the psychological needs of children who are known to have HIV, but also refers to those youngsters who are not infected themselves but who are directly affected because someone else in the family has HIV infection.

Children with vertically acquired HIV infection in the UK

- Increasing numbers are living longer, healthier lives with better care and treatments. Fewer infected babies are being born, as mother to child transmission has significantly reduced in the UK (Lwin & Melvin, 2001).
- The vertically infected group as a whole is getting older with over 25% in secondary school. More than 50% of those over eleven years are now fully informed about their diagnosis. But

there are few disclosures to schools or others outside the family or services involved in care (Dodge & Melvin, 2003).

- Most vertically infected children receive care at specialist HIV family clinics separate from adult HIV services.
- The majority live with someone from their biological family. Over 85% of the parents originate from other countries, in particular African ones, although most children have been born in the UK or lived here for many years. Many families have serious practical stresses, including immigration and residency issues.
- Most of the older children are functioning reasonably well and reported levels of emotional and behavioural difficulties are similar to those in other chronic illness; more of the younger group have complex health and disability needs (Dodge & Melvin, 2003).

Youngsters with behaviourally acquired HIV infection in the UK

- The number of young people infected or at risk of infection through sexual transmission or sharing needles in IV drug use is unknown in the UK.
- Many may be unaware of their diagnosis as traditionally there is poor uptake of health checks in adolescent groups.
- The demographics and service needs of this group are likely to be quite different from those of the vertically infected youngsters; the extent of similarities to existing adult HIV populations is also unclear.
- Most will receive care in adult services when diagnosed.

Uninfected youngsters directly affected by the presence of HIV in the family

- The number in this group is probably ten times the number of infected children. Family demographics are similar to the vertically infected group (Imrie & Coombs,1995).
- In the UK little is known about their psychological needs and adjustment, but high levels of psychological disturbance have been reported in similar groups of affected adolescents in other countries (Bauman, Camacho, Silver, Hudis, & Draimin, 2002; Brown, Lourie, & Pao, 2000, Funck-Bretano et al, 1997).

- Social studies have highlighted the extra challenges of care, secrecy and marginalisation faced by such children and youngsters (Lewis, 2001).

The tasks of adolescence

What do we know about adolescence?

Many theories of adolescence have been put forward [see Feldman and Elliot (1990) and Holmbeck and Shapera (1999), which have built upon earlier ideas (e.g., Blos, 1962)]. However, there are consistencies between different theories about the psychological processes and the accompanying tasks that dominate adolescence.

The main developmental task of adolescence is to attain independence and in so doing to acquire the freedom to take responsibility for decisions, actions, and emotions.

The following processes are important components in achieving independence:

- separating from parents and building an independent future;
- developing an identity—physical, sexual, and psychological within the context of the surrounding social and cultural context;
- establishing boundaries incorporating control and autonomy;
- heightened sense of self (body image, self-consciousness);
- establishing balance between peer pressure and family demands;
- negotiating new and intimate relationships;
- managing ambivalence and extremes of mood, impulses, etc., and finding ways of dealing with them in adequate and socially acceptable ways;
- trying to match outer realities with inner fantasies.

The presence of a chronic illness or disabling condition will influence these developments in a manner that will be discussed in more detail when considering adolescents living with HIV infection.

In order to understand the impact of HIV on adolescence there is a need to revisit what is known about healthy sexual development.

Sexual development

Sexual development can be understood to progress throughout childhood and adolescence. Infants and young children show the capacity for a wide variety of behaviours associated with pleasure from sexual organs while lacking the cognitive capacity to give these personal meaning, and have no wish for sexual contact from others (Gordon & Schroeder, 1995). While there are few physical changes associated with sexual development in these early years, children are nevertheless developing their ideas and awareness concerning sex and sexuality. Children gather information and attitudes about sexuality much as they do about everything else, through a process of socialization and as part of their natural exploration of the world.

In contrast to the lack of physical changes associated with sexual development during early childhood, with the onset of puberty the changes that occur during adolescence are tremendous. These changes happen over a relatively lengthy period of time; four to five years for boys and three to four years for girls, with puberty typically beginning earlier in girls (Gordon & Schroeder, 1995; Rutter, 1970).

The psychological and social meaning of sexual activity can be viewed as changing in parallel with processes of physical maturation taking place during early adolescence (Breakwell, 1997). Petersen and Boxer (1982) emphasized the need to regard adolescent sexual development from a "bio-psycho-social perspective" inextricably linked to the whole process of adolescence. Sexual behaviour may foster or impede the development of self-esteem and may be one of the key ways in which adolescents are able to move towards independence (Selverstone, 1989).

Healthy sexual development is also culturally defined. What is regarded as normal sexuality in one culture will be shunned in another, and what is seen as sexually acceptable also changes over time even within the same culture (Breakwell, 1997).

> Adolescents are faced with the task of assimilating, ordering and decoding the often conflicting messages which they receive about sex and sexuality. Their difficulties are magnified because so much of what society has to say about sex and sexuality is either ambiguous or treated as a series of secrets to be uncovered. [Breakwell, 1997; p. 135]

Miller and Simon (1980) suggest that one of the unique features of industrialized countries is that young people are defined as sexually mature while at the same time being defined as socially and psychologically immature. This asynchrony has the potential to generate considerable conflict and confusion for the young person and their family. Additionally, when parents have grown up in a different culture from that of the young person the potential for conflict is significantly increased.

Our understanding of sexual development in healthy adolescents comes mostly from retrospective analysis, since society restricts access to young adolescents for research into issues such as sexual activity, knowledge and attitudes (Jorgensen, 1983; Woodhead & Murph, 1985). However, many reports suggest that adolescents seem to be experimenting with sex at an increasingly early age (Heaven, 1996). Gordon and Schroeder (1995) point to research indicating links between early onset of sexual activity and involvement in delinquent behaviour (Elliot & Morse, 1989) and lack of use of effective birth control (Scott-Jones & White, 1990). Indeed, Rutter and Rutter (1993) describe early sexual activity in teenagers as a "turning point" that can significantly alter the course of their life trajectory.

Interestingly, it would seem that adults consistently underestimate children's awareness of sex and sexuality. Goldman and Goldman (1982) found that pre-adolescents were conscious of issues such as rape, child abuse, and prostitution. This is a study from over twenty years ago, and there may be greater awareness at even younger ages today. Children, therefore, may enter adolescence bombarded with a multitude of images and ideas about sex and sexuality, often acquired through the media, but which lack either a personal meaning or a context in which they can be placed. Emerging findings suggest that the most successful sex education programmes begin as adolescence approaches, in middle childhood (DoH, 2001). It seems that children can be prepared cognitively, before the physical and emotional changes take place. Such opportunities for discussion may provide some protection for adolescents, especially those who may be vulnerable or high risk. More research is needed to investigate the links between sex education provision and sexual attitudes and behaviour.

The influence of chronic illness

The general literature on the impact of chronic illness on adolescents and their families is pertinent to the specific predicament of adolescents with HIV. Improved understanding, care, and treatments have led to increasing numbers of children with previously fatal conditions surviving through adolescence and into adulthood with increasing awareness about the impact on psychological and family adjustment (Eiser, 1993; Wallander & Varni, 1998a).

While overt psychiatric pathology is rare in children with chronic physical illness, there is evidence of increased prevalence of psychological difficulties such as adjustment, anxiety, and problems in coping, with reports ranging from 10% to 37% (Audit Commission. 2002; Kush & Campo, 1998).

Restrictions caused by illness and daily treatments, often resulting in reduced self- esteem and depressive episodes, may result in youngsters feeling different to their peers or failing to connect with them (Altschuler, Black, Trompeter, Fitzpatrick, & Peto, 1991; Hardwick & Biggs, 1997).

Complex factors in the individual and in the family have been found to influence adjustment to illness. (Edwards & Davis, 1997; Eiser,1994). Poorer psychological adjustment has generally been found to be associated with:

- conditions in which there is direct involvement of the central nervous system and brain (Wallander & Varni, 1998b);
- conditions causing unexpected life threatening episodes and increase anxiety and uncertainty (Wambolt, Weintraub, Krafchick, & Wambolt, 1996);
- conditions that have a genetic or familial vulnerability or cause leading to added concerns about family blame and stigma (Thompson, Gil, Burbach, Keith, & Kinney, 1993);
- visible effects of the condition or treatments, particularly those related to growth, body shape, skin, or the timing of puberty (Patterson & Blum, 1996; Woodhead & Murph, 1985);
- demanding treatments and medications, especially those interfering with ordinary daily life and activities (Bryon, 1998).

Open communication about their condition has been found to reduce anxiety in the long term for most youngsters, suggesting there is something protective about involvement and awareness that allows a greater sense of control (Rushforth, 1999). Better psychological outcomes were reported in more flexible and sociable children from well functioning families (Paterson & Blum, 1996; Wilson, Fosson, Kanga, & Dangelo, 1996).

Studies indicate that the psychological adjustment of others in the family is also at risk when someone has a chronic or life threatening illness or disability (Altschuler, 1997; Edwards & Davies, 1997). For example, children in an affected family may experience many of the issues of difference and embarrassment described above and may also face extra caretaking duties too. This could distort their own development of identity and self-confidence and cause a sense of guilt, blame, or resentment about the restrictions on their own life and experiences. Sometimes this can lead to extreme rebellion or excessive risk taking because children believe no one cares about them or that they are worthless and don't matter. Others may become over-protective of family or neglect their own adolescent needs.

Adolescents living in the age of HIV

Adolescents and young adults are often society's most sexually active group but also often the most naïve or unaware about the possible consequences or perceived risks of this behaviour, including the risk of sexually transmitted diseases (DoH, 2001; Johnson, Wadsworth, Wellings, & Field, 1994; UNAIDS, 2002).

Young people at particular risk of acquiring HIV and/or sexually transmitted infections are those often marginalized or isolated within the surrounding community—the homeless or displaced, those whose personal networks or family structures are unavailable or destroyed, such as orphans, refugees fleeing from war or trauma, and those who are poor, struggling, or having to resort to prostitution in order to survive. While the number of youngsters whose lives fit into these categories may be higher in the developing world, there are many teenagers in the UK for whom this is a reality too. The evidence shows that existing health and sex education are minimally effective with "ordinary" adolescents, making it unlikely that there will be any chance of reducing the risks for these more marginalized young people (Ingham, 1999).

*Issues relating to personal and sexual development for
vertically infected HIV positive adolescents*

The stigma and secrecy surrounding HIV, as well as the direct effects of living with a chronic, life limiting and transmissible condition, must create considerable obstacles to the developmental processes of adolescence, particularly the gradual achievement of independence. For example, how does an HIV positive young person negotiate safer sex or know when to talk about their diagnosis? How can a parent develop confidence that their youngster with HIV can make the right treatment or friendship choices? How can a young person with HIV plan for a future with so much uncertainty? This section examines these questions in more detail.

Separation, autonomy, and new relationships

Living in silence, living with HIV

Most vertically infected young people grow up in an environment where one or several family members are also diagnosed with HIV. Living with HIV thus means living not just with a virus, but also with a whole culture (spoken or unspoken) of HIV. The *culture* of HIV is one that can be seen to pervade the family environment, the wider professional system involved in providing care for the young person, and the broader social system. At present, living with HIV also means living with the stigma associated with the condition. This means that the majority of families and young people tell few, if any, people about their diagnosis (Mellins *et al.*, 2002; Melvin, 1999).

For many families, the issue of sharing a diagnosis with their child raises fears not just about how the child or young person will cope with the information, but who they might tell and how they might be treated as a result. Moreover, a child's diagnosis is so often synonymous with at least the mother's diagnosis that there is a sense in which the information is family information rather than just the child's. This has implications for the young person who may want to share their diagnosis with others yet be concerned that this will expose the whole family. This may make relationships with others feel strained or even false.

One sixteen-year-old girl explained, "I feel like nobody actually knows me because there's this one really important thing about me that I can't tell them."

A fifteen-year-old boy put it this way: "Telling my friends about my HIV would be like 'going public' and that would be difficult for mum and dad."

For affected children there may be a similar feeling of leading a "double life" where the responsibilities of caring for other family members may dominate.

One fourteen-year-old girl whose mother is HIV positive explained, "How will I ever meet a boyfriend or go to college if I have to look after my little brother and my sick mum. It's not like I can explain to anyone what's going on."

Learning about the diagnosis can engender immense feelings of loss in the young person. An adolescent with HIV may have to deal with learning that their mother and/or others in the family also has HIV in addition to coping with their own diagnosis. Knowing that their mother is infected and has passed the infection on to them is likely to generate many feelings, including responsibility and anger as well as protectiveness and shame. It can be immensely difficult to hold all these emotions.

Many young people growing up with HIV will have learnt long before being "officially told" about their diagnosis that they are living with a condition that cannot be spoken about. Children have heard family members talking in hushed voices about "their illness" and may even have been instructed explicitly not to tell other people about their hospital appointments, medicines, and so on. Younger children's questions about their condition are also often likely to have been avoided by the adults around them so that conversations get closed down from an early age. This may also be true of children's early questions and explorations around sex and sexuality. Parents may also project their own feelings of shame and fear about their own sexuality.

Emerging sexuality

As a diagnosis of HIV is often intricately bound up in concerns about sexual transmission, a child living with HIV is likely to grow up surrounded by implicit or explicit messages associating sex with danger and illness. At a time when peers are experimenting both sexually and with their sexuality, the adolescent living with HIV can often feel increasingly different. For some HIV positive adolescents one way of coping with this may be to become removed emotionally from such feelings; this may result in some engaging in more risky sexual activities than their peers, as if denying that their condition means there are extra responsibilities in sexual practices. Alternatively, some may feel overwhelmed by the fear of infecting others and experience emerging sexual feelings as dangerous, unwanted, and something to be suppressed. The response may then be to view sex and intimacy as something that is completely out of bounds for them.

Getting intimate

There are likely to be considerable additional worries about developing an intimate relationship even for the adolescent who is in touch with their emerging sexuality. In most respects these concerns parallel those of the adult population. Young people living with HIV may be especially preoccupied with negotiating safer sex and when and under what circumstances they would discuss their HIV status with a partner. This can create considerable barriers to developing intimacy for the adolescent, when relationships are often transitory and issues of trust and how to establish it are still evolving. Moreover, sexual relationships may develop within the context of a school peer group, and so the risks of disclosure may be far higher if trust is broken.

There may also be decreased sexual desire in those with HIV infection because of a variety of physiological and psychological influences, including fatigue and depression (Nusbaum, Hamilton, & Lenahan, 2003). There is evidence too from adult populations that the combination medicines known as HAART (highly active antiretroviral therapy) may reduce sexual desire and arousal (Martinez, Collazos, Mayo, & Bianco, 1999). It is unknown whether HAART may have similar effects in the adolescent population and, indeed, such research is badly needed, especially for those vertically infected young people who have been exposed to such medication during the course of their sexual development.

Identity and awareness of self

A sense of who we are relates not only to experiences but also to personal reflections about ourselves. The thoughts, feelings, and premises that inform personal narratives are not static; they are constantly shaped and reshaped by experiences and interactions with outside world (Altschuler, 1997). All of us are exposed to varying and sometimes contradictory assumptions about how we should live our lives, modified according to gender, race, and religion. In the presence of a lifelong condition, developing a sense of self or identity separate from that condition can be elusive. *Do I exist separate from my condition? Or am I defined by the virus?*

The HIV virus inhabits not only the blood stream of the adolescent, but may also inhabit their inner world. It may become a crucial part of their core identity, either something to be hated and dismissed or something to be struggled with and understood. Those diagnosed with HIV frequently refer to themselves as *being HIV positive or infected* rather than *having* HIV. This may indicate the extent to which the virus becomes incorporated into the identity of the young person.

As one young person put it: "Am I an HIV positive boy or am I Darren, who has a virus called HIV?"

Unlike adults, whose identity develops in the absence of HIV, vertically infected youngsters have HIV as an integral part of their personal narrative right from the beginning of life. Being defined by a virus or a condition must in some way depersonalize or reduce individuality, and means identity may be defined or sometimes dominated by attributes of HIV; this, in turn, is intertwined with sexual identity and behaviour. Some attributes are externally determined and others learnt and integrated into the developing self and expressed in a variety of ways such as anger, denial, passivity, shame, or domination. Further, if the surrounding culture's attitude has negative connotations to HIV, and if experiences reinforce ideas of blame, shame, or other adverse responses, this may reflect on the sense of self worth and identity, both personal and sexual.

The existence of other influences also acts to confirm or detract from a sense of self and identity. Sometimes experiences bring gains, but they may also remind the individual about losses. For example, attendance at a support group helps reduce feelings of isolation and increases the likelihood that coping strategies can be learned. However, it can also expose youngsters to others with more severe effects of the HIV infection. If the HIV part of the self is given too much prominence, without access to other adolescent experiences, it may distort what is "normal" and give little opportunity to develop confidence in relationships with a wide range of peers.

Moore and Rosenthal (1993) suggest that adolescents develop scripts concerning appropriate sexual behaviour, acquired through conversations with their peers and, later, as a result of their own experiences. For the adolescent growing up with HIV there may be a marked conflict between the scripts acquired through non-HIV positive friends and those acquired via conversations in the clinic or in an HIV peer support group.

One sixteen-year-old girl who had known about her diagnosis for several years mentioned that she still couldn't go for long without thoughts of HIV coming into her mind. Now she doesn't get angry about it as she did at first, and now she can put it away and be a different self when she is at college or with her non-HIV friends, and has learnt to tolerate others' derogatory remarks about HIV. But she still thinks of her "real" self as that person at the clinic or with the others at the support group who know about the HIV.

Others talk about leading a dual life and feeling they are split into different people in different situations. While it is normal for everyone to assume different roles at different times, this is a more fundamental kind of splitting. Separate parts of life or identity often have to co-exist with little or no connection between them and often with considerable anxiety or fear should other parts be discovered. As yet, little is known from the UK population about the effects on later psychological adjustment, but there is little doubt about the vulnerability of identity formation and awareness of self.

Ethnic, spiritual, and cultural factors are also known to be core influences on identity formation. While some children spent parts of their early lives in another country, most were born here or have spent most of their lives here. Effects of migration, adjustment to new life styles, loss of family links and history, as well as changes in social context, will all impact on development of identity in these youngsters (Adler, 1989; Burnham & Harris, 1996; Patel et al., 2000). Parents and children may be at different points in the process of acculturation and sometimes conflicts arise, especially during adolescence, because youngsters may feel caught between two cultures or because they identify with the surrounding culture in ways parents may not understand. Some adapt closely to the dominant lifestyle in the "new" country; others remain "traditional", socializing with families and peers from the same cultural or ethnic background (Van der Veer, 1994; Woodcock, 1995).

Beatrice, a fourteen-year-old HIV positive girl of African parents, was having increasing arguments with her mother. She said her mother wouldn't let her hang out with friends or go to sleepovers. Her mother told her that when she was her age she would never have queried any decisions her parents made. All she wanted Beatrice to do was homework and study. Beatrice felt she could not be "a good African daughter" as she'd never been to Africa and her behaviour became more disaffected with family, school, and friends. Her mother threatened to send her to the boarding school she had attended in Africa.

In summary, not only does identity become determined and sometimes dominated by HIV and its associations, but also this population of youngsters often appear to develop different identities in different settings such as the home, the clinic, the school, and the support group. Coping with these different identities requires at least care and caution; it is likely to interfere with achieving independence and for some it could lead to psychological difficulties associated with a poorly developed sense of self.

HIV as a chronic condition

Uncertainty about the future

Adolescence is a time when ideas about and plans for the future become a more prominent aspect of thinking. At present there is no cure for HIV and, like other children living with a life-threatening condition, young people with HIV face uncertainty and unanswered questions about their future. Such questions may include what the course of their illness will be and whether or not the medication available can sustain their health, or, indeed, if they will survive into adulthood at all. Concerns about whether it will be possible to have children may also begin to surface for the adolescent. Indeed, this was identified as one of the most pressing questions for a group of positive youngsters who met at a participation workshop (European Forum, 2000).

Taking medicines

Feelings of uncertainty about prognosis alongside the burden of the rigorous medication regimes so often prescribed for managing HIV may lead to feelings of hopelessness about the future and consequently a reduction in, or abandonment of, adherence. Refusing to take medicines may also be a powerful way of asserting independence or control in adolescence (Bryon, 1998). In the context of HIV this is a particularly risky strategy as poor adherence may not only lead to increased vulnerability to life-threatening infections but can also result in the virus becoming resistant to the limited number of antiretroviral treatments available. Moreover, increases in viral load associated with poor adherence may further increase the risk of infecting others through unprotected sex.

Most HIV positive people take their medicines in private for fear of inadvertently alerting others to questions about their health and HIV status. Medication is also therefore likely to be an issue for young people when it comes to their relationships with others. As medicines need to be taken strictly at certain times of the day this may set boundaries around the young person's social life when it comes to impromptu invitations out, nights away from the home, school trips, or holidays. Such occasions are often missed opportunities for the development of a playful and spontaneous social and sexual self for the young person living with HIV. The spontaneous source of joy that sexuality can bring is highlighted as being important in the development of sexual identity (Selverstone, 1989).

Body image.

Concern about body image and preoccupation regarding one's sexual attractiveness is widespread during adolescence and any deviation from the norm is likely to be a cause for anxiety (Breakwell, 1997). Poor body image is likely to represent a significant impediment to the adolescent's emerging sexual identity and confidence and young people living with HIV may be especially preoccupied by issues relating to body image. Stature may be diminished and puberty can be delayed, and for some, one of the side effects of HAART is lypodystrophy (a term used to describe the redistribution of fat deposits in the body, usually from limbs and face to areas of the trunk, especially around the midriff). Social comparisons are rife during adolescence and the onset of puberty can hold particular status among young people. Adolescents may tend to withdraw from social life when they believe themselves to be physically abnormal or contaminated (Wolman, 1998). Such feelings of difference concerning growth and development may engender a heightened sense of isolation for adolescents living with HIV.

A positive mother of an adolescent with HIV expressed her anxiety. "I can see my daughter (twelve years old) beginning to get a bulge in her abdomen. The same as the changes I had to my body. And then everyone asked me if I was pregnant, if only they knew the truth. What if her friends think that she is pregnant or start to ask her?"

The connection between body image, sexuality, and illness may be especially strong for adolescents living with HIV compared with other chronic conditions. For many parents the onset of puberty in the HIV positive young person provokes an intensification of concerns about emerging sexuality and may become a cue for disclosure of the child's diagnosis. For some young people, puberty becomes associated with learning about their diagnosis and the consequent feelings of loss and fear that this engenders. This may be particularly true for girls, in whom the onset of puberty in the form of breast development and menstruation is a more obvious cue than is the case for boys. For both sexes issues about safer sex are likely to become a principal focus of conversation as they develop into a sexual person. This may leave them feeling robbed of the excitement and wonder of their emerging sexual feelings and adult body.

The family/wider context

For many parents the onset of their child's puberty and growing interest in expressing themselves sexually is a cause for anxiety as well as celebration. For families living with HIV, however, this stage in their child's life may be approached only with dread. For infected children the dread may be associated with the more pressing need for informing their child about their diagnosis and the fear of them infecting others. For the affected child the fear is likely to be associated with concerns about future children of their own being at risk of HIV infection and so repeating the cycle. For many families these very real fears and feelings of protectiveness are not articulated to the child in ways that can be understood and processed. The child therefore grows up with a sense that their sexuality cannot be enjoyed or expressed safely. This may begin early on in the child's development.

One mother said of her ten-year-old HIV positive daughter: "I can see what's starting to happen. She's started flirting, smiling at boys in this certain way. And I think 'Oh God. This is it now, isn't it'."

Parents whose own upbringing was marked by different cultural expectations and rituals may feel bewildered and overwhelmed by the influence of the dominant culture on their son or daughter at this time. With many parents in the London HIV infected population originating from other countries, especially Africa, this is often the case. Families are also frequently lacking other sources of support within the wider familial network, either because they have left them behind or lost them through HIV. A significant proportion of young people may be without a father or father figure in the home. The rituals, or people to whom parents may have encouraged a young person to turn, may therefore be lacking, making their transition into adulthood that much more difficult.

Parents are also likely to be concerned about how they will manage their child's questions about transmission and how they themselves acquired the infection. Issues around a parent's sexuality may also come into focus and can lead to embarrassment, avoidance, or feelings of shame between parent and child.

One mother expressed the anxiety she felt about talking with her HIV positive daughter about the diagnosis. "Maybe the worst thing is not whether she will blame me but maybe that she will think of me differently, think I was promiscuous or did risky things. Until I can be sure, how can I tell her?"

In others, such questions raise intolerable feelings of anxiety concerning the young person's potential to infect others (as they were themselves infected). This may mean that they become over-inclusive in what they discuss with their son or daughter as a way of avoiding the intolerable reality of the circumstances. When the young person has lost a parent or parents because of HIV and is being cared for by another family member, discussing the diagnosis with the young person may also raise questions about other family secrets that the carer feels unprepared for or unable to answer.

The stage in their development at which the child learns about their diagnosis is further likely to have an impact. If parents continue to avoid discussing the diagnosis, the heightened sense of anxiety that comes when discussing HIV for the first time can get associated with other aspects of sexuality, e.g., having a detailed discussion about transmission during the time of the youngster's first period. The young infected adolescent may have complex feelings that their sexuality is abnormal or "dangerous", or something to be ashamed about (e.g., "It can only lead to bad things"; "I can't have a sexual relationship").

Uninfected siblings may themselves have a distorted view of sexuality in the context of their family lives. Evidence is emerging from US studies concerning affected youngsters (which include such uninfected siblings) showing that they are at increased risk for a whole range of mental health problems and challenging behaviours, including high risk sexual activities (Brown, Lourie, & Pao, 2000).

Professional systems

There may be differing views in the system on what young people need to be told about their diagnosis, sex, sexuality, and future. How does the system decide who addresses these issues with the family and young person and when? It is essential for service providers to respect and be mindful of ethnic, spiritual, and cultural differences in this regard. This entails not just having a "service view" about when and what youngsters should know, but being transparent about differing views and experiences, both within the service and between providers and families.

The importance of religion in the lives of many of these families is a topic often forgotten in discussions about their care and treatments. It is something that service providers often avoid or neglect when considering both health and sex education, adherence to medicines, and even in beliefs about infection and cure. Acknowledging that there can often be crucial differences between the families' and professionals' belief systems about the cause and management of HIV infection can at least open a discussion and allow for greater understanding. The adolescent may be caught up more profoundly in this dilemma, reacting against the established family view but unsure about where to align their beliefs.

One seventeen-year-old girl lived in an African family where several family members were ministers in a Pentecostal church. Regular services preached the importance of prayer as the only way of curing HIV. During early adolescence she had rebelled and wanted nothing to do with the church but had found herself increasingly in trouble at school and with her peers. She was also a poor adherer to her HIV medicines. She had an episode of ill-health following which she rejoined the church and was able to talk to one of her uncles who was a church leader.

"He said that although it was God's will whether I got ill or not I could help by praying but also God expected me to listen and keep myself healthy too. I suppose that made me see that I could take medicines that my doctor had given me without it going against my religion."

Reduced openness in a family may elicit powerful counter-transference responses in clinicians. While trying to work in partnership with families, the professional systems can inadvertently end up colluding with a family's over-protectiveness or control towards the child, especially around issues of disclosure and sexual knowledge. This over-protectiveness may be part of the counter-transference response and could make it difficult for the system to make the necessary shift in its relationship with the family to a focus on the young person's view and to facilitate growth in independence.

Implications for practice

Multidisciplinary team working and participation strategies are crucial in managing many of the concerns raised above. The production of protocols aimed at supporting professionals as well as young people and families over issues related to transition into adolescence and on to adult services is also a priority (Viner, 1999). Psychological theories about subjects such as adolescence and stress need to inform practice, and that practice itself can build on and elaborate existing theories and knowledge derived from other chronic illnesses.

What do HIV positive adolescents need?

- First and foremost, sexual and personal development in the context of HIV needs to be normalized so that it does not become marginalized. Adolescents need to be able to celebrate and enjoy their sexuality despite living with HIV. Such adolescents can still make choices, not only about their HIV needs but also about the way they live their lives.

- Services need to provide structures and approaches that encourage thinking not only about now but also about the future, one of the main themes of adolescence referred to earlier. However, the system may avoid such conversations, anxious that this may create more upset for the young person. The future for those living with HIV is still so uncertain that professionals can feel immobilized by their inability to provide clarity. Evidence emerging from the young people themselves, through participation workshops or the first adolescent clinics, shows that these youngsters can and do want to talk about their plans for the future (European Forum, 2000). This includes having sex, having children, being successful in a job. Transitional clinics should provide both the setting and approach to enable the adolescent to feel safe and comfortable to talk about themselves and their wishes for the future.

Beatrice had always thought about when she had children of her own, but during her visits to the Family Clinic when she was fourteen had never felt she dared ask if this would be possible. Now she is in her last year at university and has linked into the adult HIV services. She visits the "paediatric" system with her established boyfriend. He is not HIV positive but knows all about Beatrice's diagnosis and they now talk together about their future plans for a big family. In this way Beatrice feels she is beginning to manage the HIV out in the adolescent/adult world.

- Psychoeducation as well as support forms the backbone of good care. For example, it is crucial to ensure that knowledge of the diagnosis occurs before the behavioural and physiological milestones in sexual development are reached (see CHIVA Guidelines on Disclosure, 2003) Proactive and "culturally sensitive" opportunities for discussing sexual issues with young people are helpful and need to include information about transmission of HIV. It would also help if we are mindful of the ways young people access all kinds of information. For example, Murdock, McClure, Large, Sarkar, and Shaw (1999) have discussed the successful use of a multimedia approach to pregnancy prevention (MAPP) with 9–14-year-olds who have asthma, diabetes, or sickle cell. Similarly, if discussions about sexuality take place only in the context of relationships with health professionals then we may, by definition, pathologize it. We know that the views of peers are especially influential at this time and there are some helpful approaches that harness these (e.g., peer groups such as Teen Spirit, based at an organization called Body and Soul in London).
- Practical, emotional and spiritual differences and dilemmas existing within the family and in relationships with peers and with the caring system have to be acknowledged in respectful and interactive ways, otherwise these adolescents' personal growth and identity will be made more vulnerable. An example would be HIV services and religious leaders having a forum to discuss support for families living with HIV.

In conclusion, throughout the journey through childhood and adolescence with all its challenges and secrets, the one recurring message is that represented by the words of the youngster at the beginning of this chapter. "We are teenagers first—not infected people or HIV positive people". They may be living with a condition that threatens their lives and whose name causes anxiety in others, but as individuals they must not be defined by the acronym

"HIV". These youngsters do not want pity any more than they want to be shunned or thought of as different or unusual. Many are coping extraordinarily well in achieving independence, but in order for other young people to do so without compromising identity and self worth, attitudes and responsibilities must change. Deconstructing and demystifying the power and fear that surrounds HIV has to be a shared responsibility in which all in society play a role and not a responsibility that individuals and families living with the condition can or should shoulder by themselves.

Note

1. A message from a young person attending a workshop organized by the European Forum for children with HIV/AIDS in 1999.

References

Adler, L. (Ed.) (1989). *Cross Cultural Research in Human Development: Life Span.* New York: Praeger.

Altschuler, J. (1997). *Working with Chronic Illness: A Family Approach.* London: Macmillan.

Altschuler, J., Black, D., Trompeter, R., Fitzpatrick, M., & Peto, H. (1991). Adolescents in end stage renal failure: a pilot study of family factors in compliance and treatment considerations. *Family Systems Medicine, 9*(3): 229–247.

Audit Commission (2002). *Child in Mind Project.* London: The Stationery Office.

Bauman, L. J., Camacho, S., Silver, E. J., Hudis, J., & Draimin, B. (2002). Behavioural problems in school aged children of mothers with HIV/AIDS. *Clinical Child Psychology & Psychiatry, 7*(1): 39–54.

Blos, P. (1962). *On Adolescence: A Psychoanalytic Interpretation.* New York: Free Press.

Breakwell, G. (1997). Adolescents and emerging sexuality. In: L. Sherr (Ed.), *AIDS and Adolescence.* Amsterdam: Harwood Academic.

Brown, L. K., Lourie, K. J., & Pao, T. (2000). Children and adolescents living with HIV and AIDS: a review. *Journal of Child Psychology & Psychiatry, 41*(1): 81–96.

Bryon, M. (1998). Adherence to treatments in children. In: L. B. Myers & K. Midence (Eds.), *Adherence to Treatment in Medical Conditions* (pp. 161–189). Amsterdam: Harwood Academic.

Burnham, J., & Harris, Q. (1996). Effects of migration and adjustment to new life styles. In: K. Dwivedi & V. Varma (Eds.), *Meeting the Needs of Ethnic Minority Children*. London: Jessica Kingsley.

CHIVA (2003). www.bhiva.org/chiva/index.html

Dodge, J., & Melvin, D. (2003). From family clinic to adolescent services: 12 years of a family HIV clinic. Paper presented at the AIDS Impact Conference. July 6–8, Milan.

Department of Health (DOH) (2001). *National Strategy for Sexual Health & HIV*. London: The Stationery Office.

Edwards, M., & Davis, H. (1997). *Counselling Children with Chronic Medical Conditions*. Leicester: BPS Books.

Eiser, C. (1993). *Growing Up with a Chronic Disease; The Impact on Children and Families*. London: Jessica Kingsley.

Eiser, C. (1994). Making sense of chronic disease. *Journal of Child Psychology & Psychiatry, 35*: 1373–1389.

Elliot, D. S., & Morse, B. J. (1989). Deliquency and drug use as risk factors in teenage sexual activity. *Youth and Society, 21*: 32–57.

European Forum on HIV/AIDS Children & Families (2000). Will Someone Listen? Please! *Newsletter Summer Issue, 10*.

Feldman, S. S., & Elliot, G. R. (Eds.) (1990). *At the Threshold: The Developing Adolescent*. Cambridge, MA: Harvard University Press.

Funck-Bretano, L., Costagliola, D., Seibel, N., Straub, E., Tardieu, M., & Blanche, S. (1997). Patterns of disclosure and perceptions of the Human Immunodeficiency Virus in elementary school-age children. *Archives Pediatric Adolescent Medicine, 151*: 978–985.

Gibb, D. M., Duong, T., Tookey, P. A., Sharland, M., Tudor-Williams, G., Novelli, V., Butler, K., Riordan, A., Farrelly, L., Masters, J., Peckham, C. S., Dunn, D. T. on behalf of the National Study of HIV in Pregnancy and Childhood (NSHPC) and the Collaborative HIV Paediatric Study (CHIPS) (2003). Decline in mortality, AIDS and hospital admissions in perinatally HIV-1 infected children in the United Kingdom and Ireland. *British Medical Journal, 327*: 1019–1023.

Goldman, R., & Goldman, J. (1982). *Children's Sexual Thinking*. Routledge & Kegan Paul.

Gordon, B. N., & Schroeder, C. S. (1995). *Sexuality: A Developmental Approach to Problems*. New York: Plenum.

Hardwick, P., & Biggs, J. (1997). Psychological aspects of chronic illness in children. *British Journal of Hospital Medicine, 57*(4): 154–157.

Heaven, P. (1996). *Adolescent Health: The Role of Individual Differences.* London: Routledge.

Holmbeck, G. N., & Shapera, W. (1999). Research methods with adolescents. In: P. C. Kendall, J. N. Butcher, & G. N. Holmbeck (Eds.), *Handbook of Research Methods in Clinical Psychology* (634–661). New York: Wiley.

Imrie, J., & Coombs, Y. (1995). *No Time to Waste: The Scale and Dimensions of the Children Affected by HIV/AIDS in the United Kingdom.* Barkingside: Barnardos.

Ingham, R. (1999). Barriers and opportunities: young people and sexual health. Paper presented at BPS Special Interest Group (HIV & Sexual Health), London, October 1999.

Johnson, A. M., Wadsworth, J., Wellings, K., & Field, J. (1994). *Sexual Attitudes & Lifestyles in Britain.* Oxford: Blackwell Scientific.

Jorgensen, S. R. (1983). Beyond adolescent pregnancy: research issues for early adolescent sexuality. *Journal of Early Adolescence, 3*: 141–155.

Kush, S., & Campo, J. (1998). Consultation and liaison in the paediatric settings. *American Handbook of Psychology & Psychiatry.*

Lewis, E. (2001). *Afraid to Say: the Needs and Views of Young People Living with HIV/AIDS.* London: Strutton Housing/NCB Enterprises.

Lwin, R., & Melvin, D. (2001). Annotation: paediatric HIV infection. *Journal of Child Psychology & Psychiatry, 42*(4): 427–438.

Martinez, E., Collazos, J., Mayo, J., & Bianco, M. S. (1999). Sexual dysfunction with protease inhibitors. *Lancet, 353*: 810–811.

Mellins C., Brakis-Cott, E., Dolezal, C., Richards, A., Nicolas, S., & Abrams, E. (2002). Patterns of HIV status disclosure to perinatally HIV-infected children and subsequent mental health outcomes. *Clinical Child Psychology and Psychiatry, 7*(1): 101–114.

Melvin, D. (1999). Psychological issues: challenges and achievements. *Journal of HIV Therapy, 4*(3): 77–81.

Miller, P. Y., & Simon, W. (1980). The development of sexuality in adolescence. In: J. Adelson (Ed.), *Handbook of Adolescent Psychology* (pp. 343–407). New York: Wiley.

Mocroft, A., Vella, S., Benfield, T. L., Chiesi, A., Miller, V., & Gargalianos, P. (1998). Changing patterns of mortality across Europe in patients infected with HIV-1. EuroSIDA Study Group. *Lancet, 352*: 1725–1730.

Moore, S., & Rosenthal, D. (1993). *Adolescent Sexuality.* London: Routledge.

Murdock, P. O., McClure, C., Large, O. G., Sarkar, D., & Shaw, K. (1999). MAPP: A multimedia instructional program for youths with chronic illness. mtsu.edu/~itconf/proceed99/Murdock.htm

Nusbaum, M. R. H., Hamilton, C., & Lenahan, P. (2003). Chronic illness and sexual functioning. *Amercian Family Physician, 67*(2): 347–354.

Patel, N., Bennett, E., Dennis, M., Dosangh, N., Mahtani, A., Miller, A., & Nadirshah, Z. (Eds.) (2000). *Clinical Psychology: "Race" and Culture. A Training Manual.* Leicester: BPS Books.

Patterson, J., & Blum, R. W. (1996). Risk and resilience among young children and youth with disabilities. *Archives of Paediatric and Adolescent Medicine, 150c,* 692–698.

Petersen, A. C., & Boxer, A. (1982). Adolescent sexuality. In: T. J. Coates, A. C. Petersen, & C. Perry (Eds.), *Promoting Adolescent Health: A Dialogue on Research and Practice* (pp. 237–253). New York: Academic Press.

Rushforth, H. (1999). Communicating with hospitalised children: Review and application of research pertaining to children's understanding of health and illness. *Journal of Child Psychology & Psychiatry, 40:* 683–692.

Rutter, M. (1970). *Helping Troubled Children.* New York: Plenum Press.

Rutter, M., & Rutter, M. (1993). *Developing Minds: Challenge and Continuity Across the Lifespan.* New York: Basic Books.

Scott-Jones, D., & White, A. B. (1990). Correlates of sexual activity in early adolescence. *Journal of Early Adolescence, 10:* 221–238.

Selverstone, R. (1989). Adolescent sexuality: developing self-esteem and mastering developmental tasks. *SIECUS Report, 18:* 1–3.

Sex Education Forum (1999). *A Framework for Sex Education.* London: National Children's Bureau.

Thompson, R., Gil, K., Burbach, D., Keith, B., & Kinney, T. (1993). Role of child and maternal process in the psychological adjustment of children with sickle cell disease. *Journal of Consulting & Clinical Psychology, 61:* 468–474.

UNAIDS (2002). Report on the global HIV/AIDS epidemic. July 2002. Geneva.

Van der Veer, G. (1994). *Counselling and Therapy with Refugees: Psychologcal Problems of War, Torture and Repression.* Chichester: Wiley.

Viner, R. (1999). Transition from paediatric to adult health care: bridging gaps or passing the buck? *Archives of Diseases in Childhood, 81:* 271–275.

Wallander, J. L., & Varni, J. W. (1998a). Effects of paediatric chronic physical disorders on child and family adjustment. *Journal of Child Psychology & Psychiatry. 39*(1): 29–46.

Wallander, J. L., & Varni, J. W. (1998b). Paediatric chronic disabilities: haemophilia and spina bifida as examples. In: D. Routh (Ed.),

Handbook of Paediatric Psychology (Chapter 6). New York: Guilford Press.

Wambolt, M. Z., Weintraub, P., Krafchick, D., & Wambolt, E. S. (1996). Psychiatric family history in adolescents with severe asthma. *Journal of the American Academy of Child Adolescent Psychiatry, 35*: 1042–1049.

Wilson, J., Fosson, A., Kanga, J. F., & Dangelo, S. (1996). Homeostatic interactions: a longitudinal study of biological, psychological and family variables in children with cystic fibrosis. *Journal of Family Therapy, 18*: 123–129.

Wolman, C. (1998). *Adolescence: Biological and Psychosocial Perspectives.* Westport, CT: Greenwood Press.

Woodhead, J. C., & Murph, J. R. (1985). Influence of chronic illness and disability on adolescent sexual development in seminars. *Adolescent Medicine, 1*(3): 171–176

Woodcock, J. (1995). Healing rituals with families in exile. *Journal of Family Therapy, 17*: 397–409.

CHAPTER FIVE

The psychodynamics of unsafe sex

Simon Thomas and Bernard Ratigan

Introduction

Why does a person engage in unsafe sexual activities and feel compelled to repeat those activities when they recognize them to be potentially harmful? Equally, if someone expresses the wish to refrain from these kinds of activities, how can we explain their inability to stop? Examples from our clinical practice include people engaging in compulsive sexual behaviour with commercial sex workers, putting themselves at risk of sexually transmitted diseases (STDs), individuals who consciously wish to infect others with HIV, and still others actively seeking out unprotected sex with people known to be HIV positive.

The dominant psychological models for understanding unsafe sexual acts and practices have ignored psychoanalytic conceptualizations and have instead focused on those derived from cognitive science and cognitive–behavioural therapy to inform preventive and clinical work. Risk-reduction interventions using these models have demonstrated some efficacy in the treatment of certain patient populations, including men who have sex with men in the US (Kelly et al, 1991) and commercial sex workers in Thailand

(UNAIDS, 1998). However, with others, for example, STD clinic patients in the UK (Parker, 1996) and the US (Branson, Ransom, Peterman, & Zaidi, 1996) these interventions have failed to achieve significant decreases in unsafe sexual behaviour. With a considerable number of patients it seems that these models are unable to adequately address the more overtly self-destructive and seemingly irrational aspects of unsafe sexual behaviour.

The aim of this chapter is to contribute additional understanding from a psychoanalytic perspective to the underlying and, we shall argue, largely unconscious, motivations and possible aetiology for sexual risk-taking. Particular attention will be paid to the implications of applying a psychodynamic model to unsafe sex for practitioners involved in attempting to understand and change such behaviours in patients or service users who are exhibiting more serious levels of disturbance in their personality organization. Composite clinical vignettes are included to illustrate theoretical conceptions as well as the clinical challenges of change-orientated interventions in this area.

In this chapter, the word "psychodynamic" is used to indicate a broad range of conceptualizations, originally derived from psychoanalysis, and here including object relations theory and self psychology.

The previous dominance of cognitive and behavioural models

Theoretical frameworks hitherto employed to inform work in this area have almost exclusively been either cognitive or behavioural. Many were originally derived from generic psychological models of attitude and behaviour change such as the Health Belief Model (Becker, 1974) and the Theory of Planned Behaviour (Ajzen & Madden, 1986). These were then further developed and adapted in order to provide an explanatory framework that could inform preventative work in HIV. Examples include the AIDS-Risk Reduction Model (Catania, Kegeles, & Coates, 1990) and the Information–Motivation–Behaviour model (Fisher & Fisher, 1992).

Such models reflect the assumptions of what Joffe (1996) has termed the KABP (knowledge–attitude–belief–practice) paradigm, to date dominant in the field of AIDS research. They are largely concerned with predicting and explaining variance in behaviour with the aim of bringing about change. Their predominant focus is therefore on attitudes, intentions, and behaviour with respect to sexual risk-taking.

The psychological interventions derived from these models and reported in the research literature share a number of characteristics (Ross & Kelly, 1999). These include: combining risk-reduction with exercises promoting positive attitudes towards safer sex; encouraging change from current high-risk sexual behaviour; teaching behavioural risk reduction skills (e.g., use of condoms and sexual negotiation); and reinforcing attempts at behaviour change.

Interventions of this kind have been criticized for paying insufficient attention to the social context within which unsafe sexual behaviour actually takes place (Joffe, 1996, 1997). For example, the same person may practise safe sex in one social situation and unsafe sex in another. Additional criticism has been levelled at these interventions for paying insufficient attention to the interpersonal and sociocultural factors involved in such behaviours (Canin, Dolcini, & Adler, 1999; Van Campenhoudt, Cohen, Guizzardi, & Hausser, 1997). Risk affects, for example, being "in love" or in a high state of arousal, may be just as— if not more—important than risk cognitions; for example, "having nothing to lose".

While meta-analytic reviews of the HIV prevention literature have provided some evidence for the effectiveness of the behavioural components to these interventions, the effects have been small in size and often not sustained over time (Kalichman, Carey, & Johnson, 1996; Sogolow et al., 1998).

From our point of view, the greatest strength of these models is also their greatest weakness, in that these social cognitive models are founded on the assumption that behaviour represents conscious activity that is based on reason and logic, and can be predicted from an examination of people's stated intentions and attitudes. While this assumption offers an approach to behaviour change that can be operationally defined, with clear targets and aims, it is an approach that appears to be wide of the mark when it comes to changing unsafe sexual behaviour with particular clients.

We would argue, as others have (e.g., Auerbach, Wypijewska, Brodie, & Keith, 1994; Friedman, 1998; Joffe, 1996), that sexual risk-taking represents an area of human behaviour that may not always be under the conscious control of an individual. It may frequently conflict with his or her stated intentions and espoused beliefs. The high incidence of unwanted pregnancies, abortions, and STDs offer convincing evidence of this discrepancy (Aggleton, 1996; McKirnan, Ostrow, & Hope, 1996). Given the irrational nature of such behaviour it is not surprising that models of prevention based on the assumptions of a rational self have been found to be of limited value in attempting to reduce risk-taking behaviour.

This view is supported by the modest conclusion that is reached by Ross and Nilsson Schonnesson (2000) in a review of the HIV prevention literature when they write:

> Despite knowing something about the variables underlying risk behaviour—personal, situational, attitudinal, affective—we need to recognise that many of these are not readily modifiable. Attempting to change personality is close to impossible, and [. . .] attitudinal changes may be overridden by affects. [Ross & Nilsson Schonnesson, 2000, p. 390]

The advantages of applying a psychodynamic model to this area become clearer. In searching for the *meaning* of human actions, this model gives due consideration to both the conscious and unconscious processes that underlie human behaviour and so attempts to provide a framework within which unsafe sexual behaviour may be understood. A psychodynamic approach recognizes that such behaviour is intimately tied up with the question of personality, and there is a small but growing body of research evidence confirming the importance of personality in sexual risk-taking (see Pinkerton & Abramson, 1995 for a review of this literature). Though it may share with cognitive and behavioural models a concern with achieving behavioural change, it sets about this in a rather different way. Rather than attempting to effect change through reasoning with or education of the client, change is sought through understanding, either directly through the medium of the psychoanalytic encounter with the patient or indirectly through the medium of psychoanalytic consultation with those caring for the patient.

The relevance of the psychodynamic model
to understanding unsafe sex

Josephine Klein has described psychodynamic psychotherapy as being "about enabling people to explore their processes, conscious and unconscious, so that they can understand better what they are doing in their lives and gain some control over the alternatives which are in principle available to them" (Klein, 1990, p. 38). This particular definition is offered here because of its emphasis on enabling the patient to achieve self-understanding and control, an aim that is clearly pertinent to working with those placing themselves at risk of HIV infection through their sexual behaviour.

The distinctive contribution of psychoanalytic psychotherapy may be summarized in three ways:

(a)   a focus on exploration of both conscious and unconscious processes;
(b)   an emphasis on analysis of how the past may be affecting the present—usually by attending to the transference aspects of the patient–therapist relationship;
(c)   the explicit processing via supervision of countertransference feelings evoked in the therapist that can then be used to inform therapeutic intervention.

The model gives considerable importance to early experience in shaping the individual's relating to the other, as part of the process of biopsychosocial development. In the interpersonal world of the infant and child, and specifically in the relationship with the primary caregiver, the intrapsychic processes are established that will profoundly, and often unconsciously, affect many aspects of the person's life.

Human sexuality is a complex of biological impulses and psychological processes in the context of particular social constructs and taboos. Besides the biologically-driven need to connect sexually, humans have a rich phantasy life that the psychodynamic model sees as stemming from early infantile experience and continuing to develop particularly during and after puberty in the context of the search for object-relations.

We shall now consider three theoretical frameworks within the psychodynamic model as they are applied to an understanding of unsafe sex.

Freud: the life and death instincts

Central to Freud's model is the concept of conflict or struggle within the psyche. Freud initially conceptualized this as a struggle between sexual instincts associated with the id and fuelled by libido, and ego instincts directed towards self-preservation. He believed that the psyche was governed by the search for pleasure, which occurred through the reduction of unpleasurable excitation or tension within the organism. The satisfaction of sexual needs through orgasm can be seen as the prototype of the "pleasure principle" in operation. Countering the drive towards pleasure is the "reality principle", mediated by the ego, that frustrates or delays pleasurable gratification of these needs. Wishes and needs cannot all be gratified immediately, as the infant soon discovers.

Subsequently, and possibly in response to the mass slaughter of men in the First World War, Freud (1920g) was forced to adapt his theory. Freud observed that people do not always strive towards pleasure, but appear to repeat, in both conscious behaviour and unconscious phantasy (such as dreams), experiences that are far from pleasurable. This repetition of aversive experiences may appear very self-destructive. In "Beyond the pleasure principle" (1920g) Freud makes his first reference to the death instinct to account for human destructiveness. The struggle within the psyche then becomes a struggle between Eros, the sexual and life-preserving instincts, and Thanatos, the death instinct, thought to be a conservative force seeking to return the organism to a state of inorganic matter through death. Active repetition of aversive experiences might then be an expression of this destructive force. For example, a person may repeat, in adult sexual behaviour, acts that echo or resemble childhood experiences of trauma or abuse. Whitmire, Harlow, Quinn, and Morokoff (1999), amongst others, have investigated the complex set of variables linking childhood trauma and HIV risk in adulthood.

Freud (1914g) had observed that experiences that could not be consciously recalled because they were repressed were often re-enacted. This "remembering" through action was evident in the transference, but was also apparent in all aspects of people's lives. Much of this "remembering and repeating" will not be in consciousness, but may be near consciousness (Freud, 1914g). In clinical practice we encounter individuals who may have some awareness that what they are doing is not safe, but they are able to push this knowledge out of consciousness, sometimes with the aid of drugs or alcohol.

Freud (1920g) wondered whether the compulsion to repeat may be seen, in part, as an attempt by the ego to master aversive experiences. By "repeating" elements of an experience of traumatic sexual abuse, for example, an individual may attempt to gain control in a situation where formerly he or she had no control over what was happening. Within Freud's later model, the compulsion to repeat unpleasurable experiences was also a more direct manifestation of the death instinct, the force within the psyche intent on self-destructiveness.

Freud's conceptualization of this unconscious conflict between *Eros* (life instinct) and *Thanatos* (death instinct) in the internal world may therefore provide a way of thinking about the forces that can push the individual into sexual risk-taking activities. Without therapeutic intervention some individuals may become trapped in a more-or-less unconscious process of repeating early psychic trauma in their adult lives as a way of "remembering" it through re-enactment, sometimes seeming to strive for mastery and understanding, but at other times seeming determined to repeat a trauma in an experience in which the negative aspects of that experience seem to outweigh any pleasure involved. This quality of destructiveness may also come to infuse the superego, so that the superego becomes particularly fierce and punitive.

CASE VIGNETTE: MR BLUE

Mr Blue was a twenty-three-year-old, single, heterosexual man who regularly attended the GUM clinic for repeat HIV testing. He believed he had placed himself at risk of infection by having unprotected sexual intercourse with women he met in bars and clubs. In his early history there was a pattern of punitive, repressive messages about sex and relationships. This was in the context of an affectionless, emotionally cold, and strictly religious family culture. In the transference there developed a similar dynamic whereby he felt judged and ashamed of his sexual impulses and behaviour, imagining that the therapist regarded him as promiscuous. This was interpreted by the therapist to Mr Blue as an unconscious projection of his own internalized judgements originating, in part, from his childhood experiences.

While at first he rejected this view, in time he came to accept this idea more and to gradually see that there was a similar dynamic underlying the pattern of his unprotected sexual relationships with women. Mr Blue was trying to manage the tension between his desire to have sex with women and his introjected, punitive views about it. His unprotected sexual intercourse with women represented an unconscious attempt to punish himself for having sexual desires. It may also have represented an aggressively defiant response to his restrictive upbringing. The therapeutic challenge was to help him work through these internal conflicts and develop a less punitive superego. This took a considerable period of time and was a difficult process for patient and therapist. For the patient it was especially distressing, as he had to radically adjust his view of his parents and his early life.

The Kleinian development

Freud's contribution to the understanding of the diversity and vicissitudes of human sexuality was extended by the ideas of Klein and those who further developed her work. Much of this is relevant to thinking about unsafe sexual behaviour. Later Kleinians have focused on the presence in adults and in children of cruelty, murderousness, and envy, concepts that have explanatory power in understanding many of the behaviours that appear in this chapter.

Recent Kleinian thinking has developed Freud's original work on the death instinct, emphasizing how it can overcome the life instinct in some people with pathological personality organizations, and in those suffering from excesses of masochism and other self-destructive character structures (Hinshelwood, 1991; Joseph, 1982; Rosenfeld, 1971; Steiner, 1993). This perspective, by seemingly focusing on the destructive and primitive processes that clearly dominate a subgroup of patients, can also illuminate pathological processes universally found in human beings. The Kleinian model does not privilege the destructive, but it does ask for it to be given equal consideration with the rational and benign aspects of human mental functioning.

Bion emphasized how human beings, from infancy, develop a capacity "not to know" (minus K) as well as "to know" (K). Significantly, for this chapter, he also linked K with L (Love) and therefore minus K with H (Hate) (Bion 1967; Money-Kyrle 1968). "Knowing", in Bion's terms, is not a purely cognitive activity, but anchors pieces of knowledge in affective experiences within and between people. In minus K, something may be "known" intellectually, but is stripped of all affective meaning. "Attacks on thinking", (Bion would suggest that these are often driven by envy within the psyche), may destroy links between conscious behaviour and an unconscious realm of experience and feeling. This concept has been helpful in understanding why some patients reporting serial episodes of unsafe sex can be so hard to treat. The capacity to simultaneously know and not know is commonly encountered in risk-taking sexual behaviour. An illustration of this is a patient who, at one moment, can be soberly acknowledging that his behaviour is "mad", while in the next moment talking excitedly about visiting a prostitute the night before. It is as if in one moment the "link" is made that his behaviour places him at serious risk (K), but in the next moment, this link is attacked or negated (minus K).

In clinical work with patients who persist in engaging in unsafe sexual practice, the Kleinian development offers a framework for thinking about this seemingly paradoxical capacity to both know and not know something simultaneously. The emphasis on destructive forces within the psyche has much to offer in thinking about patients who put themselves, or put others, at risk of possible death.

CASE VIGNETTE: MR BROWN

Mr Brown, a thirty-year-old heterosexually married, but homosexually orientated man, presented at GUM clinic in a state of extreme anxiety convinced he had become infected with HIV. Following a negative test result he remained anxious and a physician, wondering what underlay this continuing anxiety state, referred him for an assessment for psychotherapy. Assessment revealed Mr Brown to be an intelligent professional man, who often found himself involved in homosexual sadomasochistic (SM) role-playing through internet contacts. In these enacted scenarios he was always the passive partner. Although he "knew" of the dangers of the activities, both to himself and his wife, with whom he had occasional sexual relations, he found it difficult to keep the conflict in mind.

From his early years Mr Brown had managed "not to know" about the homosexual component to his nature. A member of a fundamentalist religious group, consciously he was rejecting of the complexities of his sexual make-up. A provisional hypothesis regarding Mr Brown was that he was unable to "know" about this (minus K) and his SM activities helped him to maintain a psychological equilibrium of sorts. Psychotherapy posed a number of threats to this pseudo-equilibrium, as it risked bringing to consciousness many of his fundamental conflicts and thereby plunging him into a serious depressive state. In this way K could be said to pose risks to his psychological health while minus K posed risks to his physical health.

Mr Brown was seen for psychotherapy in a specialist psychotherapy department where he had once-weekly therapy for five years. He found the process difficult and often spoke of it as if it were another of his sadomasochistic role-play sessions with the therapist "beating" him with insights or interpretations. After about a year he was able to start using the therapy and began bringing to sessions occasional dreams in which a young male child was often lost in a cold, dark, empty world. Mr Brown was eventually able to associate to the dream material and thought that the young child "might" have represented early versions of himself as he began to realize what a bleak childhood he had endured. When his dreams began to include the lost child being beaten by an anonymous adult he was able to accept links to his therapist, his sexual activities, and to his childhood. After the third year of therapy his need to engage in sadomasochistic sexual activities, which had been diminishing during the therapy, ceased. His relationship with his wife remained as a primary emotional container for him and during the therapy he was able to be more open with his wife about his homosexuality and his sadomasochistic practices. He reported his surprise that she said she had "known all along" but it had not mattered to her.

The therapist understood that Mr Brown's "not knowing" (minus K) had been gradually but persistently challenged by his "knowing" (K) of the implications of what he was doing. He was slowly able to connect his rage at his early humiliating experiences with the way these experiences were being repeated in an adult form in the SM scenes. Mr

Brown came to see that the way he treated his therapist, which included such seemingly trivial things as teasing, unannounced absences, and frequent lateness, contained a number of hidden, sado-masochistic aspects.

Mr Brown's therapy illustrates the challenge of treating patients engaging in some unsafe sexual practices when the behaviours are founded on a deep and complex history that takes time to unravel before behavioural change can begin to occur.

Kohut's self psychology

The ideas of Heinz Kohut (1971, 1977, 1984) arose in the context of ego psychology in the USA, and relate to an account of the development of the self and in particular the development of narcissism (i.e., the investment in the self), which can potentially be either healthy or malignant. Kohut places an emphasis on the individual's legitimate narcissistic needs for admiration, attention, and mirroring in order to develop a cohesive sense of self.

Development depends upon the availability of adequately admiring and appropriately responsive caretaking figures during early life. Kohut uses the term "selfobjects" to describe the way that others lend themselves to be available to the developing infant or child; the important function that others perform for the immature psyche is to be available not only as separate independent individuals but also as parts of the developing self, providing the mirroring, admiration, or attention that the child requires. Loss, unavailability, or other disruption to the functioning of selfobjects is experienced as highly disintegrative, and can be felt as a loss of part of the self, leading to a state of "narcissistic rage".

Kohut proposes that development involves the negotiation of two positions: in the first, the "grandiose self", the child feels surrounded by the admiration of the parental "selfobject" and feels him or herself to be exceptional and special in the caretaker's eyes, "the gleam in the mother's eye"; in the second position, the parent must allow themselves to be idealized by the child and to become the "idealized parental imago". As "selfobject" the parent is both the idealized other and experienced as an extension of the child, who basks in the sense of being joined with an idealized object.

Through the course of normal development reality gently intrudes, grandiosity is gradually lessened, the need for an idealized other is transformed into an ego ideal and narcissism is transformed into more mature forms (see Mollon, 2001).

This process relies on the empathic responsiveness of parental figures in their function as selfobjects. Where these are absent or otherwise unavailable, early narcissistic needs stay unmodified and are not carried through in the maturation of the personality, thus remaining in an unintegrated state. In such a situation grandiosity co-exists with feelings of shame and inferiority, and/or a persisting yet unrealistic need for the idealization of others leading to inevitable feelings of disappointment and disillusionment. This state of internal affairs may best be described as a chronic narcissistic vulnerability, in which the experiential self is constantly at risk of fragmentation.

The relevance of Kohut's theory of the self to a psychodynamic understanding of unsafe sex lies in his assertion that a common method of trying to prevent this sense of collapse in the experience of the self is to sexualize the regressive needs. In this way, sexually exhibitionistic behaviour may develop in the absence of a healthy and confident display of the self. Alternatively, humiliating experiences may be sexualized in order to transform painful injury into pleasure, thereby making them more tolerable to the self. Thus, according to Kohut, what might be regarded as perverse sexual fantasies or behaviour (and here we might include some instances of unsafe sex involving known HIV risk) are reconceptualized as "sexualised statements about [. . .] narcissistic disturbance" (Kohut, 1971, p. 71). This view is echoed in the writings of Stoller (1975).

Interestingly, other addictive behaviours such as smoking, excessive eating, and compulsively seeking stimulation are also regarded by Kohut as defences against a failing sense of self.

CASE VIGNETTE: MR GREEN

Mr Green was a recently diagnosed HIV positive gay man in his mid-fifties, who entered therapy having reached a depressive impasse in his life. He described himself as having had a very active sexual life in the past and he had often engaged in unsafe sexual practices.

There was evidence in his history of not only physical and sexual abuse, but also of severe and chronic emotional neglect by both his mother and father. This represented for him a complete lack of any empathic selfobjects for the purpose of mirroring or idealization. Some reclaiming of a healthy sense of himself as lovable was later achieved via the process of identifying as gay in early adulthood, but latterly this had been accompanied by an element of aggressive, overt sexual display and he often became involved in violent or sexually abusive relationships with others.

In therapy he came to see that his favourite term of abuse towards others—" Fuck you!"—had been transformed behaviourally into an act of self-abuse ("Fuck me!"), thus serving as an important passive–aggressive defence of his hidden insecure and vulnerable self. Unfortunately, such behaviour had also placed him at increased risk of contracting HIV. While he could now acknowledge the multiple sexual risks he had taken in the past in terms of HIV, it seemed that unconsciously this had been offset by a sense of at last being loved and wanted by others. His recent diagnosis of HIV, as well as the death of a close friend through AIDS, had finally brought about a collapse of these sexualized defences against a long warded-off narcissistic rage and associated depression.

Practice

The application of a psychodynamic model might in some instances lead to psychoanalytic psychotherapy being offered to an individual who repeatedly presents for STD testing, as well as providing a conceptual framework for clinical supervision and consultation with other multidisciplinary team members. For example, GUM clinic staff may find themselves confronting patients who continue to engage in unsafe sexual practices. At times, staff report in supervision feeling intensely angry with such patients in a way that feels out of keeping with their usual approach to counselling. Psychoanalytically-orientated supervision in such situations has often been helpful in assisting staff to think about how they can unwittingly be drawn into acting out feelings in the countertransference that originate in the patients themselves, but which are evacuated by means of projective identification into the staff member (Klein, 1946). An example of this might be a health adviser who finds herself aggressively lecturing a patient about the severe health risks they are exposed to by not using a condom. The patient may present in a passive and vulnerable way and feel attacked by this lecture, yet may remain unaware of their own aggression, enacted through compulsive, repeated high-risk behaviour. Buried, unconscious aspects of the patient's feelings can be subtly communicated and picked up by the worker, who may find him or herself expressing these to the patient, but unaware of the source of the feelings.

By clarifying the defensive purposes of these projective mechanisms—namely to avoid psychic conflict—staff can be aided in their understanding of such patients' behaviour and thereby come to adopt a more empathic and, on occasion, interpretative stance in their preventative work with these patients. Through their experience of being on the receiving end of a patient's splitting, clinic staff can be helped to recognize the distorting impact that this process can have on a patient's broader relationships with others. Scragg and Alcorn (2002) have similarly highlighted the chaos and confusion that splitting can cause in staff teams working in sexual health with patients labelled with a personality disorder.

When therapy is offered, the psychoanalytic approach to the therapeutic relationship contains an invitation to the patient to say whatever comes into his or her mind. It is designed to elicit the whole range of emotions and will often evoke socially unacceptable impulses, hateful and generous, primitive and murderous, which characterize the human mind. In the safety of a psychotherapeutic relationship patients can be helped to see, face, and understand how they are putting themselves at risk and why. The model does not explicitly attempt to change behaviour but it works toward providing the necessary conditions for change.

The examples that follow illustrate the potential impact of patients' conflicts on the staff team, the complex dynamics that may underpin unsafe sexual practices, and the detailed and sometimes long-term therapy required to understand these dynamics in the transference and in the patient's external life, which ultimately may enable them to take control of their behaviour.

Case example 1: Mr White

A thirty-five-year-old man was referred for psychotherapy three years after his older male partner had died from an AIDS-related illness. His frequent requests for HIV testing had evoked concern in the genito-urinary physician. The patient remained HIV negative but the physician was concerned that he was courting danger by having unprotected sex. Initially, the physician and a health counsellor instituted a psycho-educational approach, which appeared to be successful at its completion. However, some months later the patient was still presenting for testing. At this point he was referred for a psychotherapy assessment.

In the assessment it became apparent that he had an early history of disrupted family relationships and the patient indicated that he had been sexually abused by a number of male clients of his mother when she was working as a prostitute. As an adult he had a history of depressive episodes, self-harm, and a pattern of verbally caustic, aggressive relating to others, which usually ended up with them rejecting him. The result of this assessment was that he was put forward for psychoanalytic psychotherapy to help him understand how his early experiences had affected him and his way of relating to others.

The patient was seen for once-weekly psychotherapy for four years; the therapy was stormy, but he rarely missed sessions. Initially reluctant to trust the therapist, a therapeutic alliance did emerge gradually, but it was only after the first long summer break that the patient began to talk about cruising and cottaging during the break and having unsafe sex. At the time the therapist intuitively sensed that this was, in part, an attack on him for leaving the patient, but did not comment on this. It was not until much later in the therapy that Mr White himself came to recognize that he experienced these absences as abandonments paralleling those he experienced in his early maternal relationship. The patient was put in touch with feelings of wanting not to exist, which—when a similar pattern emerged during and after other therapy breaks—it was possible to link more fully to the pattern of seeking unsafe sexual encounters.

On an anniversary of his partner's death, the patient was able to accept an interpretation linking his wish to be joined with his partner in death with his attempting (unconsciously) to become infected with HIV. The partner (and also the therapist) had functioned as a maternal container for the hurt, abused, and neglected aspects of the patient. Caring for the sick partner had enabled the patient to act in a reparative way that temporarily obscured his own internal emptiness. Once the partner died he was then much more at risk of being overwhelmed by his chronic feeling of emptiness, and he seemed to be searching for the hoped-for bliss that he thought annihilation promised.

Similarly, the patient tried seductively to make the therapist into a perfect maternal container who would never let him down, leave him, or abuse him. When the patient was faced with a break he became anxious, depressed, and angry, leading to a search for annihilation. Any failure of understanding on the part of the therapist would plunge the patient into withering attacks. The therapist had to accept that he could not provide a "corrective emotional experience" for the patient. Much of the therapy was spent trying to understand, and work through in the transference, this rage as a defence against the deadness and emptiness that Mr White felt at the core of his emotional life. His unconscious risk-taking slowly began to make more sense to him in the context of a fuller understanding of his own internal landscape.

Interestingly the eventual impact of this insight on his behaviour was that he became "asexual" as he put it, and developed platonic relationships with other men. Although he missed having an active sex life he described feeling relieved at this outcome to his therapy.

Case Example 2: Mr Black

Mr Black was a forty-year-old heterosexually married man who presented via GUM following repeated HIV testing despite receiving negative test results. This initially caused some puzzlement in the minds of the clinic staff, who were accustomed to repeat testing in the context of overt AIDS phobia or HIV-related hypochondriasis, but in this case felt uncertain as to the underlying motivations for Mr Black's repeated requests for full STD screening.

Over the course of the next six months, Mr Black gradually came to reveal to one of the clinic's health advisers a long-standing history of compulsive, secret, sexual encounters with female prostitutes. These frequently involved unsafe sexual practices and as a result he had come to develop excessive concerns about infecting his wife and being "found out". He did not respond to the health adviser's usual information-based, psycho-educational counselling intervention, and was becoming increasingly desperate for further help regarding the prevention of his behaviour.

At a routine clinical meeting the health adviser presented his case history, wondering about his suitability for psychological intervention. A lively discussion ensued in which the clinic team found itself split between feelings of condemnation in some staff members, and feelings in others of compassion for what seemed to them a rather sad and vulnerable figure. It was agreed that he should be referred on for a detailed psychological assessment.

During the course of his assessment, which was conducted by a psychodynamic psychotherapist attached to the team, Mr Black described the sadomasochistic nature of his sexual exchanges with prostitutes. He clearly felt hugely guilty and ashamed of these behaviours, but felt equally excited by them. He reported being quite aware of the risk of HIV infection he was placing upon himself and his wife, but felt unable to stop despite wishing to do so.

The family history suggested a pattern of early object relationships characterized by both an over-involved relationship with an emotionally needy mother and a harsh and critical father who used to beat him. His description of both his personal and professional life suggested that similar patterns tended to develop in his adult relationships, whereby he became involved with emotionally dependent women (including his wife) and was frequently oversensitive to the critical comments of his boss at work.

The assessing psychotherapist was particularly struck by the parallel between the mixed feelings this man had aroused within the clinical team meeting and the ambivalent nature of Mr Black's own attitude to his unsafe sexual behaviour; on the one hand condemning himself for it, on the other feeling rather helpless about how to change.

Mr Black was offered individual, weekly, psychodynamic psychotherapy, and after a lengthy period of ambivalence early in the therapy—characterized by several missed appointments followed by profusely apologetic messages—a satisfactory working alliance developed. Mr Black was helped to acknowledge and then overcome his fearful expectations of incurring the therapist's wrath at his non-attendance.

Ongoing analysis of the transference (and the countertransference in supervision) allowed exploration of the anticipated re-enactment between patient and therapist of Mr Black's sadomasochistic relationship with his early objects; that is, his secret loathing of his mother's neediness of him while at the same time craving love from her, and (in his mind) his punishment for this in the form of his father's beatings. In time it slowly became possible to make links between these and the sadomasochistic sexual relations with prostitutes. These gradually came to be understood as his unconscious attempt to punish himself (a symbolic representation of his internalized critical father) by becoming infected with HIV and so confirming his inner feelings of badness for his unconscious craving for his mother and desire to triumph over his father.

Two contributions from the psychoanalytic literature are of relevance here to broadening a psychodynamic understanding of this man's presenting difficulties. First, Rosen's (1995) work emphasizes the aetiological role of seduction and deprivation in the constellation of sadomasochistic behaviour. Second, McDougall (1995) conceptualizes such compulsive sexual behaviour as an attempt at self-cure in the face of unbearable psychic threat. The "addictive solution" serves an important unconscious function in terms of avoiding or denying severe anxiety (often of a paranoid nature), depression (accompanied by feelings of inner deadness), or in some cases more psychotic anxieties (such as fear of bodily or psychic fragmentation).

In Mr Black's case his sadomasochistic behaviour represented an unconscious attempt to deny both his paranoid and depressive anxieties through identification with both aggressor (father) and victim (mother) of his own internal psychic drama. This drama gradually came to be played out in the therapy arena in which it could be safely observed and understood, without him becoming overwhelmed by his unconscious wish to confirm his inner feelings of badness and worthlessness that were driving him to repeatedly place himself at risk of HIV infection.

At the end of the therapy, Mr Black retained some of his anger at the world but had overcome his desire to visit prostitutes. His relationship with his wife was more harmonious and he was able to express gratitude to the therapist for the help he had received.

Concluding remarks

Not all those who engage in unsafe sexual practices need or could use psychodynamic psychotherapy. We recognize that many people have been helped, and continue to be helped, by cognitive behavioural models. However, we are interested in broadening the understanding of unsafe sexual behaviour to include the unconscious dynamics underlying unsafe sex. This may offer an alternative approach to helping those whose behaviour can otherwise remain unchanged by a more conscious and rational framework for understanding and intervention. The cases described above illustrate that this may require painstaking and long-term work, in which re-enactments of earlier conflicts and trauma, both within the trans-ference and outside the therapy, can slowly be understood and worked through.

In some patients unsafe sexual behaviours may be best under-stood as expressions of an underlying disturbance in personality organization, linked with dysfunctional ways of interpersonal relat-ing that pose great challenges to clinicians. We are interested in helping fellow professionals who work in the areas of both preven-tion and treatment to make sense of the frustrating and seemingly incomprehensible behaviours they face in some of their patients. In this way we wish to emphasize the potentially important direct and indirect contribution to interventions in unsafe sex that can be made via psychodynamic consultation to colleagues, as well as through the medium of psychodynamic psychotherapy with indi-vidual patients.

This chapter has proposed that a comprehensive model of unsafe sex needs to include space for psychodynamic conceptualizations if it is to provide an adequate and effective map that encompasses the broad range and complexity of human sexual behaviour.

Note

1. This chapter originated from a paper presented by both authors at the 1999 AIDS Impact Conference in Ottawa, and has since been substan-tially developed and revised.

Acknowledgements

ST would like to thank Derbyshire Mental Health Services NHS Trust for their support. BR would like to thank the Division of Psychiatry and Behavioural Sciences,University of Nottingham Medical School and Nottinghamshire Healthcare NHS Trust for their support.

References

Aggleton, P. (1996). Global priorities for HIV/AIDS research. *International Journal of STDs and AIDS*. 2 (suppl. 2): 13–16.

Ajzen, I., & Madden, T. J. (1986). Prediction of goal-directed behaviour: attitudes, intentions and perceived behavioural control. *Journal of Experimental Social Psychology, 22*: 453–474.

Auerbach, J. D., Wypijewska, C., Brodie, H., & Keith, H. (Eds.) (1994). *AIDS and Behaviour: An Integrated Approach*. Washington, DC: National Academy Press.

Becker, M. H. (1974). The health belief model and personal health behaviour. *Health Education Monographs, 2*: 220–243.

Bion, W. R. (1967). *Second Thoughts*. London: Heinemann.

Branson, B., Ransom, R., Peterman, T., & Zaidi A. (1996). Randomised control trial of intensive group counselling to reduce risk behaviours in high-risk STD clinic patients. Paper presented at the Eleventh International Conference on AIDS, Vancouver.

Canin, L., Dolcini, M. M., & Adler, N. E. (1999). Barriers to and facilitators of HIV–STD behaviour change: intrapersonal and relationship-based factors. *Review of General Psychology, 3*(4): 338–371.

Catania, J. A., Kegeles, S. M., & Coates, T. J. (1990). Towards an understanding of risk behaviour: an AIDS risk reduction model (ARRM). *Health Education Quarterly, 17*: 53–72.

Fisher, J. D., & Fisher, A. W. (1992). Changing AIDS risk behaviour. *Psychological Bulletin,11*(1): 455–474.

Friedman, R. (1998). Internalised homophobia, pathological grief, and high-risk sexual behaviour in a gay man with multiple psychiatric disorders. *Journal of Sex Education and Therapy, 23*: 115–120.

Freud, S. (1914g). Remembering, repeating and working-through. (Further recommendations on the technique of psycho-analysis II). *S.E., 12*: 145–156. London: Hogarth.

Freud, S. (1920g). Beyond the pleasure principle. *S.E., 18*: 7–64. London: Hogarth.

Hinshelwood, R. D. (1991). *A Dictionary of Kleinian Thought* (2nd edn). London: Free Association Books.

Joffe, H. (1996). AIDS research and prevention: a social representational approach. *British Journal of Medical Psychology, 69*: 169–190.

Joffe, H. (1997). Juxtaposing positivist and non-positivist approaches to social scientific AIDS research: reply to Fife-Schaw's commentary. *British Journal of Medical Psychology, 70*: 75–83.

Joseph, B. (1982). Addiction to near-death. *International Journal of Psycho-Analysis, 63*: 449–456 [reprinted in E. Bott-Spillius & M. Feldman (Eds), *Psychic Equilibrium and Psychic Change—Selected papers of Betty Joseph*. London: Routledge, 1989].

Kalichman, S. C., Carey, M. P., & Johnson, B. T. (1996). Prevention of sexually transmitted HIV infection: a meta-analytic review of the behavioural outcome literature. *Annals of Behavioural Medicine, 18*: 6–15.

Kelly, J., Kalichman, S., Kauth, M., Kilgore, H., Campos, P., Roo, S., Brosfield, T., & St Laurence, J. (1991). Situational factors associated with AIDS risk behaviour lapses and coping strategies used by gay men who successfully avoid lapses. *American Journal of Public Health, 81*(11): 1335–1338.

Klein, J. (1990). Patients who are not ready for interpretations. *British Journal of Psychotherapy, 7*(1): 38–48.

Klein, M. (1946). Notes on some schizoid mechanisms. *International Journal of Psycho-Analysis, 27*: 99–110.

Kohut, H. (1971). *The Analysis of the Self: A Systematic Approach to the Psychoanalytic Treatment of Narcissistic Personality Disorders.* New York: International Universities Press.

Kohut, H. (1977). *The Restoration of the Self.* New York: International Universities Press.

Kohut, H. (1984). *How does Analysis Cure?* Chicago: University of Chicago Press.

McDougall, J. (1995). *The Many Faces of Eros: A Psychoanalytic Exploration of Human Sexuality.* London: Free Association Books.

McKirnan, D. J., Ostrow, D. G., & Hope, B. (1996). Sex, drugs and escape: a psychological model of HIV-risk sexual behaviour. *AIDS Care, 8*(6): 655–670.

Mollon, P. (2001). *Releasing the Self: The Healing Legacy of Heinz Kohut.* London: Whurr Publishers.

Money-Kyrle, R. (1968). Cognitive development. *International Journal of Psycho-Analysis, 49*: 691–698.

Parker, R. (1996). Empowerment, community mobilization and social change in the face of HIV/AIDS. *AIDS 10* (suppl. 3): S27–S31.

Pinkerton, S., & Abramson, P. (1995). Decision making and personality factors in sexual risk-taking for HIV/AIDS: a theoretical integration. *Personality and Individual Difference, 19*(5): 713–723.

Rosen, I. (1995). *Sexual Deviation* (3rd edn). Oxford: Oxford University Press.

Rosenfeld, H. (1971). A clinical approach to the psycho-analytical theory of the life and death instincts: an investigation into the aggressive aspects of narcissism. *International Journal of Psycho-Analysis, 52*: 169–178.

Ross, M. W., & Kelly, J. A. (1999). Interventions to reduce HIV transmission in homosexual men. In: J. L. Peterson & R. J. Diclemente (Eds.), *Handbook of HIV Prevention*. New York: Plenum Press.

Ross, M. W., & Nilsson Schonnesson, L. (2000). HIV/AIDS and sexuality. In: Szuchman & Muscarella (Eds.), *Psychological Perspectives on Human Sexuality*. New York: Wiley.

Scragg, P., & Alcorn, R. (2002). Personality disorder and sexual health. In: D. Miller & J. Green (Eds.), *The Psychology of Sexual Health*. Oxford: Blackwell Science.

Sogolow, E., Semaan, S., Johnson, W., Neumann, M., Ramirez, G., Sweat, M., & Doll, L. (1998). Effects of U.S.-based HIV interventions on safer sex: meta-analyses, overall and for populations, age groups, and settings. Paper presented at the World AIDS Conference, June, Geneva, Switzerland.

Steiner, J. (1993). *Psychic Retreats: Pathological Organizations in Psychotic, Neurotic and Borderline Patients*. London: Routledge.

Stoller, R. (1975). *Perversion: The Erotic Form of Hatred*. New York: Pantheon.

UNAIDS (1998). Relationships of HIV and STD declines in Thailand to behavioural change. *UNAIDS* 98.2 Best practice material, Geneva.

Van Campenhoudt, L., Cohen, M., Guizzardi, G., & Hausser, D. (Eds.) (1997). *Sexual Interactions and HIV Risk: New Conceptual Perspectives in European Research*. Washington, DC: Taylor & Francis.

Whitmire, L., Harlow, L., Quinn, K., & Morokoff. P. (1999). *Childhood Trauma and HIV: Women at Risk*. Philadephia: Brunner/Mazel.

CHAPTER SIX

Refugees and sexuality

Sarah Zetler

Introduction

In the United Kingdom the response to asylum seekers, or refugees, has become increasingly entangled with national and international political agendas. Over the past decade there has been a change of emphasis regarding who is considered to have a valid right to enter and remain in the UK. This has occurred in the context of a highly polarized political debate about immigration policy. A "culture of disbelief" has infiltrated popular media and national policy about people from non-EU countries fleeing to the UK to seek safety (Asylum Aid, 1995). This controversy has often served to obscure the social and health care needs of people who have fled their country of origin.

With the spread of HIV and other sexually transmitted infections there has been an increasing awareness of the importance of addressing people's sexual health needs. The UK's National Strategy for Sexual Health and HIV (DOH, 2001) defines sexual health as follows:

> Sexual health is an important part of physical and mental health. It is a key part of our identity as human beings together with the

> fundamental human rights to privacy, a family life and living free
> from discrimination. Essential elements of good sexual health are
> equitable relationships and sexual fulfilment with access to infor-
> mation and services to avoid the risks of unintended pregnancy,
> illness or disease

The government's definition of sexual health is clear in its aims,
as well as holistic in its approach, but its ability to meet the needs
of people who are eligible for NHS treatment for sexual health
problems remains doubtful. Asylum seekers, who are eligible for
treatment while they await the outcome of their judicial process, are
one such group.

There are a number of factors that require careful consideration
when attempting to appropriately address the sexual health needs
of displaced people. This chapter will try to raise awareness about
some of the challenges clinicians face when working in this area.
Consideration will be given to assumptions that underpin the theoretical models commonly used in mainstream psychology services
in the UK. Some of the implications of applying these models cross-
culturally within the field of sexual health will be addressed. This
will be followed by an examination of some clinical issues pertinent
to performing interventions with people whose lives are marked by
uncertainty. Issues relating to power and culture are included as
additional factors that influence help-seeking behaviour and adjustment to and treatment of certain sexual health problems. Some of
the discussion will take us outside the parameters of what is traditionally viewed as the subject of clinical psychological enquiry.
Finally, some consideration will be given to the political dimensions
of the work that psychologists are involved with in order to delineate a way forward.

Definition of terms

In the UK, the term "asylum seeker" is used to describe people who
have applied for protection under the 1951 Geneva Convention,
which states that an applicant will be recognized as a refugee if
s/he is a person who:

owing to a well founded fear of being persecuted for reasons of race, religion, nationality, membership of a particular social group or political opinion, and is outside the country of his (sic) nationality or former habitual residence and is unable, or owing to such fear, is unwilling to avail himself of the protection of that country or return to it. [United Nations, 1951]

If the Home Office recognises the person as a refugee, s/he is granted refugee status and is entitled to full access to health, welfare and social services in the UK. If the applicant is refused refugee status they could still be granted humanitarian protection under the European Convention on Human Rights. It is often this clause that is invoked in the case of people who have a medical condition, such as HIV, that requires ongoing treatment. For if treatment is not readily available, returning a person to their country of origin would significantly reduce their life expectancy and potentially subject them to "acute physical and mental suffering" (United Nations High Commission on Refugees, 1951). In such cases applicants are usually granted Exceptional Leave to Remain (ELR), which allows them to remain in the host country for a defined period of time. Someone granted ELR status might not be given the same level of rights as someone granted full refugee status.

Seeking asylum in the UK

The process of seeking asylum in the UK has become increasingly complicated and problematic. Of 103,080 applications (including dependents) made during 2002, 33% were allowed to remain in the UK (Heath, Jeffries, & Purcell, 2004). Additional requirements such as Section 55 of the new Immigration and Asylum Act have resulted in applicants being denied access to shelter and essential resources because they failed to apply "as soon as is practicably possible" after their arrival in the UK. Anecdotal evidence indicates that this legislation has been very harshly interpreted, with a delay of even two days being grounds for refusal. There has been an outcry from both the statutory and non-statutory sectors regarding such requirements, as they are seen to infringe upon people's basic human rights, particularly as these requirements deny access to resources necessary for survival.

The process of seeking asylum in the UK has developed into an exercise whereby applicants, with the help of the legal profession, have to prove that they are genuinely in need of humanitarian protection. Due to the growing "culture of disbelief" (Asylum Aid, 1995) people's legitimacy to be described as refugees is constantly called into question. It is here that mental health practitioners can be asked to provide expert evidence to validate applicants' claims of having a "well founded fear of persecution" or that a return to their country of origin would result in "acute mental or physical suffering" (United Nations, 1951).

Listening to clients' stories within the consulting room can therefore take on a different meaning, as clinicians may be expected to provide medico-legal evidence based on this interaction. The disciplines of psychology and psychotherapy have developed specific ways of listening to and understanding the stories clients bring to psychotherapeutic encounters. These ways often include a focus on unconscious and symbolic communication, usually seen within the context of a developmental understanding of character formation. This special way of listening requires the suspension of assumptions and biases in order to enter into the psychic life of the client, allowing the expression of different feelings, be they contradictory or "irrational". The legal profession, however, requires a very different sort of information gathering. The process, for psychologists, of bearing witness to people's testimonies of survival, can thus take on a different meaning. Information gathered could become distorted by the context of the medico-legal system that requires "proof" that clients need humanitarian protection. Swartz and Levett (1989) have drawn attention to the potential double bind this places professionals in, as "evidence" must be gathered in ways that lend scientific credibility to the effects of being exposed to political instability, violence and endemic poverty. Such ways of gathering evidence can delimit and intrude upon the narratives that clients relay and may be countertherapeutic, as clients are expected to disclose potentially difficult events before the establishment of a trusting therapeutic relationship. Additionally, clients' narratives may be skewed to focus on what the legal system requires, rather than relaying the inherently personal meaning of their experience, both past and present.

Papadopoulos (2002) has developed a useful framework that divides refugees' experience into four distinct phases:

1. Anticipation. The knowledge of impending intrusions to survival and decisions on how to avoid this.
2. Devastating events. The phase of actual/imminent danger or violence that leads to flight.
3. Survival. When refugees are safe from danger but live in a state of uncertainty regarding their future.
4. Adjustment. The process of adjusting to life in the receiving country.

The process of seeking asylum in the UK, in terms of the legal framework, access to social support and specialized health services, tends to focus exclusively on the first two phases of the framework, namely "Anticipation" and "Devastating events". There are numerous reasons for the development of this partial focus. Some factors relate to the climate of disbelief, while others relate to the way that the effects of certain experiences are constructed, particularly experiences that are common in times of war. Psychological discourses relating to trauma, in particular post traumatic stress disorder (PTSD), have become increasingly widespread over the past few decades and have been applied across vastly different settings. Such constructs are liberally applied to asylum seekers, and discourses relating to "refugee trauma" are commonly used ways of talking about the refugee experience. Through deconstructing some of the assumptions that underlie the bio-medical model, its global applicability will be questioned, as well as the power it has to distort the way we might conceptualize our clients' needs.

Deconstructing some underlying assumptions of the bio-medical model and the way it has been applied to refugees

Notions of individuality

The anthropologist Geertz (1975) draws our attention to the western notion that people individuate autonomously and separately from each other, and from nature, as a rather peculiar idea within the context of the world's cultures. In many non-western cultures the notion of the self and its relationship to others and the outside world, including the physical and spirit world, is vastly different.

In western cultures mental distress is frequently seen as arising from internal intrapsychic experiences or pathologies that exist within the individual (Summerfield, 1995). This is contrary to the way that mental distress or illness is conceptualized in many non-western settings. The western bio-medical model has a tendency to reify certain signs and symptoms as universally occurring phenomena, attributing very specific meanings to their existence; for example, ascribing sleep disturbances and the avoidance of social situations as specific diagnostic signs of PTSD. On closer examination there may be other equally plausible explanations for such experiences that require consideration.

> Client A recounted her experience of arriving in London after fleeing from a rural village in Ethiopia as a result of being persecuted for her religious beliefs. She had been sexually assaulted by a number of soldiers in detention before escaping to the UK. She was placed in temporary accommodation in a hotel in central London, where she struggled greatly to adjust. She was unused to living with strangers in very close proximity and to sharing bathrooms and eating areas. She also felt unable to eat the ready prepared meals, which she described as "strange white people's food". Life in a very populated urban environment with its lack of open spaces felt completely alien to her. She was suffering from what might be termed panic attacks, which were precipitated by being in unfamiliar crowded spaces surrounded by people she did not know. She did not have the usual physical experiences or cognitions often seen in clients who suffer from a panic disorder, that is, fear of losing control or consciousness, or having a heart attack. Rather, her thoughts related to a fear that she was becoming invisible.

Many of the symptoms this client displayed could easily be misinterpreted as a traumatic dissociation, panic disorder, or other forms of mental illness. Through careful listening to her so-called "symptoms" they began to take on a different significance and were much more closely related to her experience of being dislocated from her village and finding herself in London than being attributable to any underlying mental disorder.

Western debate relating to the outcome of being exposed to certain experiences, such as rape and torture, which are common in times of political instability and civil war, has focused on the effects of such acts as an assault on individual integrity. This is in keeping with a western construction of identity, which tends to de-emphasize the effects of community, culture, religion, and societal norms on the construction of subjectivity. War-time experiences need to be conceptualized in terms of a dynamic interaction between the survivor and the surrounding society, and not as a confined entity located within the individual psychopathology of the victim (Summerfield, 1995). This is particularly salient in the case of people who have survived the destruction of whole communities. In the face of such devastating acts, individual brutality may be construed very differently and imbued with different meanings (Bracken, Giller, & Summerfield, 1995). For example:

> Client B from Uganda, in recounting her experience of being held in a position of forced servitude for a four-year period, did not highlight her experience of repeated non-consensual sex as particularly significant. What she pressed as the most significant part of her ordeal was her failed attempts at protecting her mother from similar advances by the rebels.

By applying a Western conception of identity across vastly different cultures, the specific cultural contexts in which certain experiences are generated, and the unique position that individuals adopt in relation to certain violations, can easily be overlooked (Papadopoulos, 2002).

The universality of responses to adverse events

There is presumptuousness in assuming that experience X will result in symptom Y, regardless of the socio-historical context in which it occurred. When focusing on people who have been exposed to large-scale organized violence, such violence is rarely aimed at specific individuals, but rather at whole groups of people who are seen to support particular views. Individual experiences of violence can thus take on very different meanings. Schlapobersky (1988) highlights how responses to stressors are highly influenced by individuals' appraisal of the situation, their capacity to process their experience, attach meaning to it and incorporate it into their pre-existing belief systems.

Theorists such as Levett (1989) have described the possible negative effects of attempting to predict what events people will experience as traumatic. This theorizing has taken place in the controversial context of focusing on the bio-medical model's prediction of how people respond to sexual experiences in childhood. I do not want to enter into the above highly contentious debate, but would like, instead, to raise readers' awareness of the pitfalls inherent in presuming what events our clients "should" experience as traumatizing and how such experiences may manifest. For example:

> Client C, a soldier in Rwanda, had participated in and witnessed multiple atrocities during the genocide in his country. He was been imprisoned and tortured for refusing to participate in continued warfare in the Congo, yet he hardly ever made mention of his war-time experiences other than to let me know he had faced death many times, including having almost been killed at the hands of his torturers. What he emphasized instead was his experience of trying to rebuild his life in the UK following an HIV positive diagnosis. He spent much time in sessions discussing problems with inadequate housing and difficulties he was having adjusting to life in what he perceived to be an environment in which he felt unwanted and devalued.

In presuming what our clients should experience as traumatic, we run the risk of imposing western interpretations of illness and health without taking cognisance of how our clients might prioritize their own needs. Although many people may present with symptomatology that can be fitted into the classic PTSD model, many others may present with problems that are expressed in very different ways. In some, the presentation of physical symptoms is marked (Losi, 2002), often in the absence of underlying organic causes that can explain their existence. Such physical symptoms may present alongside, or in the absence of, easily defined psychological symptoms; in others few symptoms appear at all.

The de-politicization of human distress and psychologization of socio-political phenomenon

Many theorists have criticized the bio-medical model for having a de-politicized framework of understanding human suffering. This may be largely due to the epistemological framework that governs most mainstream psychological theorizing and research: that is, the positivistic model of investigation. This model requires the transformation and manipulation of subjects and other variables in order to render the data intelligible within the framework. This necessitates subject characteristics to be divided into categories that are operationally definable (Gergen & Davis, 1985). Once categories have been created, relationships between these categories are investigated and emphasis is placed on certain interactions. This method of investigation is linked to experimentation in the natural sciences, where if certain interactions are seen to be repeatable, they are accepted as fact.

Harre (1987) points out that the requirements of positivistic frameworks become particularly problematic when focusing on a construct that does not exist as an entity. This is the case with research that focuses on a construct such as trauma. As the concept of trauma requires operationally definable categories, subjective experience is conceptualized in a way that is fixed, stable, and separate from the influences of time, context, and culture. The fragmentation of experience into the personal and social components required by positivistic frameworks thus fails to conceptualize subjectivity within an interactive framework that can account for the effects of context on individuals and vice versa. The western medico-legal system requires that evidence be derived from positivistic frameworks. This can pressure clinicians into applying culture-specific diagnostic models to people who come from vastly different cultures. Little cognisance is given to the culturally specific way that people may label or describe their symptoms, or how they understand the cause of their experiences. This can have far-reaching implications, for if a client fails to meet the criterion for PTSD they may be excluded from certain services or fail to be granted leave to remain, as their distress cannot be "proven" in ways that are seen as valid by the medical or legal system.

The medicalization of socio-political phenomenon has become increasingly common in UK discourses relating to refugees (Bracken, Giller, & Summerfield, 1995). Theorists such as Foucault (1980) and Rose (1989a) offer detailed analyses of how medical discourses assist in constructing subjectivity in very powerful ways that may serve to obscure underlying political and ideological processes and influences. The creation of a "refugee trauma" discourse has tended to define the distress and suffering experienced in times of war as a psychological condition that requires professional attention or treatment rather than political debate and reform (Summerfield, 1995). This is reinforced by the structure of the UK immigration system that demands proof that clients require humanitarian protection. What is not made clear, however, is that the decision-making process relating to who is a "genuine" asylum seeker in need of humanitarian protection relies on a very specific construction and interpretation of human rights, one which has undeniable political and economic underpinnings. Ironically, it is the culture-specific diagnostic categories that are integral to the internal workings of the mental health profession that get used to justify what are essentially political decisions, albeit unwittingly for many politically progressive professionals. Readers are referred to the writings of Foucault (1980) and Rose (1989b) for a detailed historical deconstruction of the complex interplay between the rise of disciplines such as psychiatry/psychology and political governance.

The possible effects of exile

Papadopoulos (2002) has very eloquently discussed some of the issues involved in losing one's home: the disorientating intrapsychic effects this can have as well as some of the difficulties in trying to establish a new home in the face of such loss. I have witnessed many clients struggling to articulate the enormity of their experience of loss in the telling of their personal histories. As one twenty-five-year-old male client from Zambia described his circumstances:

> I live in clothes that are from other people, I live in XXX [name of temporary accommodation hotel], I do not know where my family is, I am broken . . . I have nothing to offer, who will want me?

Such experiences of loss and dislocation can lead to a particular type of "frozenness" (Papadopoulos, 2002) or "cultural bereavement" (Stedman, 1999) that can diagnostically be very easy to misinterpret as mental illness. Most of the clients that I see remain frozen in the *survival phase*, which is exacerbated by the constant state of uncertainty regarding their future and the changing nature of their roles. The state of being without fixed abode, under threat of dispersal to remote parts of the UK or deportation, without access to sufficient resources or permission to work legally, would create problems for virtually anybody (Loizos, 2002). Much of the research literature regarding trauma and refugees has tended to reify the incidence of extreme violence as the central and defining experience that requires working through and has neglected other, perhaps equally important dimensions such as the effects of exile itself (Summerfield, 1995).

I have attempted to demonstrate how the theories and models that we use are not neutral and that as clinicians we, too, are operating within a specific socio-historical and political framework. This has important implications for the way we assess and respond to the needs of our clients. It is essential to include in our models an understanding of the possible effects of displacement itself when conceptualizing refugees' needs. This is particularly important when focusing on refugees' sexual health needs.

Certain pre- and post flight experiences and their possible effects on the sexual health of displaced people

Sexual assault

In times of war and civil unrest, certain sectors of society experience a loss of control over many aspects of their lives, including their sexuality. As outlined in the first section of this chapter, it is crucial not to assume that particular experiences have the same meaning and predictive outcome for all people. It is, however, useful to be aware of potential disruptions to sexual development or functioning that our clients may have experienced. Sexual violation has been reported as an endemic yet poorly visible aspect of violent conflict, usually due to the stigma and shame associated with reporting such violations (Swiss & Giller, 1993). Reports of more recent civil unrest have tended to acknowledge the extent of such violation (such as the well-publicized systematic rape of Bosnian Muslim women by Serb militia). Some have seen the rise of nationalism and militarization as playing key roles in the increase of sexual violence during times of war, especially during ethnic conflicts (Albanese, 2001). Specific therapeutic issues relating to therapy with survivors of sexual trauma are addressed in Chapter Eight of this volume. However, as the act of sexual assault is deeply embedded within prevailing social and cultural constructions, attention will be given in this chapter to the possible impact of a client's cultural milieu on their adjustment following sexual assault.

First, consideration needs to be given to how sexuality, and its violation, may be construed within a client's specific culture. This is not to detract from the highly personal ways people make sense of certain life experiences, but rather to attempt to emphasize the role that social worlds play in influencing the way people process and adjust to such experiences. Parkes (1971) introduced the concept of *assumptive worlds* as a way of understanding changes in psychosocial reality. Assumptive worlds are seen to arise from our cumulative experiences from birth and include not only assumptions about the world outside of us but also assumptions about the consequences of our actions and the actions of others to whom we may be attached (Parkes, 2001). In its broadest sense, assumptive worlds are seen as a "principle of the normative constancy of experience and belief, a constancy principle of the psychological organisation of the human world and one's experience of oneself and the world" (Kauffman, 2001, p. 2). Life events that are seen to cause the most difficult psychosocial transitions are those that violate assumptions concerning (1) *the self* as able to identify and deal with dangers; (2) *others* as able to protect the self from dangers; (3) *the world* as basically a safe place with authorities (be they God, government or the law) offering protection (Parkes, 2001). Janoff-Bulman (1992) views such assumptions as providing a mechanism by which one can preserve value-laden beliefs about the goodness, meaningfulness and benevolence of the world and of our own self-worth. She proposes that it is the *loss* of these value-laden beliefs that is experienced as traumatic. As Kauffman states:

> The assumptive world is illusion believed to be reality. And in this way human culture is constituted. What is shattered in trauma are beliefs, in the sense of vitally valued illusions, or more especially the ability to believe or assume. [2001, p. 3]

Sexual assault is an event that has frequently been seen as one that shatters people's assumptive worlds. The added difficulty for refugees is that the rebuilding of valued illusions takes place in a time of enormous change, and often in an environment in the UK that is experienced as hostile and unwelcoming. Many asylum seekers have clearly expressed knowledge of the way that the popular UK press constructs them: as infectious threats trying to take vital resources away from UK citizens. One has only to look as far as our popular media to see clear signs of racism and xenophobia; a recent headline in the *Sun* read "Polluted with disease and a threat to British lives" (All Party Parliamentary AIDS Group, 2003). Nathanson, head of the science and ethics committee at the British Medical Association, attempts to deconstruct some commonly held myths regarding the "burden" that asylum seekers place on our social and health care systems. She says the additional cost to the NHS of caring for asylum seekers is marginal.

> It [asylum seekers] adds to the strain but it didn't create it. And if they lived in better conditions they wouldn't need so much intervention from the NHS. The evidence is that asylum seekers become ill after they arrive in the UK [Aaronovitch, 2003]

There are some additional factors that may make adjustment following a sexual assault both complex and unpredictable. Heise, Pitanuy, and Germain (1994) highlight the difficulty for some women in obtaining access to safe services for termination of pregnancy, if needed, following a sexual assault. If access to terminations is unavailable or culturally prohibited, this could result in the additional burden of having to bear a perpetrator's child. Second, in cultures that place a high value on virginity, the disclosure of a sexual assault can result in women being ostracized, beaten, murdered, or driven to suicide due to the dishonour that such assaults are seen to bring upon the family (Heise, Pitanuy, & Germain, 1994). As an unmarried nineteen-year-old Muslim girl from North Africa expressed: "No-one will want me, I am spoilt . . . I cannot tell anyone, my future is without hope . . . how can I explain what has been taken away from me?"

The above client felt she was to blame for being sexually assaulted and carried a high degree of shame and guilt regarding the assault. This was despite the fact that she had been outnumbered by rebels and had no means to shield herself from their advances. She blamed herself for not being able to safeguard her virginity. She also feared being blamed by others, which in turn prevented her from disclosing the assault. She remained profoundly isolated with a secret she struggled to bear, unable to get support from friends or professionals due to feeling unable to disclose what had happened. The shattering of her assumptive world relating to herself as able to identify and deal with dangers left her feeling disorientated, highly anxious, and untrusting of herself and others, particularly men. This resulted in her feeling unable to form new friendships, leaving her socially very isolated. Furthermore, she lived in a state of constant uncertainty regarding her future as she faced the threat of dispersal. When she discussed her uncertain future, she expressed concern around her ability to find a husband, as she believed that the loss of her virginity made her less desirable and worthy. It can thus be seen that for asylum seekers in the UK, difficulties following sexual assault can extend far beyond the event(s) itself, but are also influenced by the many potentially negative outcomes determined by the social, cultural, and political milieu in which survivors may find themselves (Petrak, 2002).

HIV

The increasing prevalence of sexually transmitted infections, in particular HIV, has added an additional sobering element to the arena of sexuality. This chapter will focus on some of the ramifications that asylum seekers may face when testing HIV-positive. The spread of HIV is particularly relevant for people who come from areas with high levels of political and economic instability, as they have often had limited access to methods of protecting themselves. There are a number of factors that may inhibit access to testing and, if necessary, adherence to treatment.

Due to the way that different cultures view sexuality, especially outside of the marriage unit, young single people may find it difficult to seek out or access services. An individual's attitudes towards sexuality and sexually transmitted infections can thus be overridden by concerns for the whole family and its reputation in the community (Davidson, Fenton, & Mahtani, 2002). Once the initial hurdle of accessing services has been overcome, people may still have difficulties disclosing the extent of their sexual activity to unfamiliar professionals within a GUM setting. Coming to terms with a positive test result is very complicated for asylum seekers who belong to communities where there is a high degree of stigma associated with HIV, and research shows that people who belong to ethnic minorities in the UK have lower rates of disclosure to significant others (Petrak, Doyle, Smith, & Skinner, 1998).

While many people with HIV infection develop ways to cope with their condition, it is unfortunate that, for some, knowledge of infection can result in severe psychological distress (Petrak & Miller, 2001). Such distress can contribute to profound adjustment problems, including an inability to disclose one's status, adherence difficulties, and problems with negotiating safer sex practices (Chesney, Folkman, & Chambers, 1996). Refugees, especially from African countries, often have had first hand experience of people living with and dying of HIV/AIDS. Such exposure affects their attitudes to, beliefs in and behaviour around testing, disclosing their status, and successfully adjusting to life on highly active anti-retroviral therapies (HAART). Clients talk about their experiences of watching friends and family die very lonely and painful deaths, ostracized by their communities, without access to treatment or care. As a twenty-seven-year-old client from Ghana stated, "If you get the diagnosis you become a ghost; before death has come for you, friends and family treat you as already dead."

The lack of exposure to successful treatments can result in clients having very different views of the disease's progression as well as the efficacy of treatments available in the UK. An HIV-positive diagnosis thus needs to be related to an individual's knowledge and understanding of the illness and its treatment, as well as his/her perceptions of fear, stigma, and shame associated with a positive diagnosis. This is further complicated in men and women who may have contracted the virus through sexual assault. The added reality of the social stigma following an HIV-positive disclosure can place at further risk people who may already be vulnerable to affective disturbance or thoughts of self-harm. Increased suicidal risk behaviour is of particular importance for people who are socially isolated and/or have a history of previous affective disturbance (Catalan, Burgess, & Klimes, 1995). Recent data indicates that HIV-positive people from African communities living in the UK view psychological concerns such as anxiety and depression as their second highest priority after the immediate issue of access to resources and money (Mahtani, Davidson, Kell, & Miller, 1999).

Clinicians can find themselves in a double bind after providing extensive psycho-education around the benefits of HAART to clients who are ill and require treatment, but whose stay in the UK is uncertain. If such clients fail to qualify for Leave to Remain, their return to their country of origin, where access to HAART may be very limited, takes on a different significance. Despite being told by immigration services that antiretroviral medication should be available in their country of origin, they may not be able to afford the medication. The medical infrastructure necessary to monitor complicated drug therapies, in countries that have been devastated by war, may also not exist. Client D stated, in a session following the refusal of her appeal for ELR on medical grounds,

> Time is running out, no matter how I look at things, at first it was the XXX [name of political party] that held the watch, then I discovered it is the English Home Office, now I discover that it is the HIV . . . and there is nowhere left to run . . . I will go back to my land of death with my bad blood.

It has been well documented that giving people access to stable and consistent social support networks is one of the most important factors in helping them manage psychological distress. Cohen and Willis (1985) view social support as the most significant buffer in coping with physical illness. The UK Home Office's policy of dispersal does not allow for continuity in social support or consistency in service provision, which are known factors in helping people adjust to physical illness.

Attachment, adverse life events, and sexuality

Despite the highly individual nature of sexuality, there are commonalities that are seen to exist. Attachment theory provides a useful developmental lens through which the emergence of sexuality can be viewed. The theory is rooted in psychoanalytic theory, related to systemic ways of thinking and is a theory of both normal development processes and psychopathology (Diamond & Marrone, 2003). It is therefore seen as a useful theoretical framework to view the range of experiences that may impact on the sexual health of displaced people.

Bowlby (1977) construed *attachment* as a biologically based motivational system aimed at self-preservation. At the centre of attachment theory is the concept of a "secure base", which can be divided into the two complimentary sub-systems of *care-eliciting* and *care-giving* behaviour (Bowlby, 1977, 1988). Emotional accessibility and responsiveness on the part of the caregiver and care-receiver is seen as instrumental to this process. Holmes (2001) sees the existence of this secure base as forming the foundation for the development of a relationship with the self (such as the development of intellectual pursuits, including the ability to self-reflect and experience a sense of self-worth and esteem) and relationships with others (including friendships and sexual relationships). The theory further suggests that when people feel threatened they will seek out their secure base, resulting in an increase in care-seeking and care-eliciting behaviour that will be accompanied by a concomitant decrease in exploratory behaviour. Attachment and exploratory systems are thus seen to interact with each other so that when one is activated the other is frequently deactivated (Diamond & Marrone, 2003).

Individuals who have previously formed secure attachments are seen to be more resilient in situations where they are exposed to extreme life events, whereas insecure attachments are seen to intensify and perpetuate such experiences (Johnson, 2002). Literature that emerges from research into the specific effects of trauma suggests that chronic exposure to extreme life events may result in profound character changes and the development of a personality style that is based on psychological constriction, massive numbing, rage, and, in some cases, identification with the aggressive perpetrator (Herman, 1992; Terr, 1991; van der Kolk & Fisler, 1994). Johnson (2002), Ulman and Brothers (1988), van der Kolk (1996) and others have noted how survivors of adverse life events, be they physical or sexual in nature, often experience a general inability to take pleasure in their bodies. For some, somatization frequently occurs following the aftermath of trauma (van der Kolk, 1996). Such experiences may result in people developing a sexual dysfunction (Webster, 2002). However, the vicissitudes of these clinical observations require further in-depth exploration.

In times of difficulty, which usually follow forced displacement from one's culture, home, and secure attachment figures, how might sexuality and its expression be affected? It is hypothesized that this would strongly depend on the interaction between a person's attachment history and their pre-flight and post-flight experiences. Included in post-flight experiences should be an understanding of the degree to which the environment would be able to encourage the re-establishment of a secure base, in order to allow other motivational systems, such as sexuality, to emerge. Unfortunately, research is sparse on the impact on sexuality of extreme life events, experienced in times of political instability or war.

Some additional considerations when providing therapeutic care for displaced people in a sexual health setting

Bereavement and loss often emerge as central themes in work with displaced people. Mourning losses is obviously complicated by an atmosphere of ongoing uncertainty, which may be marked by fears of further losses. It is here that the psychoanalytically derived concepts of holding and containment are particularly useful in helping clients bear the unknown. The effects of forming attachments that may be prematurely ended due to service pressures require careful consideration, especially as refugees' experiences are often marked by multiple losses. The building of safe-enough therapeutic relationships and the choice of appropriate therapeutic goals are particularly critical for clients who have experienced severe and protracted torture involving the perversion of intimate relationships. In such cases the concept of a complete return to previous levels of functioning and ways of seeing the world can be inappropriate (Schlapobersky, 1988). The building of a relationship based on respect, acceptance, and safety is most likely to engender trust and help with the successful establishment of rapport. As cultural factors contribute to beliefs about what may help alleviate distress, it is important to explore with clients their beliefs and expectations regarding psychotherapeutic interventions.

However good a psychotherapeutic intervention may be, it cannot replace the basic and essential functions that social networks provide. It is important, therefore, to enquire about the social networks, if any, to which refugees may have recourse and to consider the social context in which they now live, and how this may relate to their recent past (Loizos, 2002). As a psychologist, one is well positioned to help clients negotiate the complicated health care and social systems that exist in the UK, across both statutory and non-statutory sectors. Helping clients address their concrete problems is seen by some practitioners as a humane and legitimate part of the therapeutic process and can be utilized as an important therapeutic tool for engaging clients (Boyd-Franklin, 1989). Maslin (2003) has focused on some of the factors that serve to enhance or inhibit the development of a successful therapeutic alliance between psychologists and asylum seeking clients in the UK. She concluded that increased feelings of confidence and competence, as well as a greater willingness to work with asylum seekers, was associated with fewer perceived, or reported, difficulties in relation to service issues, transcultural issues, professional issues, and personal ideology. This highlights the need for training courses to include modules that specifically address asylum seekers' needs, in order to increase psychologists' feelings of confidence and competence in working with this client group.

It is, however, essential to recognize the limitations of talking therapies in addressing many of the practical and existential dilemmas that asylum seekers are faced with in the UK. Therapy needs to be firmly placed within and responsive to the wider socio-political context our clients are situated in. A clear understanding of how clients prioritize their current needs seems crucial. Many clients express this in terms of the uncertainty regarding their future, or their social situation, including access to appropriate housing and food, and what the implications of not being granted leave to remain might mean. Will a return home carry with it the fear of imprisonment, sexual assault, or death? Will it mean not having access to life-saving antiretroviral therapies? Will it mean returning to a home void of family, community, friends, and access to resources? These issues serve to highlight the fact that therapeutic relationships take place in a socio-political context that has real and sometimes life-threatening implications.

A clear idea of limitations is necessary prior to embarking on an intervention. How many sessions you are able to offer, how much flexibility there is in extending the contact if needed, and what external referral options are available, are essential issues to consider when setting realistic treatment goals, especially as clients'

needs may be complex and vary over time. The cultural appropri-
ateness of utilizing standard treatments for sexual health problems
devised in western settings on people who come from culturally
diverse communities who may have been exposed to very different
life events requires consideration. For example, treatments that use
masturbation as a method of teaching ejaculatory control may be
seen as inappropriate for people who come from cultures that hold
negative views regarding masturbation as a form of sexual expression (Steggall, Gann, & Chinegwundoh, 2004). The use of certain
exposure-based cognitive-behavioural techniques also requires
careful consideration, as some clients may not yet be in a support-
ive-enough environment that can aid the processing of memories
and thoughts relating to particularly noxious events. As such
processing continues after a client leaves the consulting room, those
who are profoundly isolated may be at risk of further fragmentation, rather than the reintegration that is hoped for.

Further considerations

Muecke (1992) notes how most research regarding refugee health
tends to focus almost exclusively on illness or disease. She suggests
that a broader focus might increase our understanding regarding
the resilience that many refugees possess, including their capacity
for change and the way they understand and make sense of change.
This may allow a shift in focus from seeing refugees as vulnerable
victims towards conceptualizing them as extremely resilient individuals adept at processing and adapting to change. Research that
allows the identification of protective factors, both internal and
external, and how they might interact, is therefore much needed.

Care must be given to the assumptions that clinicians hold
regarding what "culture" is, as a person's cultural identity is a
complex and fluid construct. Cultures change and develop, people
may feel connections to a variety of cultures and may also disown
certain aspects of their own culture or adopt aspects of another
(Melzak, 1999). The interest we show regarding the way our clients
position themselves in terms of their experiences of both pre-flight
and post-flight cultures may lend an added depth to the therapeutic relationship, which has, of course, its own cultural tradition.

There appears to be a need, on a systemic level, for greater flexibility when dealing with asylum-seeking clients. Restrictive referral criteria that can exclude groups who may require costly interpreting services and medico-legal reports require reconsideration by service commissioners and providers. Such restrictions make timely access to assessment and treatment unachievable, regardless of presenting need. As English is not a spoken language for many refugee clients, access to appropriately trained interpreting services is critical, though currently difficult to obtain within the NHS.

Conclusion

Working in the current political climate with migrant populations is both difficult and highly rewarding. In the discipline of psychology there is, however, a danger in narrowing our lens of inquiry to focus only on intrapsychic events and ways that they can be measured and treated. By maintaining this narrow focus we run the risk of practising an unintentional form of solipsism. This may be due to our relative ease and familiarity with concentrating upon those relationships that fall within our area of expertise. This way of viewing refugees may be in keeping with the current political construction of human rights; however, it frequently denies our knowledge of the suffering clients have experienced and our sense of what might be required to ameliorate such experiences. Widening our lens of enquiry to include additional levels of analysis that incorporate social and political factors requires a conscious shift in thinking. Such a shift may pose a challenge to assumptions we hold about the UK's internal and external policies—that they are founded on principles of basic fairness, equality, and respect of human rights (Glenn, 2002). As this chapter has attempted to illustrate, it is the universal application of human rights that requires particular attention in the UK's approach to dealing with the sexual health needs of asylum seekers. Closer working alliances between disciplines, allowing for the building of multi-dimensional models that are able to incorporate intrapsychic, social, cultural, political, and situational variables that affect the well-being of displaced people, would afford psychologists the best chance of gaining a richer understanding of determinants of sexuality and sexual expression.

References

All Party Parliamentary AIDS Group (2003). *Migration and HIV: Improving Lives in Britain*. London: APPG.

Aaronovitch, D. (2003). Racism is what makes us really sick. The *Guardian*, 5 August, p. 5.

Albanese, P. (2001). Nationalism, war and archaization of gender relations in the Balkans. *Violence Against Women*, 7(9): 999–1023.

Asylum Aid (1995). *No reason At All: Home Office Decisions on Asylum Claims*. London: Asylum Aid.

Bowlby, J. (1977). The making and breaking of affectional bonds. *British Journal of Psychiatry*. **130**, pp 201–210.

Bowlby, J. (1988). *A Secure Base: Clinical Applications of Attachment Theory*. London: Routledge.

Boyd-Franklin, N. (1989) *Black Families in Therapy: A Multi-systems Approach*. New York: Guilford Press.

Bracken, P., Giller, E., & Summerfield, D. (1995). Psychological reponses to war and atrocity: the limitations of current concepts. *Social Science and Medicine, 40*(8): 1073–1082.

Catalan, J., Burgess, A., & Klimes, I. (1995). *Psychological Medicine of HIV Infection*. University Press: Oxford.

Chesney, M., Folkman, S., & Chambers, D. (1996). Coping effectiveness training for men living with HIV: preliminary findings. *International Journal of STD and AIDS, 7*: 75–82.

Cohen, S. & Willis T. A. (1985). Stress, social support, and the buffering hypothesis. *Psychological Bulletin, 98*: 310–357.

Davidson, O., Fenton, K., & Mahtani, A. (2002). Race and cultural issues in sexual health. In: D. Miller & J. Green (Eds.), *The Psychology of Sexual Health*. Oxford: Blackwell Science.

Department of Health (2001). *Sexual Health Strategy for Sexual Health and HIV*. London: DOH.

Diamond, N. & Marrone, M. (2003). *Attachment and Intersubjectivity*. London: Whurr.

Foucault, M. (1980). *Power/Knowledge: Selected Interviews and Other Writings*. London: Harvester Press.

Geertz, C. (1975). *The Interpretation of Cultures*. New York: Basic Books.

Gergen, K., & Davis, K. (1985). *The Social Construction of the Person*. New York: Springer.

Glenn, C. (2002). We have to blame ourselves: reefugees and the politics of systemic practice. In: R. K. Papadopoulos (Ed.), *Therapeutic Care of Refugees. No Place Like Home* (pp. 167–188). London: Karnac.

Harre, R. (1987). The social construction of selves. In: K. Yardley & T. Honess (Eds.), *Sexual Identity: Psychosocial Perspectives* (pp. 41–52). Chichester: John Wiley & Sons.

Heise, L., Pitanuy, J., & Germain, A. (1994). *Violence Against Women: The Hidden Health Burden* (World Bank Discussion Paper No. 225) Washington, DC: World Bank.

Herman, J. L. (1992). *Trauma and Recovery*. New York: Basic Books.

Heath, T., Jeffries, R., & Purcell, J. (2004). *Asylum Statistics*. London: Home Office Research Development and Statistical Directorate.

Holmes, J. (2001). *The Search for the Secure Base: Attachment Theory and Psychotherapy*. London: Brunner-Routledge.

Janoff-Bulman, R. (1992). *Shattered Assumptions: Towards a New Psychology of Trauma*. New York: The Free Press.

Johnson, S. M. (2002). *Emotionally Focused Couple Therapy with Trauma Survivors: Strenthening Attachment Bonds*. New York: Guilford Press.

Kauffman, J. (2001). Introduction. In: J. Kauffman (Ed.). *Loss of the Assumptive World. A Theory of Traumatic Loss* (pp. 1–9). New York: Brunner-Routledge.

Levett, A. (1989). Psychological trauma: a discourse of childhood sexual abuse. Unpublished PhD Thesis, University of Cape Town.

Loizos, P. (2002). Misconceiving refugees? In: R. K. Papadopoulos (Ed.), *Therapeutic Care for Refugees. No Place Like Home* (pp. 41–56). London: Karnac.

Losi, N. (2002). Some assumptions on psychological trauma interventions in post-conflict communities. In: R. K. Papadopoulos (Ed.), *Therapeutic Care for Refugees. No Place Like Home*. London: Karnac.

Mahtani, A., Davidson, O., Kell, P., & Miller, D. (1999). Psychological and medical priorities of ethnic minority attenders at a London sexual health clinic: a pilot needs assessment. Paper presented at 1999 MSSVD Conference, Edinburgh.

Maslin, J. (2003). Clinical psychology and asylum seeker clients: the therapeutic relationship. Unpublished Doctoral thesis. University of Hertford.

Melzak, S. (1999). Psychotherapeutic work with child and adolescent refugees from political violence. In: M. Lanyado & A. Horne (Eds), *Handbook of Child & Adolescent Psychotherapy* (pp. 405–428). London: Routledge.

Muecke, M. A. (1992). New paradigms for refugee health problems. *Social Science and Medicine, 35*: 515–523.

Papadopoulos, R. K. (2002). Refugees, home and trauma. In: R. K. Papadopoulos (Ed.), *Therapeutic Care for Refugees. No Place Like Home* (pp. 2–9). London: Karnac.

Parkes, C. M. (1971). Psycho-social transition: A field of study. *Social Science and Medicine, 5*: 101–115.

Parkes, C. M. (2001). Postscript. In: J. Kauffman (Ed.), *Loss of the Assumptive World. A Theory of Traumatic Loss* (pp. 237–242). New York: Brunner-Routledge.

Petrak, J. (2002). The future agenda for care and research. In: J. Petrak & B. Hedge (Eds.), *The Trauma of Sexual Assault: Treatment, Prevention and Practice* (pp. 331–346). Sussex: Wiley.

Petrak, J., & Miller, D. (2001). Psychological management in HIV infection. In: D. Miller & J. Green (Eds.), *The Psychology of Sexual Health* (pp. 141–161). Oxford: Blackwell Science.

Petrak, J., Doyle, A., Smith, A., & Skinner, C. (1998). Self disclosure of HIV serostatus to significant others: an examination of gender and cultural differences. *Abstract from the 12th World AIDS Conference,* Geneva.

Rose, N. (1989a). Individualising psychology. In: J. Shotter & K. J. Gergen (Eds.), *Texts of Identity* (pp. 119–131). London: Sage.

Rose, N. (1989b). *Governing the Soul: The Shaping of the Private Self.* London: Routledge.

Schlapobersky, J. (1988). Torture as the perversion of a healing relationship. Paper presented to the American Association for the Advancement of Science Annual Meeting, Boston.

Steggall, M. J., Gann, S. Y., & Chinegwundoh, F. I. (2004). Sexual dysfunction screening: the advantages of a culturally sensitive joint assessment clinic. *Sexual and Relationship Therapy, 19*(2): 179–189.

Stedman, M. (1999). Social and political consideration in working with refugees. *Context, 45*: 5–7.

Summerfield, D. (1995). Addressing human response to war and atrocity: major challenges in research and practices and limitations of Western psychiatric models. In: R. J. Kleber, Ch. R. Figley, & B. P. R. Gersons (Eds.), *Beyond Trauma: Cultural and Societal Dimensions* (pp. 17–29). New York: Plenum.

Swartz, L., & Levett, A. (1989). Political repression and children in South Africa: the social construction of damaging effects. *Social Science and Medicine, 28*(7): 741–750.

Swiss, S., & Giller, J. E. (1993). Rape as a crime of war: a medical perspective. *Journal of American Medical Association, 270*(5): 612–615.

Terr, L. C. (1991). Childhood traumas: an outline and overview. *American Journal of Psychiatry, 148*(1): 10–20.

Ulman, R. B., & Brothers, D. (1988). *The Shattered Self. A Psychoanalytic Study of Trauma*. Hillsdale, NJ: The Analytic Press.

United Nations High Commission on Refugees (1951). *The 1951 Refugee Convention*. Geneva: UNHCR.

van der Kolk, B. A. (1996). The complexity of adaptation to trauma: self regulation, stimulus discrimination, and characterological development. In: B.A. van der Kolk, A. C. McFarlane, & L. Weisaeth (Eds.), *Traumatic Stress: The Effects of Overwhelming Experience on Mind, Body, and Society* (pp. 182–213). New York: Guilford Press.

van der Kolk, B.A., & Fisler, R. (1994). Childhood abuse and neglect and loss of self-regulation. *Bulletin of the Menninger Clinic, 58*: 145–168.

Webster, L. (2002). Treatment for the psychosexual impact of sexual assault. In: J. Petrak & B. Hedge (Eds.), *The Trauma of Sexual Assault: Treatment, Prevention and Practice* (pp. 183–204). Sussex: Wiley.

CHAPTER SEVEN

He or she? Trying to think psychodynamically about a service for people with gender dysphoria

Bernard Ratigan

"The ego is first and foremost a bodily ego . . ."

Freud (1923b) p. 69

Introduction

The subjective experience of gender dysphoria is one of a more-or-less profound sense of dis-ease with one's body and, following Freud, with one's core sense of self. I have come to think that the psychic trauma of growing up in the "wrong body" is acute, and is heightened at puberty. When the dysphoria emerges in infancy, or no later than latency, it may be possible for the child to keep a phantasy alive that what is seen and experienced is not real. Despite having the physical characteristics of a boy, for example, the child may imagine that he will grow to become a woman. The onset of puberty can cruelly challenge this with the emergence of adult physical and sexual features.

Much of the suffering experienced by gender dysphoric children and adolescents seems to go consciously unnoticed and usually unmodified by understanding and sympathy. Indeed, the gender dysphoric child or young person may sometimes collude in an attempt to "bury" their unease with their gender. Parents, usually mothers, report a sense of things not being quite right and sometimes a half-conscious knowledge of the meaning of "dressing up" in the case of male-to female (MTF) children and clinging to boys' clothes in female-to-males (FTMs). The depths of the dis-ease are only really known to the child or young person. Following Freud's dictum, one is left wondering about the corrosive impact of the confusion and increasingly widening gap between physical, somatic, reality, and phantasy on the developing child's ego and sense of self-worth. The crisis of puberty, for the child suffering from gender dysphoria, is one where the physical evidence of sex and gender are made incarnate; mind and body are going in different directions (Di Ceglie, 1998).

Gender is a core aspect of human experience and crosses biological, psychological, social, cultural, and religious categories. It is difficult to convey the depth of feeling of bodily "wrongness" that many trans people have lived with, perhaps for decades. It is not surprising that, when they glimpse the possibility of help, clinical interviews can acquire the quality of a life-and-death struggle. The clinician may be perceived to hold the key to their salvation or to be denying them their only chance of rescue. Feelings are intense and there is often an urgent desire for action that, it is assumed, will bring relief. In such circumstances, maintaining a rational framework for thinking can become very difficult. I take it as axiomatic that service provision in this area is going to be beset by a constant struggle to keep thinking rationally in the face of unconscious attacks on thinking (Bion, 1959).

One way of responding to this severe trauma of "growing up in the wrong body" may be to get rid of any possible doubt they may have about the "wrongness" of their subjective experience. All the "wrongness" is located in their body; none can be acknowledged to reside in the mind.

My preliminary understanding is that clinicians in gender identity clinics may become the receptacles of primitive, unbearable, split-off parts of the mind that have to be got rid of and projected into them. Gender dysphoric patients often insist that they be addressed by the pronoun of their desired gender, yet clinicians often find themselves stumbling over what to call their patients, hence the title of this chapter. It is as if the naturally occurring doubt about the gender identity of the gender dysphoric patient is unbearable and is removed into the clinician. In the countertransference, I am left dazed and confused so that the patient may *not* be.

The psychoanalytic perspective has been important when addressing the subjective experience of those with gender dysphoria. Psychoanalysis, and its derivatives, psychodynamic psychotherapy and counselling, are at their most useful when they attempt to offer an understanding of human experience but they are weaker when they attempt to be aetiological or explanatory. The history of psychoanalytic attempts to "explain" such complex phenomena as human sexuality—especially culturally transgressive sexualities like transsexualism and homosexuality—is full of categorical, methodological, and epistemological problems. The condition currently named as "transsexualism" has such a diverse range of presentations and appears so heterogeneous that any broad generalization may be misguided. I will, therefore, not present an argument about the causes of transsexualism, but will focus instead on the psychological consequences and the ways these might inform service delivery within a gender identity clinic.

This chapter describes practices and structures in the working of a gender identity clinic that are founded on the *hermeneutic* aspect of psychoanalytic work. We aim to understand the subjective experience of patients with gender problems, and how this pain is transmitted and experienced by others, rather than attempting to look for the *aetiology* of the clinical phenomena. The clinic aims to offer the containing environment that may have been absent developmentally, in an attempt to "reflect, contain and modulate anxiety" (Fonagy & Target, 2000), and to assist patients towards a reasoned decision about their future.

We know from experience that simply attempting to block the move to physical and surgical procedures does not work. The internal gender dysphoric forces are so powerful that patients find their way to what they believe will help them. However, it may be possible to challenge the pressure towards hasty and impulsive action and to encourage reflection.

I will address two main issues, the importance of the assessment process in fostering thought and reflection, and transference and countertransference issues that are commonly encountered. This will be prefaced by brief consideration of the role of a psychoana-lytically-informed clinician in a gender identity clinic and will conclude by considering the implications for the development and provision of services.

In my experience, a minority of patients is willing or wishes to engage in psychoanalytic psychotherapy prior to any physical or surgical interventions. Where a psychoanalytic psychotherapist on the staff of a gender identity clinic is involved in the assessment process, I doubt whether this person could also provide psychoan-alytic psychotherapy to those patients without considerable confu-sion of boundaries. A firm and clear boundary needs to be established around any psychotherapeutic treatment, which pre-serves this as separate from the assessment process for gender reas-signment in a gender identity clinic. The role of a psychoanalytic psychotherapist that I have developed and will describe, is where the psychotherapist participates with others in the assessment of patients within the clinic, and fosters space for reflection and thought both between clinicians and patients and among staff, but does not provide formal psychotherapy. If patients specifi-cally want psychoanalytic psychotherapy they would be referred elsewhere for this.

The functioning of the gender identity clinic

The importance of the assessment process in fostering thought and reflection

Gender clinics potentially offer treatments that have irreversible physical and psychological consequences and that are in limited supply. Clinicians in gender clinics partly act as gate-keepers, regu-lating access to scarce therapeutic resources, and attempting to ensure that treatments are utilized responsibly and fairly. Awareness of gender dysphoria is patchy among the population as a whole and among GPs, who often act as referrers. Younger patients and those involved in trans-community activities will typi-cally be more aware. Less visible are the many older, often married, possible trans patients who have lived secret lives of long-suffering desperation. Those with less education, the less articulate, those with pre-existing histories of mental illness, those from lower socioeconomic backgrounds and minority ethnic communities can be particularly disadvantaged in asking for and getting help. Gender clinic protocols exist to ensure that treatment is made available on a considered basis that will be ethical and equal. Initial entry into a clinic protocol is, therefore, first for assessment and then only secondarily for treatment.

Given the range of patients who are referred for assessment, it is important to come to an understanding of what any particular patient is seeking. For some, it is very clear: gender reassignment. There are those who are suffering from psychotic illness in which there is an, often transient, delusion of being the other sex. These are not difficult to diagnose and to refer on for other forms of help. For others, perhaps a majority, it is much less clear. There are those patients who are unsure about their gender and those who have lived secret lives, sometimes for decades, and are only slowly moving toward a position of greater, but never complete, certainty. The question of certainty is one that constantly threads its way through this area of clinical work. The assessment aims to test the degree of certainty the gender dysphoric patient has for what they say they desire. The assessment needs to be of such a length to enable the patient to demonstrate some consistent certainty, or for doubts to crystallize.

From the perspective of service delivery, the assessment process may be crucial in ensuring the fair and responsible use of resources and in screening out those for whom physical intervention is inappropriate, at least at that point in time. From a psychological perspective, assessment is about prioritizing thinking rather than action. The process is designed to help understand the powerful unconscious and conscious forces at work that have been building over decades in patients. It cannot be a rapid process if it is to be thorough and to lead to safe outcomes. The length of the process can be very frustrating for some patients who, understandably, feel that they have done all the thinking they want to do before they arrive at the clinic. Thinking can be seen as dangerous and destabilizing, especially where a pseudo-equilibrium has been established. For others, it can come as a great relief that there is no immediate recourse to treatment, pharmacological or surgical, as they want time and space with trusted, safe, neutral clinicians to think about their confusion.

For the majority of people for whom assessment is indicated, the assessment takes place over a period of not less than six months and preferably longer. Central to this assessment is the construction with the patient of a developmental history. Human sexuality and gender take a long time to develop. Where a child grows up through latency and adolescence with a gradually dawning sense of gender dysphoria, this is bound to impact not only on their psychosexual development but also on their core sense of themselves. Experiences at each developmental phase will have contributed to shaping adult sexuality and gender. Crucially, how the adolescent managed the challenge of physical puberty should be considered to see how this influenced self-acceptance and ego-integration.

In middle and late adolescence it is not unusual for adult trans patients to report that they associated with, and perhaps defined themselves as, gay people. Sometimes the commercial gay scene provided the only reasonably safe space for them to experiment with their desired gender identity. More often than not, they report defining themselves as gay only temporarily. Trans patients sometimes report traumatic experiences and encounters and a growing realization that what they need is not going to be found in the commercial gay scene. Their confusion about where they belong may be compounded because, in UK society, trans-sexuality is sometimes conflated with homosexuality. This is, of course, a categorical error, as it is possible to be transsexual and gay or lesbian, transsexual and heterosexual, or transsexual and bisexual. The difficulty of establishing with whom to identify socially may be compounded by the transition from birth to desired gender, as someone who was once gay may, in effect, now be heterosexual in their choice of partner or vice versa. Comprehending this complexity can be an additional burden for patients, clinicians, families and partners.

One of the functions of assessment, from a psychological perspective, is the dislodging of masked disturbance. Growing up and living with gender dysphoria in a society such as ours is never easy. It is necessary to explore with each patient how they have come to be the person that they are now. Patients, understandably, usually want to put the best possible spin on their lives and may have become adept at hiding aspects of themselves that are felt to be unacceptable. It can be difficult, but necessary, to gently probe beneath the surface of what is presented. Having an extended assessment over at least six to twelve months can help patients and clinicians get the most extensive picture of psychological, sexual, and gender development as well as patterns of adjustment in their current life. The use of extended assessments is contrasted with the practice in some, usually private, clinical settings of making rapid assessments and starting patients on hormone therapy almost immediately.

A proportion of patients come to the assessment with histories of complex and long-standing mental health difficulties. For some, there is a sense that gender dysphoria is so disruptive to the developing psyche that it has contributed to mental distress. With others one is reminded that trans-people, like any others, are subject to the exigencies of life such as loss, trauma, abuse, and deprivation, and the gender dysphoria may have played a subsidiary role. Trans-patients may have learned as children, adolescents, and adults to hide shameful aspects of themselves and a mental illness career may offer a way of obscuring their enduring unease about themselves. In such a complex area, extreme caution is necessary in assigning causal links. A history of mental illness, even sometimes severe mental illness, does not in itself disqualify a person from gender treatment including reassignment. The difficult assessment task is to develop the best possible understanding of the meaning of the (mental) illness behaviour.

Patients are invited to prepare, by way of homework assignment, an autobiographical essay, "My Story". Patients attending gender clinics are on momentous journeys that have their origins many years before they arrive for a first meeting. To give patients a sense of agency and personal development the task is set. Some return with a single page, others with hundreds of pages, typed, illustrated, and bound. The length is unimportant; what is important is to enable patients, if they need to, to feel like actors, even heroes and heroines, and not helpless victims in their own life stories.

Involving more than one clinician in the assessment process is invaluable. In such a powerful and delicate matter as gender, where patients have often become very skilled at hiding shameful aspects of themselves, different clinicians can attract very different projections from patients. The gender of the clinician can be significant in attracting different projections, but clinician personality, sexual orientation, training in psychodynamics, and degree of awareness of the trans condition can also be very significant. Psychiatric and psychological assessments conducted by different people are there-fore brought together in multi-disciplinary discussions and peer supervision.

After the two clinical interviews, the preparation of the auto-biography and the passage of about six months, a network meeting is convened. To this meeting come the patient, those from his/her social system, family, friendship circle who are invited (by the patient), and both clinicians. The purpose of the network meeting is to communicate to the patient that he/she is not a single indi-vidual but part of a social world upon which gender transition will impact. It can show the patient (and the clinicians) the reality of the support, or lack of support, that they actually have. It is clear from experience that the network meeting can be powerful, painful, and supportive, and may reveal needs beyond those of the identified patient. Two significant relationships stand out as needing thought: partners (including wives/husbands) and children. Network meet-ings can be emotionally very tense when the non-patient partner finds a voice to express sometimes years of hurt, pretence, waste, guilt, support, and love. Ideally, adult family therapy should be available to assist in ongoing work of reconciliation or help with separation. Similarly, with the children of adult trans patients there are often unidentified needs that require attention. The gender clinic may be able to help with providing some group or individual support, intra- or extra-murally, if indicated. It is helpful for adult gender clinics to have input from a child psychotherapist.

The end of the assessment phase of involvement with the gender clinic can be entry into the Real Life Experience with regu-lar clinic reviews and physical check-ups. The latter are essential because of the possibility of a serious toxic reaction to hormone treatment in a small minority of patients. For those not yet ready, further assessment and support in preparing for entry into the RLE, referral for specialist psychotherapy outside the gender clinic, withdrawal from the assessment protocol for a period of time, or discharge are all available options.

Thus, the assessment process aims to halt the pressure towards impulsive action; to screen out those who by virtue of a serious mental illness would be considered unsuitable at the present time; to take time for thorough exploration of the client's past and present relationships and the history of the gender and sexual development; to empower the patient to take responsibility for his or her own life; to reflect on their relation to the clinic and different staff within the clinic; and to establish the degree of conviction and consistency in their desire for gender reassignment.

Transference and countertransference processes

Gender dysphoria is about pain: the pain of believing that you are living in the wrong gender and body. Whatever its genesis, assessment needs to attend to this pain and understand its roots and effects, both physical and psychological, before attempts are made to intervene. Experience has shown that not all patients who are referred for assessment will want to stay in the protocol. Some decide they cannot be bothered with extensive assessments and go elsewhere, usually to the private sector, abroad, or to the internet, where assessment protocols are shorter or non-existent and hormones can be readily obtained. Others change their mind and decide they want something else first or instead. These people are often referred for assessment in specialist NHS psychotherapy services.

Among those who stay it is possible to observe both the anguish of their predicament and defences against that pain. Clinicians and the clinic itself may be drawn in as receptacles for the projection of feelings that are unbearable, and powerful transference and countertransference reactions are not uncommon.

Denial is a universal mechanism of ego defence used to manage the gap between that which is wished for and that which exists. Combined with play and fantasy it stands as a major method of coping with the losses, trauma and tragedy that inhabit all human lives eventually. Freud (1927e) distinguished between "scotomization", the process whereby a perception is entirely wiped out so that the thing is simply "not seen", "repression", where the affect attaching to an idea is removed from consciousness, and "denial" or "disavowal"[1] in which an idea, which has been perceived, is obliterated from consciousness. It is this latter mechanism that seems to apply in some cases of gender dysphoria. The person both knows that they are anatomically male or female but is unable to accept this emotionally, and would believe and convince others that this is not true.

> X, a twenty-one-year-old biological male, was referred for assessment in a gender clinic by a psychiatrist who considered that X had a personality disorder but did not suffer from an Axis I disorder on *DSM IV*. Physically and socially, X presented in an androgenous, somewhat feminized manner. The youngest of a sibship of four, he reported that his elderly and emotionally unavailable father had figured very little in his upbringing.

> Intellectually, X knew that he was a biological male but his use of a female name could be seen as his use of denial as a mechanism of defence. He believed that he had convinced his mother, siblings, and others to endorse this denial of his biological maleness. His father, through his distance from the close emotional world of mother and children, seems to have resisted this pressure towards denial of X's anatomical maleness.

The crisis of the emergence of adult anatomical features in the child who will grow up gender dysphoric has to be managed somehow. Many patients report histories of latency and adolescent secret cross-dressing, often wearing the mother's clothing. I am less concerned at this point with the significance of the ownership of the clothing than with the mechanism of denial to which it points. It can be seen as an outward activity acting as an overlay on internal, primitive anxieties that it may be attempting to mask or rectify. However, it is an illusion that the internal dysphoria can be so readily healed. The dress does not make the boy a girl; in the dressing-up, the problem is both expressed and effectively denied. A pattern of denial may become entrenched as a major mechanism of ego defence in the adult's functioning.

At a deeper level, where there is more severe psychic trauma, perhaps linked with profound maternal or paternal emotional unavailability, there may be a preponderance of splitting and projection as the child or adolescent is unable to tolerate feelings that have failed to be received and metabolized by an effective parental container. In a condition as profoundly disturbing as severe gender dysphoria it is not surprising that an emotional "blind eye" is turned to the internal distress of the child, and in this context the processes of splitting and projection may come to saturate mental functioning in adult life. For example, others may be perceived to be hostilely attacking towards the individual, or to be impervious to the individual's distress.

Projective identification may be observed as a major form of communication in the gender dysphoric patient as he or she struggles to manage and rid themselves of psychic distress; the clinician may then come to feel critical, rejecting, or impervious to the individual's distress, when this is at odds with his or her usual clinical attitude. Clinicians working in the field do not need reminding of the powerful dynamics they may become party to as they stand in for emotionally closed-off parents or a transphobic society; they are seen as nay-saying gatekeepers; or are criticized for being patronizing and assuming they know better than patients. It requires considerable skill, plus the support of colleagues, not to get drawn into unconscious identificatory responses to hostile or seductive projections.

The linked concepts of projective identification and container–contained, derived from the work of Klein and Bion, are invaluable in reflecting upon the management of the minority of seriously disturbed gender dysphoric patients. As Bion (1959) and Money-Kyrle (1978) describe, projective identification may serve as a means of communicating intolerable affects, or of evacuating those affects so that they are disposed of and denied. If clinicians are able to reflect upon projected feelings in the countertransference, these may be transformed into a useful source of communication.

> Y, a thirty-year-old biological male, was referred for assessment for gender reassignment by a GP. A freelance computer programmer, he had a background as a member of a religious faith known for its negative attitudes to any form of sexual transgression and for deeply conventional views about the role of men and women. Y now lived alone, had no contact with his family, and conducted most of his professional transactions by Internet, e-mail, fax, and telephone. At assessment, Y reported a very early history of gender confusion that he kept secret and that persisted through latency, adolescence, and into adulthood. Apparently this did not evoke comment or conflict with his family.
>
> His highly intelligent, verbal, and amusing presentation left both assessors with a confused countertransference that they shared with each

other after individual meetings with Y. They were left wondering where was the pain and hurt in Y's story; he presented his life as an idyll from the day he was born. Y's seemingly droll account of his current life seemed to gloss over his almost total social and emotional isolation from family and from friendships.

The male assessor pointed out how Y was almost a hermit, albeit a professionally successful one. The female assessor reported that she had felt uneasy at Y's seeming failure to be troubled by any aspect of his situation. The assessors also reported to each other that they were left feeling bleak and sad when Y told his superficially cheerful story. In consultation with a third member of the clinic staff, who was acting on this occasion as a peer supervisor, the assessors considered that Y's internal world may have been so bleak that, in the context of the clinical interview, the assessing clinicians had become receptacles for the unbearable split-off parts that he had to get rid of; they had been able to introject and identify with the sadness, emptiness, and worry about his life. With this understanding, the assessing clinicians felt better able to help Y see just how bleak his internal world had been and how he had constructed his current life in such a way as to reduce the likelihood of relationships and thereby keep the risk of emotional injury or narcissistic challenge to an absolute minimum.

The gender clinic itself may function as a container, via projective identification, for the unbearable anxieties of being in the wrong body. The clinic may come to represent the wished-for "good breast" that will bestow the comfort, containment, or understanding that the individual longs for; alternatively it may become the withholding "bad breast", and be metaphorically "bitten" in the process. Clinics therefore need to be carefully set up, staffed, supported, and supervised in order that conflicting projections can be processed and utilized constructively.

As part of the psychodynamic assessment, the pattern of relationships of the patient will be considered. This is revealed in both the history the patient gives and in how the patient relates to the clinic and its staff. Where there is a history of solid, containing parenting and ego-relatedness this can provide the basis for a relatively trouble-free transition and a relatively trouble-free relationship to the clinic. However, such is the explosive toxicity of "boys not being boys" and "girls not being girls" in some families and communities that no amount of "good enough" early emotional nourishment and containment are going to make for an easy transition. Part of the function of the assessment is to help understand the emotional damage done to trans patients, especially in childhood and adolescence. The past cannot be changed but awareness and understanding can sometimes make it more bearable.

A valuable assessment tool is Luborsky's (1998) Core-Conflict Relationships Themes, which documents the patterns that emerge as the patient tells his/her story. This can help the assessor see patterns more clearly and highlights the patient's relationship with his/her body, with his/her family and social system and with the gender clinic.

It is with trans patients with personality difficulties and disorders that assessment is most arduous. Growing up with gender dysphoria is for some trans patients so traumatic that personality can become skewed and disordered. It is not surprising that, for some, verbal duelling is more than protective badinage; the seeking-out of relationships that hurt and damage and sometimes the resort to violence can repeat early patterns of actual violence, or emotional violence as the gender dysphoric child struggles with increasingly unbearable internal conflicts. Relationships with clinic staff can be very fraught with the need for constant watch by clinicians to avoid hostile acting out in the countertransference (Ratigan, 1991; Winnicott, 1975) in the face of sometimes withering attacks.

Where a would-be trans patient has unconsciously sublimated their gender difficulties over decades and has been seen to be suffering from a personality disorder or severe mental illness, it is very difficult to disentangle the various strands in the patient's psychology. I have come to the view that much work needs to be done in educating clinicians in a deeper understanding of human sexualities and the diversity of gender. If a patient has spent years in the mental health system and not found the words to speak of their gender dysphoria, it may be seen as their failure and their responsibility. Gender dysphoria is, or can be, deeply disturbing, not just to patients but also to clinicians. Perhaps, sometimes, the patient cannot bear to speak about that which the clinician cannot bear to hear. An informed countertransference is essential in this work as trans patients challenge the core of our understanding of ourselves as gendered human beings. If gender, which may be taken as a given, is actually a construction that is sometimes fragile, confused, or capable of change, then our most fundamental assumptions may be questioned and the clinician needs to be aware of the discomfort this arouses.

Where there is a split countertransference among assessing clinicians towards an individual patient, this always needs detailed discussion and understanding if the patient is to be maximally helped. Different aspects of the internal world of the trans patient may resonate with each of the assessing clinicians, with one, perhaps, convinced of the patient's certainty and readiness for reassignment, and another full of doubt and uncertainty. Often this reflects some unacknowledged split between different parts of the patient's self, which they may be helped to own and integrate.

> Z, a twenty-two-year-old biological female, was in assessment for gender reassignment. She came from a materially poor but emotionally expressive and warm, large, working-class family. Z had been living independently as a male since leaving school and currently worked as a "delivery man". In assessment, by two psychiatrists, there was a marked difference between Z's treatment of the male assessor with whom s/he had an apparently matey, if combative, stance, and his/her denigrating, almost withering attitude to the female assessor. When Z met with both assessors, together with Z's female partner and Z's brother, the differences in approach were very clear. Z's female partner remonstrated with Z in the meeting and said to the female assessor, "That's how he treats me and his mum as well."

> In later meetings with clinic staff, Z was able to explore how she had taken on rather stereotyped male attitudes to men and women in an attempt to pass more convincingly as male. It perhaps also reflected a deeper need to distance him/herself from anything female or feminine and to rid him/herself of any lingering doubts about gender reassignment. Z went on to have successful surgery and continued in his relationship.

Concluding remarks and implications for services

The role of formal psychotherapy in the treatment of gender dysphoria

Views differ about the role of formal psychotherapy in the treatment of gender dysphoria; there are those who see it as the only appropriate treatment and others who hold a more sceptical position.

Pre-operative patients often do not want formal psychotherapy, as it may threaten the certainty of what they desire. Post-operatively, formal psychotherapy may be more acceptable for those patients who find that they can never absolutely acquire the body of the desired gender. Therapy or counselling can then help in adjusting to the loss of the hoped-for outcome. I have come to think that pre-operative trans patients who ask for or consent to referral for formal psychoanalytic psychotherapy, individual or group, are much less likely to go forward to physical reassignment. Those patients who have refused formal psychotherapy pre-operatively can sometimes use it post-operatively to good effect, especially over questions of loss. For optimum patient care, a gender clinic needs to have an easy referral route to a specialist NHS psychotherapy clinic.

Where a clinic, or a clinician, has a well known view on trans-sexualism, for example, that it is sometimes a delusion (Hakeem, 2002), it may well be that the patients who get referred there are more likely to accede to that view, albeit perhaps reluctantly. Others take a more pragmatic view that while it may well be desirable that pre-operative transsexual patients might benefit from formal psychoanalytic psychotherapy, some or many would-be patients are unwilling or unable to entertain or tolerate it.

One of the key roles of the assessment is to examine the text of the patient's history and inner world and the countertransferences of the assessing clinicians. This thinking with the patient and the assessing team can assist in establishing the fullest understanding of the patient's gender dysphoria, its physical and/or psychic genesis and the likelihood of it being treated by psycho- rather than pharmaco-therapy and/or surgery. In my experience, for the clinician, the point at which the patient moves on from thought and reflection to action is often accompanied by feelings of regret yet of acceptance and acquiescence. The sadness is compounded in encounters with post-operative transsexual patients who have realized that what they wanted they do not have, nor cannot have.

Supervision and consultation: a necessity not a "frill"

One of the contributions made by psychoanalytic thinking to both psychiatry and clinical psychology is to stress the need for supervision and consultation as part of continuing professional development and clinical governance. Such are the dynamics operating between patients and clinicians in this much-contested area that specialist help is indicated for a number of reasons. Most clinicians in the area are not specialist psychotherapists and, even if they are, they will need the help of consultants or supervisors to help them understand the feelings evoked in them, and the unconscious pressures to action in the clinical process with patients. Gender identity clinics need to include specialist psychotherapists with expertise in gender and related areas and/or easy access to outside consultation facilities. The model with children and young people is now well established with the Gender Dysphoria Service in the Tavistock and Portman NHS Trust, acting as a national resource (Di Ceglie, 1998) and putting into effect the Royal College of Psychiatrists' guidelines. What is needed now is a similar model of service provision, including supervision and consultation, for adult gender identity clinics.

The need for supervision and consultation is most strong when working with trans patients who have families and children. Introducing children into the clinical equation brings new strains into the assessment and into the countertransference of clinicians. Another area requiring supervision is where there is a history of sexual abuse, as this is now widely recognized as having a lasting impact on the development and functioning of thought and emotions. The patient may have been abused as a child, he/she may be an abuser or it may be suspected that s/he may be using transitioning as a cover, consciously or otherwise, to facilitate access to children. Such cases are complex and arouse powerful emotions in clinicians. Similarly, where patients are in the prison system, special care is indicated in managing the assessment because of institutional dynamics affecting clinical judgement.

Supervision may also be important in monitoring the attitudes communicated to patients. As with homosexual patients, having grown up in deeply homo-negative cultures such as Britain, trans patients can be very sensitive to others' real or imagined hostilities. Clinicians working with trans people need to be similarly aware of the "reading" that will be going on between themselves and the patient. It is even more important when the clinician is in a gate-keeping role. It may also help to explain the combative stance adopted by some trans patients during assessment in gender identity clinics.

The dangers of single-handed, unsupervised clinical work in the area of gender identity work cannot be over-emphasized. As has been constantly reiterated in this chapter, it is my experience that such are the unconscious forces at work in trans patients it is simply not sound practice to work without the support of supervising colleagues and peers.

The role of the psychoanalytically-orientated clinician

The central task, from a psychoanalytically-informed perspective, in providing a gender identity service is helping with the restoration of the clinicians' capacity to think under fire. This chapter takes it as axiomatic that the clinical process is one in which the capacity to think will be continually being lost and then regained through supervision and consultation.

From the point of view of the patient, a gender clinic can potentially be a transitional space (Winnicott, 1971) for the patient and clinicians to think together about:

> from where the patient has come;
> where they are now;
> to where they want to go;
> what they desire.

Bion (1992) spoke of the importance of the analyst entering every session without "memory, desire or will". This rather ascetic, and perhaps persecutory, injunction has particular resonance for clinicians working in gender clinics, as what can be certain in the mind of the patient at one moment can sometimes be reversed quite rapidly. If one is drawn into wanting a specific outcome for them, this may soon appear inappropriate. The range of patients now coming forward for assessment include those with clear gender dysphoria who are already well on their way to a smooth transition, those who are more-or-less certain and then change their minds, those who are confused and need space and time to think about matters that have troubled them all their lives, as well as the occasional person who is clearly suffering from an Axis 1 (*DSM IV*) disorder. There is a duty of care to all referred patients, including the uncertain and those who need space to think but not necessarily to act.

This chapter addressed the vicissitudes of running a gender identity service that is sensitive to the powerful unconscious dynamics in the patients' internal worlds and between patients and clinicians. It has stressed the contribution of clinicians' informed countertransferences in the dynamic assessment of gender dysphoric patients in NHS gender clinics and has emphasized the need for supervision and consultation for all clinicians working in the area.

Note

1.   Laplanche and Pontalis (1973) suggest that "disavowal" may be the clearest translation of the German word "Verleugnung", used by Freud, since denial may suggest a more emphatic negation; however, disavowal and denial are often used interchangeably

References

Bion, W. (1959). Attacks on linking. *International Journal of Psycho-Analysis, 30*: 308–315.

Bion, W. (1992). *Attention and Interpretation*. London: Maresfield Library/Karnac.

Di Ceglie, D. (Ed.) (1998). *A Stranger In My Own Body: Atypical Gender Development and Mental Health*. London: Karnac.

Fonagy, P., & Target, M. (2000). Attachment and borderline personality disorder: a theory and some evidence. *Psychiatric Clinics of North America, 23*(1): 103–122.

Freud, S. (1923b). The ego and the id. *S.E.,. 19*. London: Hogarth.

Freud, S. (1927e). Fetishism. *S.E., 21*. London: Hogarth.

Hakeem, A. (2002). Transsexualism: a case of the emperor's new clothes? *Frame: Newsletter for the International Association for Forensic Psychotherapy, 6*: 34–40.

Luborsky, L.(1998) *Understanding Transference: The Core Conflictual Relationship Theme Method*. New York: APA Books.

Laplanche, J., & Pontalis, J. B. (1973). *The Language of Psychoanalysis.* London: Hogarth [reprinted London: Karnac, 1988].

Money-Kyrle, R. (1978). Cognitive development. In: D. M. & E. O'Shaughnessy (Eds.), *The Collected Papers of Roger Money-Kyrle* (pp. 416–433). Strath Tay, Perthshire: Clunie Press.

Ratigan, B. (1991). On not traumatising the traumatised: the contribution of psychodynamic psychotherapy to work with people with HIV and AIDS. *British Journal of Psychotherapy, 8*(1): 39–47.

Winnicott, D. (1975). Hate in the counter-transference. *Through Paediatrics to Psychoanalysis: Collected Papers.* London: Karnac.

Winnicott, D. (1971). *Playing and Reality.* London: Routledge.

PART III

INNOVATIVE THERAPEUTIC APPROACHES

CHAPTER EIGHT

Psychological treatment for survivors of rape and sexual assault

Anne-Marie Doyle

Introduction

The aim of this chapter is to describe aspects of an integrative psychological treatment approach for survivors of rape and sexual assault that draws upon insights and techniques from the fields of contemporary cognitive science, behavioural psychology, and psychoanalysis. The aim of the therapy is to help the individual bear the emotional pain of the experience, to reintegrate dissociated schemas and to facilitate adaptation and positive change. The context for the clinical work is the UK National Health Service: therapy is generally brief (e.g., sixteen sessions), takes place on a weekly basis, and individuals do not pay directly for services. Following an introduction to the subject of rape, key aspects of therapy will be discussed.

There are growing psychoanalytic and cognitive–behavioural literatures on theoretical and clinical approaches to working with trauma. While these two fields of psychology are clearly distinct, increasingly influences between the two have been recognized (Bucci, 1997; Shevrin, Bond, Brakel, Hertel, & Williams, 1996). Both cognitive and analytic approaches acknowledge one of the central tenets of therapy: the importance of elucidating the meaning of the event for the individual. Therapy that is theoretically underpinned by these two approaches gives rise to a broad conceptual understanding of an individual's problems with attention paid to developmental issues, cognitive and affective systems, unconscious processes, hidden meanings, and dynamics within the therapeutic relationship. It is widely recognized that the therapeutic relationship itself is a key factor in the resolution of problems and progress in therapy (Safran and Muran, 2000; Sandler, Dare & Holder, 1973).

Cognitive and behavioural therapies are generally characterized as short-term, time-limited, problem-focused, structured, and psycho-educational. Clients are encouraged to undertake work between sessions. The therapeutic stance is positive, supportive, active, and educational. The basis of cognitive therapy is the premise that distressing emotional reactions arise from one's interpretation of events, that is, the way one thinks about events determines how one feels about them. The rape incident leaves a cognitive representation, which has sound, smell, and visual associations, each of which is associated with affect. The representation itself is subsequently appraised by the individual and will include, for example, beliefs about causal factors, issues of responsibility, and changes to perception of self-identity. A trauma-induced cognitive schema leads a person to attend to evidence that is consistent with the schema and ignore evidence that is inconsistent. Evidence consistent with threat perception triggers a fear response and escape/avoidance behaviours.

The emphasis of cognitive–behavioural therapies is on exposure to the feared stimulus; for example, the memory of the event, and minimization of avoided fear and avoidance behaviour. It also aims to identify and challenge maladaptive beliefs. The therapy promotes the development of skills and change. There are a number of rape-specific cognitive–behavioural treatments including Prolonged Exposure Therapy (Foa, Rothbaum, Riggs, & Murdock, 1991) and Cognitive Processing Therapy (Resick & Schnicke, 1993). Patient suitability criteria for cognitive-behavioural therapy includes ability to access and identify thoughts and feelings, acceptance of the cognitive-behavioural model, motivation to change, commitment to therapy and commitment to the tasks of therapy (Safran & Segal, 1990).

Psychoanalytic treatment approaches are characterized as longer-term and more exploratory in nature. The therapeutic stance is non-directive and analysis of the positive and negative transference forms the basis of a developing understanding of the patient's complex internal world of object relations. Consistency of the therapy setting is important; that is, place, time, frequency, and duration of session. The content of sessions is guided by the client's material and the focus is often on the present. Communications about external events are taken as a communication about internal reality as well as external reality. Attention is paid to breaks, disruptions, and separations during therapy. The approach is based upon the idea that early relationships shape mental life and character and have a continuing effect on the internal world. For this reason greater attention is paid to developmental issues. A trauma such as rape is considered to re-evoke earlier unresolved conflicts of childhood. An understanding of early traumatic experiences and the unconscious ways in which an individual has attempted to resolve these conflicts provides insight and understanding into the individual's current response. Recommended criteria regarding suitability for psychoanalytic-based therapy include motivation for insight and change, a childhood history of at least one good relationship, flexible use of psychological defences, sufficient ego-strength, and commitment to therapy and the process of self-understanding. Exclusion criteria include poor impulse control and substance abuse (Coltart, 1988a,b).

Distress following rape

In beginning to understand the psychological sequelae and the process of recovery following rape it is important to consider the broad nature of the trauma. Rape is an offence involving a victimizer and a victim; the knowledge that another person has wilfully and maliciously chosen the individual as the object of an assault can add to the disturbing nature of the event. Kilpatrick *et al.* (1985) have suggested that the effects of victimization are worse than the effects of other kinds of disasters or crises. Rape is a physically and psychologically intrusive sexual attack that may last from minutes to hours or days. In the cases of abusive relationships, assaults can take place over years. During an attack the person is typically controlled, threatened, and abused. The assault is likely to induce significant feelings of fear and helplessness. There may be actual physical injury and/or threat of injury; there may also be perception of threat to life. The attack may be carried out by a stranger, friend, work colleague, or partner. The effect of sexual assault tends to be more severe if the offender is known to the victim; this has an impact on the survivor's trust in his or her own judgement and trust in others, and increases feelings of vulnerability. The event may be clearly remembered, partially remembered, or not remembered at all. Survivors may be under the influence of alcohol or drugs administered by themselves or by the assailant. There have been increasing reports of drug-assisted rape over recent years (Slaughter, 2000; Sturman, 2000). Drugs such as flunitrazepam, a benzodiazepine marketed under the trade name Rohypnol, render an individual unconscious. For medical purposes the drug is used in the short-term for insomnia and as a sedative hypnotic and preanaesthetic medication. It has similar effects to diazepam (trade name Valium) although it is several times more potent. It is not unusual in cases of drug rape with flunitrazepam for individuals to report very brief windows of consciousness followed again by loss of memory. There is often great distress associated with not being able to remember the complete sequence of events.

In the immediate aftermath following sexual assault medical care may be necessary for physical injuries, screening for and treatment of sexually transmitted infections, and emergency contraception. Some women find themselves pregnant as a consequence of rape. Clearly this adds significantly to distress. Many women decide to terminate the pregnancy, some choose to continue with the pregnancy. In cases of high HIV risk, post-exposure prophylaxis can be administered, although treatment needs to be started within seventy-two hours of exposure. The HIV test is carried out three months after the time of risk, leaving individuals with an anxiety-provoking waiting period. For women who suspect drug-assisted rape, urine and blood tests need to be taken within seventy-two hours. If an assault is reported to the police the survivor will undergo a forensic medical examination and give a detailed witness statement. Distress evoked by police and forensic procedures has been acknowledged in the literature (Temkin, 1996).

The nature of the distress following rape and sexual assault has been increasingly documented over recent years (Baker, Skolnik, Davis, & Brickman, 1991; Burgess & Holstrom, 1974; Foa & Steketee, 1987; Kilpatrick, Best, & Veronen, 1984; Koss, 1983; Lees & Gregory, 1993; Mezey & Taylor, 1988; Nadeson, Notman, Zackson, & Gornick, 1982; Resick, 1993; Shapland, Willmore, & Duff, 1985; Veronen, Kilpatrick, & Resick, 1979). Whilst levels of distress following a sexual trauma have been shown to decline over time, symptoms within the initial weeks and months typically include features of depression, anxiety, and PTSD, as well as sexual dysfunction and drug and alcohol misuse. Problems also relate to self-blame, guilt, shame, and a decreased sense of trust, safety, and control. Following rape, the qualitative nature and extent of distress will vary according to a number of factors. These include the relationship to the assailant, the circumstances and nature of the assault and the cognitive appraisal of the assault.

Mental health services

Although increasing social awareness of rape over the past thirty years or so in Western societies has resulted in many survivors feeling that there are now legitimate reasons to seek help from mental health services, there continues to be much secrecy and shame surrounding the subject of rape. Similarly, using NHS mental health services and being viewed as a "mental health patient" or "psychiatric case" remains stigmatizing. An individual may be treated within a range of NHS mental health services including primary care, trauma services, sexual health services, psychological therapies services, and community mental health teams. While rape may provide the entry point to mental health services, some individuals will have pre-existing mental health problems and some of these may be long-standing and complex. Survivors often present with multiple problems and histories of prior abuse (Kilpatrick, Edmonds, & Seymour, 1992; Wyatt, Guthrie, & Notgrass, 1992). It may prove difficult to address wider or long-standing problems during a time-limited therapy and it may be helpful to acknowledge the limitations of the work with the client.

> Miss A was referred to the psychology service by a specialist registrar following a sexual health check at a genito-urinary medicine clinic. She had been raped by a neighbour. She was a twenty-seven-year-old single woman with a history of childhood sexual abuse by her father, chronic depression, deliberate self-harm, suicide attempts and eating disorder (anorexia). The rape by her neighbour was the most recent event in a long history of abuse, victimization and vulnerability.

For a more detailed description of assessment issues in rape and sexual assault see Doyle and Thornton (2002).

In the psychiatric literature, rape and sexual assault-related problems are often classified under the diagnostic terms Acute Stress Disorder (ASD) and Post-Traumatic Stress Disorder (*DSM-IV*, American Psychiatric Association, 1994; *ICD-10*, World Health Organization, 1992). Those diagnosed with PTSD are twice as likely to meet the diagnostic criteria for another psychiatric disorder as those without (Helzer, Robins, & McEvoy, 1987). While the diagnosis of PTSD groups together a list of frequently recurring symptoms within a specified definition of time, it ignores many other aspects of a person's response to trauma. In cases of moderate to severe PTSD symptoms, pharmacological treatments that may prove helpful include selective serotonin re-uptake inhibitors (SSRIs) such as paroxetine and sertraline. Medication may prove a helpful adjunct to psychological therapy.

Psychological treatment

Early stages of therapy involve establishment of the therapeutic relationship, containment, validation and elucidation of the meaning of the rape experience for the person. In cognitive–behavioural terms this means identifying the predominant emotions and the main cognitive themes. What are the worst aspects of the event? What are the areas that elicit most distress? What is the nature of the intrusive thoughts and images? It is important to match patients to an appropriate style of therapy; using an integrative approach enables the clinician to respond flexibly. Some clients will benefit from a more structured approach, others from a more client-led agenda with links and interpretations made by the therapist. It is helpful to inform clients that distress is likely to increase during the initial stages of therapy as individuals move from a more avoidance-related coping style to trauma-focused strategies to help process feelings and thoughts related to the trauma (Nishith, Resick, & Griffin, 2002).

Containment and holding

The concepts of "holding' and "containment' originate in the work of Winnicott (1960) and Bion (1962a). Winnicott's concept of holding is based in the physical relationship of mother and infant—the infant feels safe in her mother's arms. Winnicott extends the concept of holding to the total emotional and physical environment created by the mother; on the basis of the security the infant feels, she can begin to separate and discover the world into which she has been born. Using this concept in relation to therapy, holding refers to those provisions within the environment that protect the individual and offer consistency, reliability, and a safe supportive space. The establishment of a holding environment involves reliability of the therapist's presence, consistency of the setting, reliable time-keeping and the maintenance of boundaries. An attack such as rape can shatter an individual's sense of safety.

> Mrs B was a thirty-five-year-old woman who had been raped by an acquaintance. She started once-a-week therapy two months after the assault in the autumn. She came to the first session after a three-week Christmas break and revealed that she felt "empty" and had no feelings. She said, "I don't want to kill myself but I don't want to live." Immediately prior to the break she had reported feeling worse with increased symptoms of depression, including suicidal ideation and anxiety. The break in therapy had been difficult for Mrs B and had the effect of exacerbating her distress. On her return to therapy she reported a sense of depersonalization. While this is a common response following trauma, in this instance it can also be seen to relate to the experience of attachment to the therapist, issues of dependence, and an experience of being left by the therapist. Feeling abandoned by a good object can leave a person feeling at the mercy of a bad object; depersonalization can be a defence against this. These ideas are described by Bion (1962b) in relation to the infant and the breast.

Bion's concept of containment is based on the idea that the infant projects feelings into the mother that are distressing, frightening, painful, or in some other way unbearable for the infant at that level of development. The mother is affected by the infant's feelings, as discomfort, fear, or agitation are evoked in her. If she can process or transform these feelings by recognizing them, thinking about them, acting on them and not being overwhelmed by them, she can then "return" the feelings to the infant in a modified form. In theory, the infant can then reintegrate them as her own. It is not the infant herself that is contained, it is the feeling that the mother experiences that derives from the infant.

The concept of emotional containment in therapy refers to the idea that the therapist contains what has been projected into him or her. Through the therapist's understanding, transformations can take place that enable the patient to mentally process an event. In this way the therapist temporarily acts as a mental container for the patient's emotional vulnerability and disturbed state of mind. Containment takes place when the therapist absorbs and thinks about difficult feelings and experiences and then puts these feelings into words, in so doing, allowing the experience to become more manageable for the patient. Individuals can experience considerable relief from identifying, talking about, and processing these painful emotional states.

Transference and countertransference

Freud (1912b) identified the concept of transference and distinguished both positive and negative types. Transference can be defined as the experiencing of feelings and attitudes towards a person, which are a repetition of reactions originating in relation to significant relationships in early childhood. It is an actualization of internal object relations within the analytic relationship. Countertransference is the therapist's emotional response to the client. It is used as a way to understand the meaning of the client's unconscious communications. An awareness of transference and countertransference issues involves close monitoring of the emotional relationship between the therapist and the patient. Essentially, transference phenomena involve re-enactment of previous experiences, especially those related to trauma.

Therapists drawing upon psychoanalytic theory are likely to make a high number of transference statements and respond more fully to patients' references to the therapist. From a psychoanalytic point of view, transference is not extinguished if therapists do not recognize or acknowledge it. Although cognitive–behavioural therapies do not generally involve comment on the therapeutic relationship, it has been suggested that inattention to interpersonal issues in CBT may potentially weaken the therapeutic relationship and lead to resistance behaviour and treatment non-compliance (Beach & Power, 1996).

At the start of therapy, the therapist may be perceived as an idealized figure, offering care when the patient feels very vulnerable. As therapy progresses, there is likely to be further development of both positive and negative transference. In the negative transference, patients can feel humiliated, experience aggressive urges towards the therapist, and may make attempts to disparage the therapy. In more extreme cases survivors may act out in sadistic, masochistic, or intrusive ways towards therapists.

An understanding of countertransference involves monitoring the unconscious emotional reaction to the patient. Related to this, it is important to be able to distinguish between those feelings that relate to the therapist's internal world and those that derive from the survivor. In cases of rape and sexual assault, it is not uncommon for the patient to evoke a very caring and protective response in the therapist. Feelings of empathy and identification may also be located in the therapist. The countertransference can involve feelings of anger at the abuse the patient has experienced. Negative countertransference towards the patient can sometimes be split off and located in a supervisor or the wider mental health team. This can lead to neglect of the patient's aggressive feelings within the therapeutic relationship, as well as neglect of their potential to evoke aggression in others.

Basic routines and self-care

Through therapy, the patient can be helped to establish basic self-care routines and to re-establish normal routines of sleep, eating, and daily activities. Identification of personal goals regarding daily and weekly activities can lead to behavioural changes in small, graded steps. Individuals who are experiencing guilt, shame, or even self-hatred may unconsciously neglect their bodies as a form of self-punishment. They may not feel deserving of time or money spent on their medical, emotional, or physical needs.

Problems that relate to a basic sense of security such as housing or finance problems may also need to be addressed initially. Depending on the circumstances of the rape and the identity of the assailant, survivors may feel unsafe in their home and feel compelled to move home and/or change job. There may be a fear of reprisals from the assailant and/or the assailant's family and friends. Perception of the threat to safety can be appraised during therapy and will be discussed later (see cognitive re-structuring).

Normalization

A key aspect of therapy is to place the patient's responses to rape and subsequent distress within an understanding of normal expected reactions to traumatic events. Individuals can feel frightened and confused by their reactions and fear that they are losing control or "going mad". An explanation of normal reactions after a trauma including, for example, information about thought-intrusions, emotional numbing, and hyper-arousal can help survivors understand normal physiological and psychological reactions.

Mourning

A primary task of therapy is to allow the person to mourn, that is to feel truly sorry for themselves, what has happened and what has been lost. Anger is an important part of mourning. Rape may involve losses on many levels: practical, emotional, spiritual, philosophical. Any mourning will also take a person back to early mourning experiences. Klein (1932, 1935) described the experience of the "loss of the breast" as the "template for mourning". According to Klein, the loss of the breast relates to the loss of a phantasy of omnipotent control over the "breast" or the caregiver, which may or may not coincide with actual weaning. In rape, the individual's sense of control over her life is likely to suffer a severe blow; there may be a loss of a sense of safety, control, dignity, and self-respect. There may be a loss of a sense of integrity of the physical self and loss of a sense of being inviolable and in control of decisions about events involving the body. The losses incurred in rape may resonate with earlier, and even infantile, experiences of loss; this may lend the experience a quality of being primitive, overwhelming, or impossible to put into words.

Cognitive re-structuring

The aim of cognitive re-structuring is to help survivors identify and change dysfunctional thoughts and beliefs (Beck, 1967, 1976; Beck, Rush, Shaw, & Emery, 1979). The focus is on thoughts, beliefs, and expectations. According to Beck's theory, individuals develop stable cognitive structures, including beliefs about the self, others, and the world, that help organize life experiences. These schemas are developed through experiences in early life. Cognitive therapy helps individuals learn how thoughts, feelings, behaviour, and physiological experiences are linked, and focuses on targeting dysfunctional patterns of thinking that lead to exaggerated emotional responses. The aim is to develop more effective ways of thinking. During the course of therapy it becomes possible to identify irrational, negative self-talk and replace it with more positive, coping statements.

Cognitive processing therapy (CPT, Resick & Schnicke, 1992) is different from Beck's cognitive therapy in important ways. It does not assume that rape elicits previously existing distorted and dysfunctional thinking patterns, as in depression or anxiety. Instead, it proposes that difficulties are usually caused as a result of conflicts between pre-existing schema and new information arising from the rape experience. The focus of CPT is on identifying these "stuck points". CPT also recognizes that problems may arise for three other reasons. First, as a result of others' responses to the rape; for example, a person may be blamed for the rape by those expected to provide support. Second, a person's coping style may be avoidant, so that she is unable to psychologically process the event. Last, there may be no relevant schema in which to store the new information; that is, the event is outside her range of experience and cannot be comprehended.

Following rape, the sense of current threat is appraised and may need to be modified. After rape there is frequently a loss of a sense of safety, increase in a sense of vulnerability, loss of trust in others, and over-negative view of likelihood of attack. It is not uncommon for survivors of rape and sexual assault to overestimate future risks to themselves, although the possibility of real danger needs to be considered carefully.

Thought suppression is a way of coping with upsetting thoughts or images; nevertheless, it acts over time to increase thought intrusiveness. It is helpful to explain this to patients and to reduce avoidance by actively considering the problematic thoughts and images. Through imagery work it is possible to change the nature of the memories by asking the survivor what they would have liked to have done or to have happened at different points during the event. In this way the memory can be elaborated and changed, and the overall nature of the representation altered.

Responsibility and self-blame

Feelings of guilt and shame are common in rape survivors and are related to a sense of responsibility and self-blame. It is helpful to identify and address these areas before carrying out more focused exposure work. Therapy needs to focus on cognitive representations of the self and relationships to others. Clearly, both shame and fear-based reactions can co-exist in the same person (Adshead, 2000). In cognitive–behavioural terms, issues related to self-blame and the attribution of responsibility fall under the remit of cognitive restructuring.

As self-blame can relate to a person's behaviour or to a person's character, it is helpful to consider the extent to which the person placed himself or herself in a position of risk initially. In order to do this it is relevant to consider both Freud's (1920g) concept of the death-instinct—that is self-destructive forces—as well as the phenomenon of "repetition compulsion". He considers repetition compulsion to be an occurrence whereby a person places him or herself in a risky or distressing position, thereby repeating a previous unpleasant or even painful experience in an attempt to gain mastery over the experience; the individual may not recognize the unconscious motivation for this. In sexual abuse cases this can be seen clearly; the phenomenon of individuals with histories of repeated abuse is well recognized (Kilpatrick, Edmonds, & Seymour, 1992; Russell, 1983; Wyatt, Guthrie & Notgrass, 1992). If a rape or sexual assault is the person's first experience of an abusive situation, there is a risk that the person will unconsciously place themselves again in circumstances reminiscent of the assault situation, which may serve as a way of unconsciously working through the trauma.

> Ms C was a twenty-one-year-old woman travelling in France who was running short of money and needed somewhere to stay for the night. A recommended hostel was full, but when she explained her predicament to a man she met outside, he invited her to stay for the night. Judging him to be friendly and of good character, and feeling safe with him, she accompanied him on a short bus ride to his home, which he shared with three male friends. After a meal she rejected his sexual advances. He was insistent and gradually became more and more controlling and aggressive, in the end threatening her with a knife. She was multiply raped by the four men throughout the course of the night. She believed that she would be killed.

> During the course of therapy a significant incident occurred whereby she invited an eighteen-year-old man whom she had recently met at work to her home for supper. There was a significant physical resemblance between this colleague and one of her attackers in France. After the meal, not knowing him very well at all, she told him about the attack, about the assailants, and about the fact that they were from the same ethnic background as him. The man, clearly upset and disturbed by the information, left her home shortly afterwards. The incident reveals how the young woman had unconsciously re-created a situation that was reminiscent of the night of the assault. However, in the recreated scenario she was in control, and it can be seen as an attempt at mastery over a situation in which she felt terrified and helpless. In fact, in the re-worked situation she became the persecutor when she recounted her ordeal to a young man who inadvertently and unwittingly had been caught up in her emotional trauma.

In therapy, breaking down a situation into component elements can clarify the extent of a survivor's responsibility. In the case of Ms

C above, clearly she had placed herself in a position of risk by going to an unknown person's house. In this way she did carry a degree of responsibility for placing herself at risk. By disentangling this behaviour and responsibility from any other subsequent events and responsibilities she was helped to understand differences in the nature and severity of events/behaviours. It is often a relief for survivors to be able to define and see the limits of any responsibility they may have, and to delineate this from other events and other's responsibilities. Examples of alternative or coping thoughts include the following: I did not cause the rape; I am not responsible for the rape no matter where I was; the rape is not a punishment because of something I did in the past; blaming myself won't make the memories disappear; I may not be able to change what has happened but I can take positive steps towards caring for myself.

Guilt and shame

The terms "guilt" and "shame" are often used interchangeably without distinguishing between the two internal, affective states. An influential reconceptualization by Lewis (1971) views guilt as an emotion linked to the idea of "bad behaviour" and shame as an emotion linked to the idea of "bad self". A guilt experience that is fused with shame embraces both remorse about a specific behaviour as well as more global feelings of self-contempt and self-disgust. Guilt can be viewed as both adaptive or maladaptive; maladaptive guilt is characterized by chronic self-blame and an obsessive rumination over some objectionable behaviour. Feelings of guilt are more likely to become maladaptive when there is an overlay of shame, which can lead to interminable rumination and self-castigation (Tangney, 1996).

Self-blame can be seen as functional in that it can help a person to avoid more painful feelings. It helps to maintain a view that the survivor is in control and that the external world is manageable. The core helplessness is therefore avoided. To face the situation of feeling helpless without support, as in the rape situation, can feel worse than feeling to blame.

In the initial denial and shock during a rape event it is easy to make what later appear to be "mistakes", or to act in a manner that later confuses a person and causes them to doubt and criticize themselves. What appear to be reasonable decisions at the time are later judged to be errors of judgement by the person, thereby fuelling self-blame.

> Miss D was a twenty-five-year-old woman who was being held in her own flat by an assailant and had been told by him to take her clothes off. He had said that he would not leave until he had had sex with her. Before he raped her he asked her to go to the kitchen to get a drink. With hindsight she feels that at that point she had the opportunity to escape from the flat. At the time she felt unable to leave because she was undressed and felt embarrassed to be seen by her neighbours. Through therapy she was helped to see that it was reasonable to have had these kinds of concerns but that, importantly, at the time she was in shock and denial about what was about to happen.

At times, being in shock and denial can leave individuals feeling unable to think. Survivors then feel to blame for not taking steps to avert a course of action. Many survivors are fearful for their lives and the over-riding goal then becomes survival. In this way, not putting up resistance to rape can be a way of minimizing assailant aggression and increasing chances of survival. In situations of terror individuals can act in unexpected ways. Through therapy, the force of the survival instinct, set against the backdrop of terror, shock, and disbelief, can be understood and acknowledged.

Revictimization

McCarthy (1986) describes three levels of victimization facing a rape survivor. The primary trauma effects following rape include loss of invulnerability, loss of a sense of an orderly world and loss of a positive self-image. Secondary trauma effects include a sense of isolation, difficulties related to the forensic examination and criminal justice system, and negative social attitudes. Negative attitudes and reactions of others include denial and discounting of difficulties, stigma, denial of assistance, victim-blaming, and ignorance. The third level of traumatization relates to identification as a victim whereby the survivor moves to a psychological position involving acceptance of the victim label and internalization of society's negative view.

It is recognized that a significant proportion of rape survivors present with histories of multiple victimization (Rush, Amodeo, Leon, & Gartrell, 1991; Wyatt, Guthrie, & Notgrass, 1992). Survivors may experience greater difficulty than others in asserting their rights, pursuing their goals, or putting a stop to further abuses. A passive role may be assumed because such a position was a survival tactic during a previous trauma. Self-blame can contribute to the acceptance of further victimization. Therapy can help the person become aware of all the instances in life, large or small, in which the role of victim is assumed.

Identification with the aggressor

Identification with the aggressor is a defence mechanism identified and described by Anna Freud (1936) whereby the victim changes a passive experience into an active one; the victim becomes the abuser. In this circumstance, the victim identifies with the assailant and as a result may feel responsible for the rape, as though this was something they did to themselves or knowingly allowed to happen. They may even feel that they deserved this "punishment". Crucially this is a defence against helplessness and enables the victim to feel empowered (along the lines of "if you can't beat them, join them"). In this process the body may become objectified as the victim, as the mind becomes identified with the aggressor. The person may then be prone to further enactment of abuse towards the self or others.

> Ms E was a thirty-two-year-old woman who took to hitting her head following a rape incident. Her behaviour in part related to a distraction mechanism to rid her mind of intrusive sounds in her ears of the assailant's voice, yet she also believed she was worthy of punishment herself. She had been terrified during the rape ordeal and thought she would be killed. Following the rape she described the symptom of pain in her right ear and said she could hear the shouting voice of the assailant, as it had sounded on the night.

The deliberate form of self-harm can be seen as a bodily re-enactment of a trauma. In this case, Ms E expressed a striking lack of anger towards the assailant and in fact felt sorry for him because he was in prison serving a sentence for rape. Her appraisal of the man's violence was in contrast to the therapist's sense of the man. The therapist considered the man's attack to have been physically and emotionally violent, cruel and sadistic. He had raped the woman on a number of occasions during the course of a night, taunted her with threats of death, and had told her details of murder cases involving young women. Ms E had no sense of her own anger and was unable to perceive the extent and seriousness of her assailant's aggression. Her own anger and destructiveness remained unconscious and was expressed in the form of sado-masochistic behaviour as an unconscious need to inflict harm upon herself.

Traumatic dreams

Traumatic dreams have long been recognized as a phenomenon associated with real-life trauma (Freud, 1900a). These dreams frequently include a repetition of the actual trauma. Freud (1914g) recognized that the unconscious mind repeated experiences all the time and that repeating in itself was nothing new. What was striking, however, was the compulsion to repeat something that was unpleasurable. Later (Freud, 1920g) he revised his theory of mind, which was based on a notion of the pursuit of pleasure, and suggested that repetition of unpleasurable experiences either serves to achieve mastery over a trauma or reflects a self-destructive wish.

> Ms F was raped by an acquaintance. He had held her hostage in her home overnight and raped her three times. During the course of the night he threatened to kill her. On several occasions he put his hands around her neck and partially strangled her. During therapy Ms F described a dream in which she was at a funfair with her cat. She saw some friends she hadn't seen since her schooldays who came towards her. She was initially pleased to see them but soon realized that her friends intended to kill the cat. She attempted to protect the cat but her friends then tried to kill her. Her friends were on top of her and she felt unable to breathe, as if she were suffocating.

The events in the dream can be seen at the most basic level to be a representation of the real-life trauma. The friends represent the assailant who attacked Ms F and the attack on the cat represents the assault on Ms F's mind, body, and sexuality. In the dream Ms F is unable to breathe, which is a repetition of her lived experience when the attacker attempted to strangle her. At another level, anger is projected on to the school-friends, who are not violent people and who wouldn't ordinarily abuse Ms F. The dream is important in that it may represent the start of Ms F beginning to recognize her own anger and rage, rather than believing that the aggression remained solely located in the assailant. In this particular case, one of the factors likely to have placed Ms F at risk of attack initially was that she was not in touch with her own or others' aggression; although signs of aggression and mental instability were identifiable in the assailant before the attack, she had been unable to pick these up.

Traumatic dreams can be seen as a symbolic representation of a concrete trauma. During therapy a client can be asked if there are any thought or feeling associations to the dream and enquiries can be made about the client's ideas regarding the meaning of the dream. This may illuminate aspects of the trauma that had previously been obscured, or aspects of the client's feelings about themselves, others, or the therapy.

Anxiety management

Principally fear-based reactions following rape and sexual assault benefit from a therapy that addresses the management of fear and anxiety. Anxiety-management includes relaxation skills training, for example progressive muscle relaxation (Jacobson, 1938), breathing control exercises, and guided imagery. During therapy clients can be introduced to basic cognitive–behavioural theory (the five component model of cognitive, affective, behavioural, physical, and environmental factors) and learn to distinguish between thoughts, emotions, physical sensations, and behaviour. The concept of an anxiety spiral can be explained; that is, the way in which reciprocal interaction between anxious thoughts and monitoring of physical sensations leads to an increasing state of anxiety, as well as avoidance (cognitive, affective, and behavioural) acting as a maintenance factor. Clients are helped to identify triggers of intrusive memories and to distinguish between stimuli that occurred around the time of the event and those that occur currently. A series of coping thoughts and behaviours are developed to facilitate a more adaptive response in general, and more specifically in relation to rape-related anxiety triggers.

Reliving the trauma

It is recognized that for an individual to be encouraged to give an account of the rape before the therapeutic relationship is established is likely to prove unhelpful and feel overwhelming. This is particularly so if issues of shame, guilt, and self-blame are paramount and have not been addressed initially. However, when the patient is ready, this stage of therapy involves talking about what has happened, including how the person felt and what the person thought during the event. The memory of the assault needs to be integrated into previous and subsequent experience.

For some survivors the court appearance may be experienced as being as traumatic as the assault itself. This is because of self-blame, shame, difficulties talking about the rape in public, fear of being disbelieved, reliving experiences, answering the defence barrister, and seeing the assailant again. The majority of women find their experiences in court humiliating and distressing (Lees, 1996). For others, it may be the forensic examination that evokes considerable distress (Temkin, 1996).

This stage of treatment involves fully processing all aspects of the trauma, including thinking about and discussing it in detail on a number of occasions. Intense exposure work, although effective at bringing about eventual habituation, is likely to bring about an immediate increase in avoidance symptoms (Nishith, Resick, & Griffin, 2002). Techniques of reliving and cognitive restructuring can be usefully combined as in Cognitive Processing Therapy (Resick & Schnicke, 1993).

Exposure can be accomplished through a number of techniques, including systematic de-sensitization, *in vivo* exposure, and imaginal exposure. Imaginal exposure, or "reliving" (described by Foa &

Rothbaum, 1998), requires the client to recall the memory of the rape in the present tense, in the first person, including details of how they felt and what they thought at different points in time. Initially, reliving starts from just before the event until a time when person was safe. Later there can be a focus on particularly upsetting aspects. Clients can be asked to rate their level of distress at different times throughout the memory recall, and from recall to recall. This procedure becomes less distressing as exposures are repeated. The Subjective Units of Distress Scale (SUDS; Wolpe, 1969) can be used to monitor distress levels and generate a hierarchy for *in vivo* exposures. *In vivo* exposure requires clients to face trauma-related cues; for example, by visiting the site of the assault. Clients can be encouraged to undertake this work between sessions.

In Prolonged Exposure Therapy (Foa *et al.*, 1999) clients are asked to generate a hierarchy for *in vivo* exposures that may include a variety of places implicated during the rape situation. The *in vivo* exposure situations are subsequently assigned as daily homework tasks. The imaginal exposures are conducted over several therapy sessions and each is tape-recorded. Homework also includes listening once to the tape of the entire session and listening daily to the taped imaginal exposure.

The exposure component of Cognitive Processing Therapy (CPT) involves writing and reading a detailed account of the rape. Clients are asked to write an account of the rape including all of the sensory details, emotions, and thoughts. They are also encouraged to experience their emotions fully while writing and reading over the account (Resick & Schnicke, 1992).

Conclusion

Rape triggers a series of complex psychological responses, which in turn warrant a comprehensive treatment approach based upon depth, complexity, and a sensitivity of understanding. Unconscious and conscious defence mechanisms operate to facilitate survival and, in particular, operate in situations of extreme vulnerability. The importance of understanding such defences is not to be underestimated when helping an individual manage responses to an experience such as rape. The trauma requires mental processing in order to facilitate integration of a painful abuse experience into a previously held set of lived experiences and beliefs about the self, others, and the world. It takes place in the context of a therapeutic relationship in which the therapist understands the difference between "relationship", "sex", and "abuse". The aim of the therapy is to help the person to process the experience and to facilitate as functional and constructive an adjustment as possible. Through the experience of the therapist and the therapy, the experience and meaning of the event is transformed into something that, while still painful, can be considered and managed.

References

Adshead, G. (2000). Psychological therapies for post-traumatic stress disorder. *British Journal of Psychiatry*, 177: 144–148.

American Psychiatric Association (1994). *Diagnostic and Statistical Manual of Mental Disorders* (4th edn). Washington, DC: American Psychiatric Association.

Baker, T., Skolnik, L., Davis, R., & Brickman, E. (1991). The social support of survivors of rape: The differences between rape survivors and survivors of other violent crimes and between husbands, boyfriends, and women friends. In: A. Burgess (Ed.) *Rape and Sexual Assault III*. New York: Garland.

Beach, K., & Power, M. (1996). Transference: an empirical investigation across a range of cognitive–behavioural and psychoanalytic therapies. *Clinical Psychology and Psychotherapy*, 3(1): 1–14.

Beck, A. T. (1967). *Depression: Clinical, Experimental and Theoretical Aspects*. New York: Harper and Row.

Beck, A. T. (1976). *Cognitive Therapy and the Emotional Disorders*. New York: International Universities Press.

Beck, A. T., Rush, A. J., Shaw, B. F., & Emery, G. (1979). *Cognitive Therapy of Depression*. New York: Guilford Press.

Bion, W. R. (1962a) A theory of thinking. *International Journal of Psycho-Analysis*, 43. Reprinted in *Second Thoughts* (1967) London: Karnac.

Bion, W. R. (1962b). *Learning from Experience*. London: Karnac.

Bucci, W. (1997). *Psychoanalysis and Cognitive Science: A Multiple Code Theory*. New York: Guilford Press.

Burgess, A., & Holstrom, L. (1974). Rape trauma syndrome. *American Journal of Psychiatry*, 131: 981–986.

Coltart, N. (1988a). Diagnosis and assessment for suitability for psycho-analytical psychotherapy. *British Journal of Psychiatry, 4*: 127–134.

Coltart, N. (1988b). The assessment of psychological mindedness in the diagnostic interview. *British Journal of Psychiatry, 153*: 819–820.

Doyle, A. M., & Thornton, S. (2002). Psychological assessment of sexual assault. In: J. Petrak & B. Hedge (Eds.), *The Trauma of Sexual Assault*. Wiley.

Foa, E. B., Dancu, C. V., Hembree, E. A., Jaycox, L. H., Meadows, E. A., & Street, G. P. (1999). A comparison of exposure therapy, stress inoculation training, and their combination for reducing posttraumatic stress disorder in female assault victims. *Journal of Consulting and Clinical Psychology, 67*: 194–200.

Foa, E. B., & Rothbaum, B. O. (1998). *Treating the Trauma of Rape. Cognitive-behaviour Therapy for PTSD*. New York: Guilford Press.

Foa, E. B., Rothbaum, B. O., Riggs, D. S., & Murdock, T. B. (1991). Treatment of post-traumatic stress disorder in rape victims: A comparison between cognitive behavioural procedures and counselling. *Journal of Consulting and Clinical Psychology, 59*(5): 715–723.

Foa, E. B., & Steketee, G. (1987). Rape victims: Post traumatic stress responses and their treatment: A review of the literature. *Journal of Anxiety Disorders, 1*: 69–86.

Freud, A. (1936). Identification with the aggressor. *Writings, 2*: 109–121.

Freud, S. (1900a). The interpretation of dreams. *S.E., 4–5*. London: Hogarth.

Freud, S. (1912b). The dynamics of transference. *S.E., 13*: 104. London: Hogarth.

Freud, S. (1914g). Remembering, repeating and working-through. *S.E., 12*: 147–156. London: Hogarth.

Freud, S. (1920g). Beyond the pleasure principle. *S.E., 18*: 1–64. London: Hogarth.

Helzer, J. E., Robins, L. M., & McEvoy, L. (1987). Post-traumatic stress disorder in the general population: findings of the epidemiologic catchment area survey. *New England Journal of Medicine, 317*: 1630–1634.

Jacobsen, E. (1938). *Progressive Relaxation*. Chicago: University of Chicago Press.

Kilpatrick, D. G., Best, C., & Veronen, L. (1984). Factors predicting psychological distress among rape victims. In: C. R. Figley (Ed.), *Trauma and its Wake* (pp. 133–141). New York: Brunner/Mazel.

Kilpatrick, D. G., Best, C. L., Veronen, L. J., Amick, A. E., Villeponteaux, L. A., & Ruff, G. A. (1985). Mental health correlates of criminal victimisation: a random community survey. *Journal of Consulting and Clinical Psychology, 53*(6): 866–873.

Kilpatrick, D. G., Edmonds, C., & Seymour, A. (1992). *Rape in America: A Report to the Nation.* Arlington, VA: National Victim Centre.

Klein, M. (1932). *The Psycho-Analysis of Children.* London: Hogarth.

Klein, M. (1935). A contribution to the psychogenesis of manic-depressive states. *International Journal of Psychoanalysis, 16*: 145–174.

Koss, M. (1983). The scope of rape: implications for the clinical treatment of victims. *The Clinical Psychologist, 36*: 88–91

Lees, S. (1996). *Carnal Knowledge. Rape on Trial.* London: Penguin.

Lees, S., & Gregory, J. (1993). *Rape and Sexual Assault: A Study of Attrition—Multi-agency Investigation into the Problem of Rape and Sexual Assault in the Borough of Islington.* London: Islington Council.

Lewis, H. B. (1971). *Shame & Guilt in Neurosis.* New York: International Universities Press.

McCarthy, B. (1986). A cognitive behavioural approach to understanding and treating sexual trauma. *Journal of Sex and Marital Therapy, 12*(4): 322–329.

Mezey, G., & Taylor, P. (1988). Psychological reactions of women who have been raped. *British Journal of Psychiatry, 152*: 330–339.

Nadeson, C., Notman, M., Zackson, H., & Gornick, J. (1982). A follow-up study of rape victims. *American Journal of Psychiatry, 139*: 1266–1270.

Nishith, P., Resick, P. A., & Griffin, M. G. (2002). Pattern of change in prolonged exposure and cognitive-processing therapy for female rape victims with posttraumatic stress disorder. *Journal of Consulting and Clinical Psychology, 70*(4): 880–886.

Resick, P. A. (1993). The psychological impact of rape. *Journal of Interpersonal Violence, 8*: 223–255.

Resick, P. A., & Schnicke, M. K. (1992). Cognitive processing therapy for sexual assault victims. *Journal of Consulting and Clinical Psychology, 60*: 748–756.

Resick, P. A., & Schnicke, M. K. (1993). *Cognitive Processing Therapy for Rape Victims.* Newbury Park, CA: Sage.

Ruch, L. O., Amedeo, S. R., Leon, J. J., & Gartrell, J. W. (1991). Repeated sexual victimisation and trauma change during the acute phase of the sexual assault trauma syndrome. *Women and Health, 17*(1): 1–19.

Russell, D. E. H. (1983). The incidence and prevalence of intrafamilial and extrafamilial sexual abuse of female children. *Child Abuse and Neglect, 7*: 133–146.

Safran, J. D., & Segal, Z. V. (1990). *Interpersonal Process in Cognitive Therapy*. New York: Basic Books.

Safran, J. D., & Muran, J. C. (2000). *Negotiating the Therapeutic Alliance*. New York: Guilford Press.

Sandler, J., Dare, C., & Holder, A. (1973). *The Patient and the Analyst. The Basis of the Psychoanalytic Process*. New York: International Universities Press.

Shapland, J., Willmore, J., & Duff, P. (1985). *Victims in the Criminal Justice System*. Aldershot: Gower.

Shevrin, H., Bond, J. A., Brakel, L. A., Hertel, R. K., & Williams, W. J. (1996). *Conscious and Unconscious Processes: Psychodynamic, Cognitive and Neuropsychological Convergences*. New York: Guilford Press.

Slaughter, L. (2000). Involvement of drugs in sexual assault. *Journal of Reproductive Medicine, 45*: 425–430.

Sturman, P. (2000). *Drug Assisted Sexual Assault: A Study for the Home Office under The Police Research Award Scheme*. London: Home Office.

Tangney, J. P. (1996). Conceptual and methodological issues in the assessment of shame and guilt. *Behaviour Research and Therapy, 34*(9): 741–754.

Temkin, J. (1996). Doctors, rape and criminal justice. *The Howard Journal of Criminal Justice, 35*(1): 1–20.

Veronen, L. J., Kilpatrick, D. G., & Resick, P. A. (1979). Treatment of fear and anxiety in rape victims: implications for the criminal justice system. In: W. H. Parsonage (Ed.), *Perspectives on Victimology*. Beverly Hills, CA: Sage.

Winnicott, D. (1960). The theory of the parent–child relationship. *International Journal of Psychoanalysis, 41*: 585–595.

Wolpe, J. (1969). *The Practice of Behaviour Therapy*. New York: Pergamon.

World Health Organization (1992). *The International Classification of Mental and Behavioural Disorders (ICD-10)*. Geneva: WHO.

Wyatt, G. E., Guthrie, D., & Notgrass, C. M. (1992). Differential effects of women's child sexual abuse and subsequent revictimisation. *Journal of Consulting and Clinical Psychology, 60*(2): 167–173.

CHAPTER NINE

Systemic therapy techniques for sexual difficulties

Naomi Adams

S exual activity carries a myriad of expectations, hopes, restrictions, and taboos that help to shape our sexual lives and the sexual lives of our clients. The meaning of sex for a particular individual might be influenced by multiple contexts: their gender, their religion, the culture they grew up in, their current relationship status, their health, their sexuality, and their age, to name but a few. Sex is also, generally, an activity that takes place in relation to another person. Thus, to truly understand our clients' experiences, we need to understand their own personal contexts and the context of their sexual relationships. It is my view that systemic therapy approaches, with their explicit acknowledgement of context and relationships, can help to bring these wider social, cultural, and political contexts into therapy in a helpful and therapeutically meaningful way.

This chapter does not attempt to provide a comprehensive review of all of the early, Milan, post-Milan, narrative, and postmodern systemic therapies, which are well described elsewhere (Hayes, 1991; Stratton, Preston-Shoot, & Hanks, 1990; Tomm, 1984), but attempts to describe some of the theoretical principles underpinning systemic approaches and, through a series of case examples, their application in psychosexual therapy.

The systemic approach: an introduction

Systemic theory holds that problems arise not in individuals but in systems. A "system" might include the individual client, their partner or partners, families, friends, but also their wider social contexts, such as their class, religion, culture, ethnicity, sexual orientation, or age. According to early systemic theorists (Watzlawick, Weakland, & Fisch, 1974), problems occur when a system gets "stuck" in a particular pattern of action and (re)action, while later narrative approaches (White, 1989) focus more on meaning and the problem-saturated stories that are told about the problem. With either approach, individuals cannot be seen to have a problem in isolation from a system. Thus, understanding the context in which a problem exists is essential to understanding the problem with which the client presents, or, "no context, no meaning" (Bateson, 1972).

Sexual problems from a systemic perspective are also understood as problems not in an individual client, but in the relationship between the members of the client's system, where "relationship" refers to any interaction between people in the system, who need not be in an ongoing relationship in the traditional sense.

Systemic formulations

Within a systemic formulation, beliefs and behaviours are not considered to be right, wrong, or dysfunctional. Instead, they are viewed as more or less helpful, according to the extent that they maintain a stuck system. The therapist does not directly challenge the belief or behaviour, but maintains curiosity about where these beliefs come from and the effect that the belief or behaviour has on the other members of the system. Therapeutic change is brought about through the use of therapeutic questions, which encourage the members of the system to reflect on their position and become "observers to their own system". This process is believed to create change through the opening of new, alternative possibilities for meaning and interaction.

Central to the later systemic approaches is the idea that the client or clients are seen as bringing their own areas of expertise and the solution is therefore actively co-created between the client(s) and the therapist rather than prescribed to a novice client by an "expert" therapist (Anderson & Goolishian, 1987).

Systemic hypothesizing

Like most forms of therapy, therapeutic questions are generated from hypotheses about the problem with which the individual or couple presents (Stratton, Preston-Shoot, & Hanks, 1990). But for a hypothesis to be truly systemic it must:

> *Include all members of the system and multiple perspectives on the problem.*
> The hypothesis must include all sexual partners and their views on the problem (assuming the client is sexually involved with at least one other person) and may include others, such as family members, friends, or other professionals.

> *Be circular not linear (e.g., A leads to B, B leads to A, rather than A leads to B)*
> A hypothesis is linear if it describes one event (A) leading to another (B). For example, "When Andrew says he wants sex, Nick gets upset" is a linear hypothesis because Nick getting upset is constructed as a direct consequence of Andrew saying that he wants sex. A circular hypothesis includes the first action (A leads to B) but also the subsequent (re)action (B leads to A), thus forming a reflexive loop. An alternative, circular hypothesis might be "When Andrew says he wants sex, Nick feels angry because he feels pressured. When Nick shows his anger, Andrew feels rejected and seeks reassurance by asking Nick to have sex. Nick feels more angry because he feels Andrew is not listening and withdraws". The circular hypothesis includes the effect of each person's behaviour on the other, but does not imply responsibility of one person over the other.

> *Talk about relationships, not individuals (e.g., X shows anger to Y, rather than X is angry)*
> A hypothesis that talks about individuals, for example, "Nick is angry", does not show the feeling or behaviour in context and therefore individualizes the problem. A hypothesis that

talks about relationships, for example, "Nick shows his anger to Andrew by withdrawing", allows the anger to be shown in the context of the relationship. Talking about relationships, rather than individuals, encourages a discussion about context, communication and meaning.

Be "meta" to the system, i.e., at a different level to the clients' ideas about the problem
For change to happen within a systemic framework, the therapist must help to introduce difference into the system, hence the systemic concept of "the difference that makes a difference" (Bateson, 1972), as "difference" allows the system to become "unstuck". But in order for this to happen, the therapist must have hypotheses that are different to those of the client or clients, or the system will be maintained.

Positively/logically connote all members of the system
All of the actions of individuals in a system are seen as positive and/or logical, in that they make sense from the individual's point of view (Cecchin, 1987). The therapist logically connotes the actions of all members of the system, by describing actions as an attempt to find a solution. For example, the hypothesis "Andrew wants to have sex as a way to comfort Nick and seek reassurance" helps us to understand the meaning of Andrew asking for sex as something functional and positive (caring, communicating, reassuring). Equally, the hypothesis that "Nick withdraws to protect himself and Andrew from his feelings" helps us to understand Nick withdrawing as something protective for himself and Andrew. By logically connoting actions, clients are enabled to understand the problem "as an attempted solution" (Burnham, 1986), rather than a failure of the relationship or an attempt at deliberate harm by a partner.

As with all therapeutic approaches, there will be some actions, such as domestic violence or child neglect, where it may not be appropriate to focus on logically connoting behaviour. At these times the therapist will need to step out of this role and act according to legal or professional guidelines.

Maintain the neutrality/transparency of the therapist
Early systemic theorising held that the therapist must take a position of neutrality in relation to the client's concerns (Boscolo, Cecchin, & Prata, 1980). Neutrality in this sense refers to the notion that the therapist does not have an agenda with regard to the outcome of the sessions. However, more recent approaches (Cecchin, 1987) recognize that neutrality is not possible and this notion has been replaced with the ideas of "transparency" (of thinking) and "curiosity" (holding all ideas open to enquiry and change) (see below under Therapist Contexts).

Systemic therapy with psychosexual difficulties

Within my own psychosexual therapy practice, I have found systemic models and techniques useful with both individuals and couples. By working with the system in which the client presents, sexual partners become an essential component in the therapeutic process, be they inside or outside the room. In the following sections, I have attempted to show how systemic therapy ideas can be incorporated into therapeutic work with individuals or couples, before therapy begins and during therapy itself.

Before therapy begins

THERAPIST CONTEXTS

It is essential to remember that during therapy the therapist also becomes part of the system. The therapist brings his or her own beliefs and contexts into the work and needs to maintain curiosity about the ways these beliefs interact with those of the client(s) (Cecchin, Lane, & Ray, 1994).

Many textbooks on sex and relationship therapy recognise the importance of the gender of the therapist in the therapeutic process (Jones, 1993). Systemic approaches also recognize the importance of gender, but place equal emphasis on other contexts and beliefs. Given the multitude of moral, religious, and social sanctions for and against certain sexual behaviours and types of relationships, the therapist's beliefs about sex, sexuality, and relationships and the desired outcome of therapy may be some of the issues that merit particular attention.

The professional context is also a powerful one and as therapists we are likely to be significantly influenced by the way in which our profession has historically conceptualized sexual difficulties. Many writers have criticized the assumptions that underlie the American Psychiatric Association's classification of sexual disorders (American Psychiatric Association, 1994) and the way that this may unfairly represent the concerns of women and sexual minorities in particular (McNally & Adams, 2000; Ussher, 1993). As professionals, we have a responsibility to think critically about the work that we do and whether the frameworks we may use draw on particular social discourses at the expense of others. It is worth noting that systemic approaches have been described as particularly helpful when working with lesbian, gay, and bisexual clients, as they are non-normative, non-pathologizing and take account of the experience of homophobia (Simon & Whitfield, 2000).

Maintaining neutrality and/or curiosity about outcome is essential (Jones, 1993) and the therapist needs to constantly revisit the identified goals of the client(s) to ensure that a shared understanding of the hoped for ending is maintained. Maintaining curiosity also remains equally important when working with clients who are perceived to be more similar to the therapist, as when working with clients with significantly different beliefs.

One valuable training technique for exploring beliefs and contexts is the mapping of a cultural genogram, similar to a family genogram, but one which incorporates the wider contexts such as of class and ethnicity [see Hardy & Laszloffy (1995) for a full description]. This encourages clinicians to consider contexts that may be less visible, or in systemic terms, not privileged or "foregrounded" in the room. This can also be a useful exercise with clients in the first few sessions, as it brings multiple contexts into the room from the very beginning of therapy.

WHO TO INVITE?

Before the first session, it is my preference to write to the identified client and invite them to bring along anyone who they feel would be helpful. This begins the process of identifying the client's system and the client's views of the problem. This does not, however, preclude seeing partners individually, either during the first session or at a later date.

Starting therapy: setting the scene

WHOSE PROBLEM?

In their paper "The problem of the referring person" (Palazzoli, Boscolo, Cecchin, & Prata, 1980), the Milan group talk about the importance of identifying who the problem is a problem for. Our clients may be referred or seek help for many reasons and it is essential to understand their motivations and hopes for the session to ensure a positive therapeutic relationship and a sense of shared goals.

In psychosexual therapy, many clients may come with a belief that their sexual problems are physical in origin and with strong ambivalence about seeing a therapist. Their General Practitioner or other medical professionals may have referred them, perhaps when their attempts to provide a medical diagnosis or treatment have failed. Or they may have been asked to come by a partner who has given them an ultimatum for resolving the problem.

Before the first session it may be useful to contact the referrer and ask questions about their best hopes for the referral. Questions such as "Who is concerned about this problem?"; "Whose idea was it for the referral to be made?"; and "What do you think they were hoping for?" may be useful to ask of the referrer and the client. This helps to establish at an early stage whether or not the client really wants to engage in therapy or has doubts or fears about the process that may need to be addressed before any other conversations take place.

RELATIONSHIP TO HELP

It can often be difficult for clients to ask for help with sexual problems, because they feel embarrassed, or they hold a belief that they are alone in their difficulties or they are simply unaware of the services that might be available. However, some clients may have seen many health professionals or other therapists before they are referred. By asking questions early on in the therapy about previous experiences of help, the therapist gains a better understanding of what is known as the "relationship to help": the beliefs the client has about what has been helpful, what has not been helpful and what might or might not be helpful in the future (Reder & Fredman, 1996).

Help in this context need not be professional help. It can be useful to ask about everything that has been tried by the client or couple in the past and advice that they may have received from non-professionals, friends, family, or other sources of information, such as books or magazines.

TALKING ABOUT TALKING

It is often difficult for clients to ask for help with sexual difficulties and it may also be difficult for clients to talk about their sexual difficulties once in the room. Jones (1993) describes the amount of emotional investment couples make in their sexual relationships and the concomitant threat to self-esteem that facing sexual difficulties can represent. She describes clients feeling intense shame or guilt, anger towards themselves or their partners and those who see their sexual difficulties as a sign of significant personal failure. The therapist in this position can be seen as an intruder in a very personal area of life and risks being seen as potential judge and jury rather than facilitator.

When working with couples, it is often useful to start therapy with a conversation about the process of talking. Clients often have anxieties about expressing strong emotions in the therapy session, particularly the fear that this will escalate into an argument and they will leave feeling worse than when they arrived. They may also have fears about the therapist witnessing an argument and taking sides, either explicitly or implicitly.

It may be helpful to have a series of "ground rules" or to negotiate a contract with clients about how to discuss distressing subject matters. Questions such as "How would I know if this was getting too difficult for you?"; "Would you be able to let me know if you were finding this upsetting?"; "What would I notice happening if you were feeling embarrassed/angry/upset?"; or "What would be the most useful thing for me to do if I noticed that happening?" can help the client feel in control of the session while giving the therapist the freedom to ask questions that may be useful. It also invites the client to become an active participant in the therapeutic process, an essential component of effective systemic therapy.

STAYING IMPARTIAL WITH COUPLES

Fears in a couple about the therapist "taking sides" may come from the client's beliefs about the therapist's own personal values. These fears may be influenced by the therapist's gender, age, perceived sexuality, or marital status, ethnicity, or class, be they similar or different to those of the client.

When working with couples, the challenge to remain neutral and avoid forming an alliance with one partner or another is more present in the room than when working with individuals. In my experience it is difficult to achieve. The therapeutic process is dynamic and fluid and the therapist cannot maintain an equal level of communication with both partners simultaneously. Nevertheless, a therapist can show impartiality over a session through a careful "balancing act" of empathy, attention, curiosity, and questioning (Jones, 1993).

Simply stating explicitly at the beginning of therapy that your role is not to take sides is also helpful. This can be framed as the only way in which you can be sure that you will stay helpful to both individuals and also emphasizes your role as facilitator to help the couple to find their own solutions.

Starting therapy

IDENTIFYING THERAPEUTIC GOALS

At some point during the first session it is important to establish a shared understanding of the therapeutic goals. Questions such as "How would you like things to be different"; "Where would you need to be at the end of therapy to feel that this had been useful"; "If this problem was not in your life, how would you know"; and "How would your life be different if this problem no longer existed" help to establish hopes for therapy. Once this has been agreed, questions such as "What ideas do you have about what would need to happen for this problem to be resolved" and "relationship to help" questions (see above) may begin to connect the perceived problem with a solution (Reder & Fredman, 1996).

RESOURCES

As we have described, the process of coming for psychosexual therapy can be a very emotionally loaded experience. By highlighting the strengths and qualities of the client and/or their relationship, we can help our clients to become aware of the resources they already have and stay connected to hope and the possibility of change. This approach also helps the couple to see the relationship itself as a resource (as below) and is consistent with the solution-focused ideals of most systemic therapies (Iveson & Ratner, 1990; Molnar & De Shazer, 1987).

In the first session with a couple it may be helpful to spend a significant amount of time hearing about the positive aspects of the relationship. I often ask clients to say what they think their partner likes about them and then invite each partner to comment and/or expand on what they have heard. In this way clients not only hear their positive qualities, but also have the opportunity to correct any misunderstandings or add qualities that have previously been unexpressed. Even after many years together, partners are often (pleasantly) surprised by what they hear.

If the experience of discussing the positive aspects of the relationship seems helpful, I will sometimes invite clients to write these down in a letter or card. Making a ritual of exchanging these affirmations can act as a symbol of the investment in the relationship and a commitment to working on the sexual difficulties together.

TRACKING THE PATTERN OF INTERACTION

Once the basic ground rules have been established, the therapist and clients begin to map out the system and the pattern of interactions that maintain the problem.

As ongoing problems are understood systemically in terms of "stuck" systems, it is often useful to identify one episode when the problem shows itself and then "track the pattern of interaction" to map out the sequence of thoughts and actions (Burnham, 1986; Jones & Asen, 2000). Clients are invited to describe a typical episode "frame by frame", slowing it down so that they can step outside the process, observe the sequence and begin to notice where the system gets stuck. Partners are encouraged to report on each other's experiences to encourage empathy and understanding of the other's position, help them to positively connote the partner's response and therefore reduce blame. Once clients can let go of a sense of responsibility or blame they are often able to communicate more freely about the problem and more likely to find a way of moving forward together.

Sometimes simply becoming aware of the pattern of interaction and "naming the game" can be enough to prevent the couple from maintaining the pattern (Stratton, Preston-Shoot, & Hanks, 1990). It is also helpful to encourage couples to notice whenever the cycle begins and to try and "do something different", to see whether this has an impact on the problem. However, intervention at the level of meaning, rather than solely action, is usually essential to introduce change (Tomm, 1984).

Most disagreements between couples are not at the level of action, but the level of meaning. In other words, couples will usually agree about what happened, but may disagree about the intent. The process of tracking the interaction allows the couple to see that regardless of intent, being misunderstood is problematic for both partners and therefore a problem that both people can help to resolve.

At this point it may be helpful to share the idea of the "problem as an attempted solution" (Burnham, 1986). As described earlier in the chapter, this idea assumes that the problem exists because each individual in the relationship is attempting to protect themselves or the other person. For example, one partner experiences sexual pain, the other stops initiating sex to avoid putting pressure on their partner. The other experiences the change as a lack of interest and also stops initiating sex, which further reinforces the partner's idea that they don't want sex and so on.

If partners are finding it difficult to step outside of their own experience and remain stuck in a pattern of blame and recrimination, the technique of "interviewing the internalised other" can sometimes be helpful (Tomm, 1984). In this approach, the client is interviewed while they role-play their partner. They are addressed by their partner's name and encouraged to respond in the first person. The other partner is then given the opportunity to comment on what they have heard and whether their viewpoint has been adequately represented.

EXTERNALIZING THE PROBLEM

Sometimes, despite these techniques, it is difficult for partners to come to a shared understanding of the problem. In these circumstances, it may be enough to name the common ground—that both agree there is a problem. Moving on to a discussion of the therapeutic goals may be more useful than staying with the "stuck" system, but the technique of "externalising the problem" may also help to detach blame and allow the partners to begin to work towards a solution together.

The notion of externalizing the problem was initially developed by White (White, 1989; Carr, 1998) for use with children with continence problems. By giving the identified problem a name and a personality (in this case, "Sneaky Poo"), White encouraged the client to see the problem as a person outside of him or herself and therefore as something he or she could have control over. By talking about the problem as other, White allowed the child to acknowledge parts of him or herself that he or she wanted to change, without feeling shame or blame. Without this same sense of shame, the child is empowered to fight against "Sneaky Poo" and to find a solution.

Similar techniques can be used with sexual difficulties, by talking about "the problem" and asking how it affects both clients and their relationships. In this way the problem is not seen as a problem *in* an individual, nor as a problem *in* the relationship, but as a problem *for* the relationship. Externalizing questions in this context might include "When does the problem show itself?" "What effect does the problem have on you?" or "What effect does it have on your partner, or on your relationship?" (See case study three, below, for further illustration.)

Within this perspective the relationship itself can be seen as a resource that the couple can draw on to help them find a solution to the problem. The couple can thus become united against a common enemy, rather than seeing the other or the relationship as the problem. If the problem is seen to reside in the other or the relationship, this is usually a much greater threat to the long-term survival of the relationship than if the problem is seen to be a problem for the relationship.

WIDER CONTEXTS

The clinical reality may often be that shifting from a position of blame and responsibility to a united approach takes some time. It may, indeed, become the main focus for the therapeutic work. However, externalizing problems while also placing them in their wider contexts can become a very powerful intervention. I have found this particularly useful in gendered discussions about blame.

Men and women often feel blamed and constrained by social discourses about gender and sexual performance; for example, "Men should want sex all the time", "Women should be sexually passive". By locating these discourses in their wider social contexts, clients are encouraged to re-examine the varied social and cultural factors that influence sexual attitudes and consider the inequalities and gender politics of the world at large rather than feel blamed for perceived personal inadequacies (Boyle, 1993; Ussher, 1993).

Individuals and couples may also be influenced by family beliefs about sex and relationships. Clients' experiences of their parents' relationship(s) and/or the relationships of other significant people in the family can have a significant effect on their fears and hopes for their own. Byng-Hall (1988) talks about the power of family "scripts and legends" and how stories that are told and retold can act as both a resource and a constraint on members of that family.

The Co-ordinated Management of Meaning approach (Cronen & Pearce, 1980) is one way of teasing out the impact of these wider contexts with clients. CMM invites clients to take an idea or belief and consider what different contexts might say about that belief. For example, a second generation British-Asian woman considering her ideas about sex might want to consider discourses relevant to her gender, marital status, religion, family culture, youth culture, the media, her parents, siblings, and friends. By looking at the range of contexts that inform their views of sex, clients can begin to understand tensions or contradictions and start to choose which views they wish to agree or disagree with.

Interventions: case examples

The following case examples are intended to give a flavour of some of these systemic techniques in practice. Working systemically does not preclude the use of traditional psychosexual therapy techniques, such as self-examination, sensate focus, stop/start techniques or Kegel exercises (pelvic floor exercises); rather these are used as part of the range of interventions that might be used with individuals or couples [for further discussion see Burnham (1992)].

Case study one: externalizing the problem, tracking the pattern of interaction, the relationship as resource, family scripts

Sarah was referred for low libido, which she attributed to her chronic fatigue. Patrick, her partner, was very supportive and keen to attend sessions, but he also identified the problem as "Sarah's problem". Through tracking the pattern of interaction throughout an evening when Sarah had wanted to have sex, some of the disadvantages of locating the problem in Sarah became apparent. Sarah felt blamed by Patrick and this made her feel unable to communicate about her chronic fatigue. This made it more difficult to say when she felt able or unable to have sex and she therefore tended to avoid sexual contact. Patrick felt hurt by Sarah's apparent rejection but felt unable to express this because he did not wish to be seen as focusing on his own needs and therefore being unsupportive about Sarah's health problems. Both parties tried to protect themselves from further hurt by avoiding initiating sex, which resulted in an increased sense of rejection on both sides.

However, after some discussion of this cycle, there also seemed to be some advantages for the couple in continuing to see the problem as a problem in Sarah. Both partners had come from families where their parents had divorced and both were terrified that conceptualizing the sexual problem as a problem for both of them meant that there was a problem with the relationship itself. In both cases, their parents had separated after one parent had had an affair and they assumed that this meant that their parents' sexual relationship had been poor. Seeing the problem as a problem for Sarah enabled them to maintain confidence in the future of their relationship.

The first step towards working on their sexual difficulties involved looking at the family stories about sex and relationships and some of the other reasons why their parents' relationships might be different from theirs. After some discussion, it seemed that there were many reasons why the parental relationships might have failed. This understanding freed us from the fear of looking at the effect of the problem on the couple and allowed us to reframe the problem as a problem for the relationship. Identifying the problem as a problem *for* the relationship rather than a problem *in* the relationship also helped Sarah and Patrick to feel united in their desire for a better sexual life. Sarah was able to feel less blamed for the situation and Patrick was freer to discuss his feelings. Both Sarah and Patrick were able to feel more confident about their long-term future and identified a long list of resources they were able to use in the rest of their relationship that they might be able to bring to working on the sexual problem. At the next session, for the first time, they reported having discussed their problems outside of the session and reported feeling much more optimistic for the future.

Case study two: contexts of meaning: Co-ordinated Management of Meaning, looking at different discourses about sex and gender

Colin presented to the psychosexual clinic with his partner Samantha, who was concerned about Colin's erectile difficulties. After several sessions of meeting together, Colin disclosed that he was looking at a lot of pornography on the internet and that he felt a great deal of shame about this. Colin felt that he needed to address his behaviour as he felt it was contributing to his erectile problems.

After further discussion, it emerged that Colin believed that he had become unable to experience sexual attraction for someone he loved because he associated sex and sexual fantasies with pornography. He could imagine "making love" with his partner but not "having sex". I was curious about the different discourses that might be influencing Colin's views about sex and gender and so we spent some time mapping these out together. Colin identified his key contexts as his partner Samantha, her family, his family, his religion, his male friends at work, the social circle he and Samantha shared, and media and feminist discourses about pornography and women's sexuality. I then asked Samantha and Colin to write down the stories that each of these contexts had about men and women's sexuality and bring them to the next session.

During the next session, I encouraged Colin and Samantha to look at the similarities and differences between their stories and to have a conversation about which stories they agreed with and which they disagreed with. From this, we went on to discuss what their different views were about "making love" and "sex".

It emerged that Colin felt one of the main reasons that Samantha had been attracted to him was because she described him as a "New Man". For Samantha, this mean that Colin was good at communicating his feelings and was happy to take an equal share of housework responsibilities. But for Colin, this meant that he shouldn't really want to look at pornography and by wanting to have "sex" rather than "make love" he was letting Samantha down by objectifying her, as "sex" to Colin meant something dirty, cold, and emotionless. Samantha did not share this view and felt that having "sex" rather than "making love" was more about being sexually adventurous than being less intimate. However, Samantha had assumed that being more sexually assertive would put pressure on Colin and, since the onset of the erectile problem, had become more passive sexually, which Colin had taken as evidence that she only wanted to "make love".

Through identifying the different contexts that influenced both Colin's and Samantha's views of sex and gender, they were able to discuss their differences in a non-threatening way and come to a agreement as to what felt comfortable for them both. Colin was able to let go of his guilt about his sexual fantasies and share some of them with Samantha, and Samantha then felt more free to share her own sexual fantasies. Finding out that Samantha had sexual fantasies of her own was very liberating for Colin and helped him to bridge the gap between his experience of love and respect for partner and his sexual desires. Samantha felt more confident about herself and able to be more sexually adventurous, and this led to further discussions about which sexual activities they were willing to try.

Case study three: Constance and Andy: construction of sex, relationship to body, ideas about coping, externalizing lichen sclerosis

Constance, twenty-five, presented with concerns about lack of sexual activity and painful penetrative sex. She had a ten-year history of lichen sclerosis (a dermatological condition causing itching, splitting, and scarring of the skin) around her vulva and perineum, which made penetration painful and often impossible. Constance described feeling angry and frustrated that she was unable to have penetrative sex and felt that her partner would not wish to remain in the relationship if their sex life did not improve.

When Constance and her partner, Andy, attended together, we used externalizing questions to map the effect of the problem, lichen sclerosis, on Constance, on Andy, and on the relationship. Shifting the focus of the problem away from Constance allowed the couple to think about the ways in which they could work on their problem together, but also helped Constance to feel sympathy, rather than anger, towards her body. Lichen sclerosis, rather than her body, became the problem and the challenge. Constance became able to feel protective towards her body and therefore to consider what she needed for her to maintain her health and her sexual pleasure.

We also spent some time deconstructing the idea of sex and what it meant to both partners. Talking through stories about what activities constituted "real sex" while at the same time talking about what they both enjoyed and valued about sex, allowed them to let go of the idea that only penetrative sex was "real". After weighing up the advantages and disadvantages of continuing to try to have penetrative sex, they decided that they were more likely to have a satisfying sexual life by no longer seeing this as the focus of their sexual activity. Through talking, massage exercises, and gentle exploration of non-penetrative genital contact, Constance and Andy felt able to enjoy non-penetrative sexual activities without feeling that they were having an "incomplete" sexual life.

Summary

In this chapter I have attempted to summarize some of the main features of systemic therapy approaches and how these can be put to use when carrying out psychosexual therapy. It is my view that the very nature of sex means that we cannot afford to ignore the context in which sex is happening and, in my view, the systemic framework provides an open invitation to explore this for both ourselves as practitioners and for our clients. This chapter provides only an introduction to systemic practice, but I hope that readers feel inspired to include some of the ideas and techniques illustrated here into their own practice.

References

American Psychiatric Association (1994). *Diagnostic and Statistical Manual of Mental Disorders* (4th edn). Washington, DC: American Psychiatric Association.

Anderson, H., & Goolishian, H. (1987). *The Client is the Expert: A Not-Knowing Approach to Therapy*. London: Sage.

Bateson, G. (1972). *Steps to an Ecology of Mind*. New York: Ballantine.

Boscolo, I., Cecchin, G., & Prata, G. (1980). Hypothesising—circularity—neutrality: three guidelines for the conductor of the session. *Family Process, 19*: 3–12.

Boyle, M. (1993). Sexual dysfunction or heterosexual dysfunction? *Feminism and Psychology, 3*(1): 73–88.

Burnham, J. (1986). *Family Therapy: First Steps Towards a Systemic Approach*. London: Tavistock.

Burnham, J. (1992). Approach—method—technique: making distinctions and creating connections. *Human Systems: The Journal of Systemic Consultation & Management, 3*: 3–26.

Byng-Hall, J. (1988). Scripts and legends in families and family therapy. *Family Process, 27*: 167–179.

Carr, A. (1998). Narrative therapy. One perspective on the work of Michael White. *Family Therapy Networker, 12*: 14–24.

Cecchin, G. (1987). Hypothesizing, circularity and neutrality revisited: an invitation to curiosity. *Family Process, 26*(4), 405–413.

Cecchin, G., Lane, G., & Ray, W. A. (1994). *The Cybernetics of Prejudice in the Practice of Psychotherapy*. London: Karnac.

Cronen, V., & Pearce, W. B. (1980). *Communication, Action and Meaning: The Creation of Social Realities*. New York: Prager.

Hardy, K. V., & Laszloffy, T. A. (1995). The cultural genogram: key to training culturally competent family therapists. *Journal of Marital and Family Therapy, 21*, 27–43.

Hayes, H. (1991). A reintroduction to family therapy: clarification of three schools. *Australia and New Zealand Journal of Family Therapy, 12*: 27–43.

Iveson, G., & Ratner, H. (1990). *Problem to Solution. Brief Therapy with Individuals and Families*. London: BT Press.

Jones, E. (1993). Working with couples. In: E. Jones (Ed.), *Family Systems Therapy: Developments in the Milan Systemic Therapies*. Chichester: Wiley.

Jones, E. & Asen, E. (2000). *Systemic Couple Therapy and Depression*. London: Karnac.

McNally, I., & Adams, N. (2000). Psychosexual issues. In: C. Neal & D. Davies (Eds.), *Pink Therapy 3: Issues in Therapy with Lesbian, Gay, Bisexual and Transgender Clients*. Buckingham: Open University Press.

Molnar, A., & De Shazer, S. (1987). Solution-focused therapy: towards the identification of therapeutic tasks. *Journal of Marital and Family Therapy*, 13(4): 348–358.

Palazzoli, S., Boscolo, I., Cecchin, G., & Prata, G. (1980). The problem of the referring person. *Journal of Marital and Family Therapy*, 6: 3–9.

Reder, P., & Fredman, G. (1996). The relationship to help: interacting beliefs about the treatment process. *Clinical Child Psychology and Psychiatry*, 1(3): 457–467.

Simon, G., & Whitfield, G. (2000). Social constructionist and systemic therapy. In: D. Davies & C. Neal (Eds.), *Pink Therapy 2: Therapist Perspectives on Working with Lesbian, Gay and Bisexual Clients*. Open University Press.

Stratton, P., Preston-Shoot, M., & Hanks, H. (1990). *Family Therapy, Training and Practice*. Birmingham: Venture Press.

Tomm, K. (1984). One perspective on the Milan Approach, Parts 1 & 2. *Journal of Marital and Family Therapy*, 10(2): 113–125 & 253–271.

Ussher, J. (1993). The construction of female sexual problems. In: J. Ussher & C. Baker (Eds.), *Psychological Perspective on Sexual Problems*. London: Routledge.

Watzlawick, P., Weakland, J. H., & Fisch, R. (1974). *Change: Principles of Problem Formation and Problem Resolution*. New York: W. W. Norton.

White, M. (1989). *The Externalising of the Problem and the Re-authoring of Lives and Relationships*. London: Dulwich Centre Newsletter.

CHAPTER TEN

Borderline sexuality: sexually addictive behaviour in the context of a diagnosis of borderline personality disorder

Deirdre Williams

Introduction

C lients with a diagnosis of borderline personality disorder (BPD) are highly likely to have had a history of sexual abuse (Bryer, Nelson, Miller, & Kroll, 1987; Herman, Perry, & van der Kolk, 1989). It is not surprising, therefore, that their sexuality is shaped and often complicated by their earlier traumatic experiences. Many female clients with a diagnosis of BPD experience sexual problems or are disturbed by some aspect of their sexuality. Anecdotally, there would appear to be an increased incidence of the common forms of sexual dysfunction (e.g., vaginismus, dyspaneuria or anorgasmia) in this client group, and confusion about sexual orientation or gender dysphoria is also prevalent.

In this chapter, the broader spectrum of sexual problems will not be addressed. Instead, the particular problem of sexually addictive behaviour will be discussed. Within the *DSM-IV-R* diagnostic criteria for BPD (American Psychiatric Association, 1997), the criterion of impulsivity includes acts of sexual risk-taking and promiscuity. The explicit inclusion of these sexual behaviours within the diagnostic criteria reflects the high incidence of this problem within this client group. The impulsivity criterion also includes a range of other behaviours such as substance misuse, binge drinking, gambling, and overspending. All these behaviours, including the named sexual behaviours, share at least three things in common: they are associated with strong and usually specific urges that are responded to impulsively; they are used primarily in an affect-modulating way; and (as stated as a prerequisite for meeting the criterion) they are potentially self-damaging. A further feature that links these behaviours is that they can all be seen to some extent as addictive, and I will use the term "sexually addictive behaviour" to refer to sexual behaviour that would generally be included within this "impulsivity" criterion.

It has been argued that sexually addictive behaviour is not exclusively associated with the diagnosis of Borderline Personality Disorder and there is now a lobby for the inclusion of "sexual addiction" within *DSM-V* as a separate diagnostic category (see Delmonico, 2001). It remains to be seen whether the majority of people who show sexually addictive behaviours meet the diagnosis for BPD, or even have borderline character structures in the psychoanalytic sense, but it is not uncommon for borderline clients to have problems with sexual addiction or, indeed, to get involved with sexual partners who engage in these behaviours themselves.

There is a current debate as to how well the analogy with other addictive behaviours holds up. Certainly within a literal interpretation of early psychoanalytic literature the concept of a "sexual addiction" is self-contradictory and paradoxical, since addiction was viewed primarily as an autoerotic activity and as a substitute for mature adult sexual relations. But is this as contradictory as it first appears? In most formulations of sexual addiction, and in the one that I use within this chapter, a sexual addiction can be as much a pseudosexual activity as any other addiction when the main function of the activity is not sexual at all, but affect-regulating and defensive.

In the discussion that follows, a client who had a diagnosis of BPD and a history of sexually addictive behaviour will be described. This client was treated with Cognitive Analytic Therapy (CAT) (Ryle, 1991, 1997), a therapy that attempts an integration of cognitive and psychoanalytic thinking in the formulation and treatment of psychological problems. This brief therapy has been shown to produce relatively good outcomes for clients with a diagnosis of BPD (Ryle & Golynkina, 2000). For a detailed introduction to CAT see Ryle and Kerr (2002).

CAT and BPD

CAT is a continuously evolving therapy and more recent versions of it have based their formulations around an essentially dynamic or object relational concept, that of the Reciprocal Role. In order to follow the clinical discussion below, an outline will be given of the concept of the Reciprocal Role in general and its relation to BPD.

The basic idea of a Reciprocal Role is that during development we internalize our earliest dyadic relationships with caregivers and these become a template for interpersonal and, crucially, intrapersonal relationships in adulthood. Reciprocal roles are dyadic in that they focus on pairs of roles; they are also reciprocal in that one pole very much implies or constrains the other. For example, a child who is exposed to a largely nurturing and protecting caregiver will feel nurtured and protected with respect to that caregiver, the Reciprocal Role here being "Nurturing-to-Nurtured". This experience will, by a process of internalization, set the child up to both be able to give nurturance to, and to receive nurturance from, themselves and others in adulthood.

This emphasis on what is dyadic and relational in development is prefigured by Winnicott's now infamous remark "There is no such thing as a baby" (Winnicott, 1940, cited in Khan, 2003). The self, and particularly the self-in-development, cannot be viewed outside its relational context. The concept of the reciprocal role differs from many psychoanalytic concepts of development in its attention to what is dyadic and relational instead of focusing on internal processes of ego development. In this way it bears many similarities to earlier concepts in the literature on attachment, in particular Bowlby's concept of an internal working model of relationships (Bowlby, 1988). This conceptualization contrasts with a drive-based psychoanalytic model of development in terms of its emphasis on a fundamentally relational self.

A model of development based on the concept of the reciprocal role also differs from many object relations models by partially

de-emphasizing the importance of the very earliest years in development. Reciprocal roles are often inferred from the conscious and
remembered qualities of the client's core relationships and also on
reported history. Reciprocal roles will thus only by extrapolation
incorporate those early and pre-verbal experiences with caregivers.
This fits in with the clinical observation that the most significant
childhood trauma for the client often does not occur in the infantile, pre-oedipal, or oedipal phases at all, but much later (see
Westen, 1990). This may be particularly the case in borderline
personality organization where there is so often some sexual or
other trauma after infancy (Herman, Perry, & van der Kolk, 1989).
Of course, it can always be argued that the very existence of this
trauma might imply a certain amount of neglect or pathological
relatedness on the part of caregivers that would have been present
in the earlier relationship too.

The concept of the reciprocal role is particularly useful in formulating the difficulties of clients with a diagnosis of BPD (Ryle, 1997).
These clients have often been subjected to a very restricted range of
mainly negative roles by their primary caregivers in childhood.
They may also have been subjected to rapid and extreme shifts of
mental state or role in primary caregivers with extreme or borderline pathology themselves. This means that, in their relationships
with other people, borderline clients have a more restricted range
of roles from which to draw than neurotic clients, and thus appear
to be more rigid or inflexible in their mode of relationship. A further
problem, which has been formulated elsewhere as a deficit of
"mentalization" (see Fonagy & Target, 2000), is that these clients
have less ability to self-reflect and therefore less flexibility and
control over moving into certain roles. Deficient in reflective self-
awareness, these clients find it extremely difficult to override the
compulsion to assume certain roles with respect to themselves or
others. Roles are also often highly differentiated from each other
and the person can experience rapid state shifts, or even dissociation, when switching between roles. This, coupled with a lack of
mentalization or self-observation, means that often these roles do
not become integrated into a coherent sense of self.

The reciprocal role is a key formulation tool in CAT. Using what
has been called the Procedural Sequence Object Relations Model
(see Ryle, 1997, for a full description), groups of reciprocal roles and

the procedures or behavioural sequences that link them and emanate from them are built up into a dynamic formulation of the client's difficulties. The formulation is then summarized verbally in the form of a Reformulation Letter addressed to the client from the therapist. The formulation is also visually represented as a "diagrammatic reformulation" which is a diagram showing the client's presenting problems (target problem procedures or TPPs in CAT) and dominant modes of relating (reciprocal roles).

CAT conceptualizes a client's problems for the most part as defensive avoidance of certain poles of reciprocal roles, often those poles associated with their original trauma as a child. For example, someone who has been abused in childhood by a primary caregiver, may well have the reciprocal role of Abusing-to-Abused as one dominant mode of relating. In order to escape from feeling abused, the client may use the defensive procedure of seeking to avoid relationships in order to avoid further victimization. Within relationships, they may also flip defensively into a mode of becoming abusive in response to feeling vulnerable, as this is preferable to being trapped in the abused pole once more. Specifying the client's behaviour in this way leads to a discussion of its likely or actual effect on others, including the therapist if it is enacted in the therapy. In response to these defensive procedures, the therapist's countertransferential responses can be classified into identifying countertransferences (where the therapist takes up the pole that the client identifies with, often the child pole of the reciprocal role, in this case the abused victim), or reciprocating countertransferences (where the therapist takes up the disavowed and often adult pole of the reciprocal role, in this case the abusing parent).

In Klein's formulation of the paranoid–schizoid state (Klein, 1946), which has become a model of borderline personality organization, projective identification is the primary or modal form of defence. Projective identification is encapsulated in the CAT model of BPD as well because, in comparison to neurotic clients, borderline clients find certain poles of reciprocal roles much harder to tolerate and certain poles of reciprocal roles more essential to disavow (see Ryle, 1997). In CAT, projective identification is not a magical process where clients mysteriously put their feelings into the other: instead, it is a mechanical process that is specified in terms of actual and proceduralized behaviour on the part of the client and the therapist. To this extent, it closely resembles Sandler's concept of "role responsiveness" (Sandler, 1976), which goes beyond the concept of projective identification in that not only does the analyst take the feeling and identify it as their own, but they are also tempted to "act it out", effectively being forced into a role by the analysand.

In CAT, as in many models of psychotherapy, the task of the therapist is to reflect on and empathize with the client's emotional experience and hand feelings and projections back to the client in a processed and digestible form. In this respect, the therapist performs something like Bion's "alpha function" of a containing mother who can "metabolize" the hostile projections of the baby and soothe the baby through intense emotional experiences (Bion, 1962). In order to be able to do this, the therapist needs to be aware of projective identifications or of being drawn into or manoeuvred into certain roles in relation to the client. In Sandler's terminology, the analyst must resist role responsiveness in order to make sure that they do not act out (or what Sandler calls "act in") in the therapy. Similarly, in Ryle's model, the CAT therapist must refuse "to join the dance" in terms of not allowing themselves to be positioned in the reciprocal roles of the client. In CAT this process is explicit and transparent: the therapist reflects on their own countertransferential responses in relation to the client's reciprocal roles and procedures, often using the diagrammatic reformulation to locate therapist and client in their current enactments of certain roles.

In the discussion that follows, a case study will be described of a client with a diagnosis of BPD who was seen for twenty-four sessions of CAT. The client's sexually addictive behaviour will be examined with reference to the psychoanalytic literature on borderline and narcissistic character structures and on addiction. In order to protect the client's confidentiality, potentially identifying information has been changed, and aspects of other cases have been borrowed to produce a fictionalized case composite.

Case study

Linda was an attractive heterosexual woman in her early thirties. She grew up with her parents and with a much younger sister and brother.

Her mother had been a model, and Linda felt that the women and girls in the family were valued on the single dimension of physical appearance. Although she was not sexually abused by her father, from her early teens he would make sexually provocative and humiliating remarks about her appearance and her developing body, and speculate about her future sex life. He would often do this in front of other men in the extended family, and Linda felt that she was paraded and handed about between them.

Linda's father was an abusive alcoholic who was violent towards Linda and her mother. Linda's mother was often ill with migraines and would sometimes take to her bed for days at a time. Linda suspected that her mother's migraines were contiguous with the beatings she suffered and she felt in retrospect that they might have been some kind of protest directed at her father. Linda said that she became her "mother's little helper" and often nursed her through these bouts of illness.

Linda learned to cope with her family situation by trying to placate people and anticipate their needs and desires, and by sometimes escaping from the family home when things got too much for her. Her teens were characterized by truanting from school and drug-taking. She also began to self-harm in the form of cutting during this period.

Linda dropped out of school and college, and in her twenties became involved in a series of relationships, generally with older men who had alcohol or substance misuse problems. These relationships were generally non-monogamous on Linda's part. Throughout her twenties Linda continued to take drugs, particularly amphetamines and "club drugs", but was also briefly addicted to heroin. She became increasingly involved in the sex industry, initially by becoming a cabaret dancer, but eventually becoming involved in making pornography.

After the end of one particularly significant relationship, Linda left the country to live and work abroad as a club dancer in a holiday resort. She described herself going on what she described as a year-long "sex and drug binge" that culminated in a violent rape. This precipitated her return to England and made her determined to "clean up". At the time I saw her she had been free of drugs for three years. She was in her first stable and mainstream job, and had a partner of two years' standing who was an ex-alcoholic.

At the time of referral, she described her main problem as depression and as dissatisfaction with her relationship with her current partner.

She felt bored and sexually disinterested and was worried that she would often feel violent rages towards her partner and had on two occasions hit him. She had been having strong urges to be unfaithful to her partner, but she also was aware of the potential destructiveness of this behaviour and recognized this pattern of unfaithfulness as one that had been present in her other relationships and as one that she wanted to break.

Formulation of Linda's procedures in CAT

In the course of the first five sessions leading up to the reformulation letter, we settled on three target problem procedures to work on. The first of these was a lack of assertiveness and a tendency to placate others. The second was a tendency to withdraw or act on urges to flee from situations when she felt criticized or exposed. The third problem procedure that we identified was her need for extraneous sexual contacts outside her primary relationship and her difficulty in maintaining a relationship that was both sexual and intimate.

Reformulation letter

Here is a fragment from Linda's original reformulation letter, pertaining to this third procedure and formulating the defensive functions of her sexually addictive behaviour:

A problem which you have brought up is how you have generally used sex to feel powerful and in control in your relationships. Feeling afraid of being dependent and intimate with someone, you have tended to seek out casual sexual encounters outside your relationship, often under the influence of drugs. This has been damaging to your relationships and led to their breakdown, confirming your sense that you need to be fearful of getting close to and dependent on people. A way out of this procedure for you would be to try to put sex and feelings of intimacy together, instead of escaping into illicit affairs or drug-fuelled sex. It will be important for us to find other ways for you to deal with the anxiety that being intimate or feeling dependent causes.

In CAT reformulation letters, there is usually an anticipation of how procedures might manifest themselves within the therapy. The client and therapist can then work together on avoiding collusive acting out in the therapy. In the original letter, there was no mention of how Linda's third procedure might come into the transference in an eroticized or sexualized way (although this may have been more apparent with a male therapist), but it was linked to how she might feel driven to flee the therapy if she began to feel dependent on it in any way.

> As we work together and get to know each other better, you might also at times feel like shying away from intimacy here or distancing yourself, or using sex, drugs and alcohol to get away from vulnerable feelings. These times may give us a chance to work together on new ways for you to tolerate the difficult feelings of dependency that relationships stir up in you.

> It has seemed to me that you have been "half in and half out" in most of your relationships, yet despite this it has been hard for you to leave them and you have found the endings almost impossible to bear. The ending of therapy may also be difficult for you but I hope that you do manage to be more than "half in" the therapy and that we can work together on coping with any feelings that the ending might stir up.

Fragment of a diagram

Figure 1 shows Linda's Sequential Diagrammatic Reformulation. The three procedures are represented on this diagram, including the procedure that relates to sexual addiction or chronic unfaithfulness.

Linda's diagram illustrates that her sexually addictive behaviour was formulated as a largely narcissistic problem at this point in her treatment. Narcissistic difficulties are often represented as a "split egg" diagram (see Ryle & Kerr, 2002), which separates off an idealized self that is associated with the reciprocal role admiring-to-admired, and a debased self that is usually associated with the reciprocal role contemptuous-to-contemptible. In addition to being a key feature of Narcissistic Personality Disorder, this narcissistic pattern is very commonly observed in BPD as well. Linda had an idealized self which was sexually powerful, and an abased self which was vulnerable and contemptible and disgusting. Relationships, which stirred up fears of dependency and abandonment, caused Linda to flip into the top half of the diagram, particularly into an idealized sexual self, caught up with another person in a bubble of mutual sexual admiration. Linda referred to this state

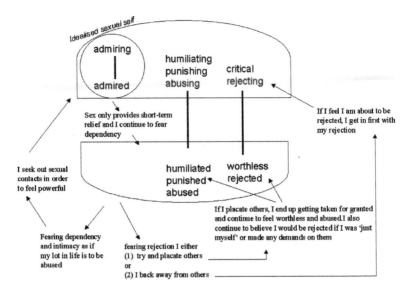

Figure 1.   Linda's diagrammatic reformulation.

as "sex goddess", and clearly described how powerful she felt in it and how in control.

Procedural enactment in the transference and countertransference

At times, I felt Linda wanted to draw me into the admiring-to-admired state with her. She felt that she was the envy of her female friends who, from her description, tended to glamourize her sexual behaviour. She also glamourized her experiences in the sex industry and was at times at pains to emphasize the financial gains and freedom it brought her, although at other times she was deeply ashamed and upset about how it also met some of her own needs to be sexually admired. When she glamourized her behaviour within the session, with the diagram before us, I was able to point out that maybe she would prefer me to be in the admired-to-admiring bubble as well, like her friends, because she was afraid of being judged and because this protected her from other feelings she herself might have about the behaviour. I also tried to name, as sensitively as I could, the way she might be fleeing in the session from more vulnerable feelings represented in the lower half of the diagram.

At other times, I felt pushed into the abused and disparaged pole in relation to her sexual behaviour. She was switching between accepting interpretations of her sexual behaviour as avoidant of intimacy and dependency, and insisting that her behaviour was normal. I felt beaten down by her intellectual arguments that in effect monogamy was a social construct, and by her citing of the dysfunctional relationships of other people she knew in order to justify and normalize her behaviour. In terms of her reciprocal roles, I felt I was sometimes being positioned as pathetically "square" and the object of her contempt, and at other times as critical and judgmental and overly bound by the norms of society. I sometimes felt useless as my attempts to formulate her problems with her and my attempts to empathize with her were often rejected. Even when feeling like a "pathetic square", it was hard not to be aware of a great degree of shame on Linda's part about the behaviour that drove her into this narcissistic disparagement. With the CAT diagram before us, we were able to point out how by refusing to enter the admiring-to-admired bubble with her, she either perceived me as contemptuous and rejecting or had to become contemptuous and rejecting herself to escape from her more vulnerable feelings of worthlessness and shame.

Later sessions and reformulation in the light of further disclosures

Keeping us out of the admiring-to-admired bubble, while maintaining that Linda was not contemptible, seemed to have the effect of leading to a flurry of disclosure of sexual trauma. At the time of the reformulation letter, Linda had just started to confide about the extent of sexualization at home, but had not divulged any sexual trauma beyond this. As therapy progressed, Linda began to tell me about having being molested by her cousin, about a gang rape she suffered when she was fifteen, about trauma she suffered in the sex industry, and about the extent of violence and abuse within her previous sexual relationships. The extent to which her own sexual behaviour could be seen as revictimization, in the sense of being an attempt to replay her trauma, could then be explored.

This led to radical reformulation as it became clear that Linda used some casual sexual contacts in a way that was less narcissistic and more borderline. Triggers to using sex in a more borderline way seemed to be the ending of relationships, or conflict within them, after which she would go on what she called "sex binges". When she was in this state she said that she would sleep with people under the influence of drink or drugs. She found herself unable to say no to anyone's sexual advances, which led to her sleeping with men who were unattractive to her or even potentially dangerous. She identified that choosing these sexual partners was akin to an act of self-harm. This was less about an idealized self than about an abased self that she was punishing. We did not remodel the diagram, but instead looked at the way she enacted the reciprocal role punishing–abusive to punished–abused towards herself in response to feeling worthless, ashamed, and rejected.

When the extent of violent and sexual abuse within her previous relationships was revealed, this allowed us to formulate her choice of sexual partners as an additional procedure, there being a discernible pattern for her to be attracted to substance-abusing and abusive men (like her alcoholic father). We looked at her choices of abusive objects as familiar and therefore comfortable, and also at her fantasy that she could gain control and mastery over a situation that she had had little control over as a child. We examined how the choice of abusive partners was potentially unexposing for her: it allowed her to disown her own propensity to be abusive, gave her a righteous cause for her anger, and provided some justification for her infidelities. It seemed that the most discomfiting thing for Linda about her current relationship was that she now found herself in the role of the abuser within the relationship rather than in her preferred role of the abused victim, which had defended her until now from her own potential for violence and abuse.

Working on exits: experimenting with other ways of relating and sexual relating

Generally, after reformulation in CAT, the focus is on getting the client to observe when the procedures are being enacted and to experiment with "exits" from these procedures. Exits are alternative ways to relate to the self and to others that do not maintain the problem, or do not maintain reliance on the procedure as the dominant or only way of solving the problem.

With borderline clients, there is usually a significant amount of formulation after the reformulation letter. This is partly because reformulation generally occurs very early in treatment (typically the fourth or fifth session). Often, as in Linda's case, this does not give time to have formed a sufficiently trusting relationship where the client feels able to divulge the extent of their trauma or to talk about aspects of themselves and their behaviour that they consider to be shameful and unacceptable. It is also because, again as in Linda's case, clients with a diagnosis of BPD are generally very poor at self-monitoring and often come into therapy being unable to observe and label the emotional states that impelled them towards certain behaviours.

Borderline clients in particular need help with learning to observe their emotions before exits can be found or a formulation can be derived. Some of this self-observation is probably learned through modelling by the therapist over the course of therapy, but CAT uses various tools and written forms of self-monitoring in order to help clients externalize and stand back from their feelings. In Linda's case this was essential, as apart from feeling "overwhelmed", she was often unable to label her feelings or see triggers for them, unless we replayed situations in the therapy and speculated as to how she might have felt in that situation. It was also the case that she sometimes somaticized her urges to have sexual contacts ("I just have a high sex drive") and at other times was more receptive to psychological formulations.

The first exit we worked on was therefore to promote Linda's awareness of her emotions. In tandem with using the various self-monitoring tools of CAT (such as procedural diaries), we worked on using mindfulness to observe and label emotional states. Mindfulness is a form of Buddhist meditation practice that is increasingly being used in the cognitive–behavioural treatment of mental health problems (see Baer, 2003, for a review; Segal, Williams, & Teasdale, 2003) and which forms a core component of Dialectical Behaviour Therapy in its treatment of borderline self-harmers (Linehan, 1993a). Mindfulness can help to promote awareness of affect, but also to promote tolerance of affect and to help draw a distinction between, and therefore decouple, urges and actions. Linda did find mindfulness helpful in improving her capacity for self-observation, and commented at the end of therapy (in her "goodbye letter") how the very idea that she could have feelings without acting on them had been liberating for her.

We worked hard on finding ways for Linda to improve her capacity to soothe herself when distressed or anxious, or when experiencing strong urges to seek out extra-relationship sexual contacts, or use alcohol or drugs. The exits we used here were again influenced in no small way by Linehan's treatment program for Borderline Personality Disorder with its emphasis on self-soothing skills as a means of distress tolerance (Linehan, 1993b).

Another exit was to try and find ways for Linda to gain power and self-esteem that were not based on sexual admiration or sexual prowess. These ways were "everyday" or ordinary ways for her to feel good about herself and in control, such as completing personal tasks, putting herself forward for further training at work, taking classes in things she was good at, like dance. This came with the acknowledgement that she would not get the highs from these activities that she got from sex, but that she might over time gain a sense of herself as a competent person whose value was not just dependent on her sexuality and looks or reliant on the admiration of others.

A final exit was to try to get Linda out of the abusing and punishing role towards herself, and instead encourage a more compassionate stance when she was being self-critical or feeling vulnerable. Again, self-soothing skills were paramount here, as was Linda using imagery of being a kind, attentive, nurturing parent towards herself. This was framed as a way of setting up a new reciprocal role for herself of nurturing to nurtured.

Discussion

Early psychoanalytic descriptions of the dynamics of drug addiction would appear to have some relevance to sexually addictive behaviour in Linda's case and more generally.

In Rado's early psychoanalytic formulations of drug dependency, drug-taking provides a narcissistic illusion of self-sufficiency (Rado, 1933). He suggested that once someone has happened on drug use as a means of escaping from dysthymia, he discovers that the "elation has reactivated his narcissistic belief in his invulnerability" (Rado, 1933, p. 61) and it is this that becomes addictive. Although the effect of drug-taking was to evoke disregard for affectionate relationships, he did not see drug addiction as primarily an escape from mutuality and dependency, but as an escape from negative emotions. He insisted that following each "pharmacothymic elation", the addict experiences a resultant "pharmacothymic depression", which is partly an experience of being thrown back on the very feelings or situation that he originally sought to escape through drugs, and partly a result of increased guilt about the damage done to relationships and about opting out of responsibilities in general.

Rado's description of the dynamics of drug addiction illuminates the narcissistic way in which Linda used sex when she was in a relationship. Sex was used to escape from feelings of boredom and emptiness, which were probably themselves a defence against fear of dependency and fear of abandonment. For Linda, sex in this mode promoted strong feelings of blissful union, yet paradoxically of autonomy, and of being in control. The consequence of this behaviour, once the liaison was over, was a descent into guilt and self-abasement.

This view of drug addiction as a narcissistic act is prevalent throughout the psychodynamic literature. In CAT too, substance misuse is commonly framed as a narcissistic procedure: a way of escaping from unwanted states or roles into an autonomous euphoric and grandiose state associated with the reciprocal role admiring-to-admired. Interestingly, there is also a statistical association between addiction to certain kinds of drug, particularly cocaine and amphetamines, and a diagnosis of narcissistic personality disorder (see Ronningstam, 2000, for a review).

Rado's view of the course of drug addiction may also be relevant to Linda's case and more generally to the problem of sexual addiction. He feels that dependency comes about, not because of physiological addiction, but because depressive and guilt-ridden states are potentiated by the use of the drug, which, in turn, increase the demand for its use. He proposed that tolerance occurs when there is a growing awareness that the drug is providing only a temporary escape, which makes drug use seem increasingly insubstantial and hollow. These phenomena create a downward spiral where the client needs more and more of the drug but it produces less and less of an effect. In effect, the drug becomes used increasingly masochistically as the addict loses their grandiose expectations about the drug but becomes more aware of the negative consequences of its use.

It could be interpreted that what Rado is describing is how a behaviour, which initially is used in a narcissistic way, ends up gradually being used in an increasingly borderline way. This did seem to have been the case for Linda. Initially, she used sex to feel powerful, but over time she became painfully aware of the damage caused to the healthier of her relationships, realized that her sexual behaviour only offered temporary respite from her problems, and experienced further and cumulative sexual trauma along the way. This had left Linda feeling worse about herself and had led her to use sex in a more desperate self-harming and borderline way, and less in a way which was about excitement and admiration. Other clients in our service who appear to use sex compulsively have also exhibited this pattern over time: what they initially describe as a behaviour used "for kicks" becomes a behaviour that is recognizably, even to themselves, self-destructive. It is often the case that the sexually addictive behaviour has to bring them to a crisis point of some kind (e.g., destroying a potentially helpful relationship, leading to sexual trauma, or leading to multiple pregnancies and terminations) before clients will present it as a problem to be worked on.

Another psychoanalytic theorist, Rosenfeld, made the distinction between two ways of using drugs (Rosenfeld, 1960). He described "manic drugging" as using the drug in order to merge with a fantasized idealized object and feel omnipotent. He described "destructive drugging" as using the drug in response to sadistic and persecutory impulses that are directed mainly towards what is felt as the bad self. Rosenfeld saw these processes occurring in parallel or simultaneously in drug addiction. Although Linda tended to present the two forms of her sexual behaviour as distinct, this separation was not always clear. It is probably safe to assume that sexually addictive behaviour is generally "overdetermined" (Laplanche & Pontalis, 1973) as a symptom; that is, it is multiply caused and can fulfil a number of defensive functions simultaneously even when these are apparently contradictory.

Another idea within the psychoanalytic literature that is useful in thinking about Linda's addictive sexual behaviour relies on the idea of drug addiction as an attempt at self-medication (Wurmser,

1974). It was suggested that people who are temperamentally either hypo- or hyper-aroused may be more vulnerable to becoming addicted to substances or other behaviours that either increase or decrease affect respectively (Jacobs, 1986). Drugs or addictive behaviours can be used to produce sensations of euphoria and of being alive if the resting state is one of being numb and cut off. They can also be used to block out extreme feelings of rage, anxiety, or shame if the resting state is one of having an excess of affect. This idea would seem to be particularly applicable to the treatment of clients with borderline personality disorder who, regardless of their temperamental baseline arousal levels, commonly flip between a state of being either emotionally overcontrolled and cut off or a state of being extremely emotionally dysregulated. This adds to the complexity of formulation with borderline clients since they (like Linda), can use the same behaviour (in this case sex) to perform different functions in different states of mind.

One of the advantages of CAT is that it explicitly tracks the behaviours that link states of mind and that cause state shifts in the form of Reciprocal Role Procedures. These are then embodied in a diagrammatic formulation that helps the client to understand and track their own behaviour and state of mind and, potentially, identifies the point in this sequence when they may be more likely to resort to the use of drugs or "self-medicating" behaviours.

Some psychoanalytic theorists like Krystal (1978) believe that the fundamental deficits leading to drug addiction are alexithymia (or an impairment in being able to differentiate and verbalize emotions) and an inability to tolerate affect due to a deficit in the capacity for self-care. Krystal also talked about the drug-dependent individual as relying on projection and projective identification through his "inability to claim, own up to, and exercise various parts of himself". This would seem to imply that the main characterological vulnerability factor is not obviously narcissistic but is more recognizably borderline in nature.

One consequence of alexithymia is that affect is likely to remain "dedifferentiated" for the client and is therefore more likely to be somaticized (Krystal, 1978). This is apparent in many drug addictions where the urges and cravings are experienced as distinct physiological entities rather than being linked to any affective state. This is perhaps more true for sexually addictive behaviour where the impulse for the behaviour can conveniently be attributed to a natural biological urge.

This inability to be aware of emotions, tendency to somaticize, and inability to soothe oneself when distressed, was very apparent in Linda's treatment. In the course of analytic treatment, clients are likely to learn how to reflect on their feelings and then attend to them appropriately, through behavioural modelling of the analyst who initially performs these functions for them. One of the strengths of CAT, perhaps along with other therapies like Dialectical Behaviour Therapy, is that it explicitly recognizes this deficit and tries to remedy it in a more directly targeted and active fashion. This is done partly through the use of tools that promote self-reflection (like the reformulation letter, the diagram, and diaries) and partly through the teaching and rehearsal of procedural exits that often involve some form of self-soothing. It is interesting that Krystal himself believed that clients who presented with these problems were probably unsuitable for psychoanalytic treatment but needed "a preliminary stage of the treatment where the patient's affective functions are dealt with" (1997, p. 110).

Summary

The above case study and the psychoanalytic literature examined suggest that borderline and narcissistic processes may govern sexually addictive behaviour, sometimes serially and sometimes simultaneously. In addition, these processes may be linked to a fundamental emotional deficit in these clients which has been conceptualized variously as "alexithymia" or as a "lack of mentalization".

With its focus on formulation in terms of reciprocal roles, CAT may be a therapy which is particularly well placed to help clients explore and understand the narcissistic and borderline functions of their addictive behaviour in a collaborative way. With the main part of the therapy focused on finding exits from procedures and engaging in active processes of change, CAT directly addresses identified deficits such as alexithymia and problems with affect tolerance and self-soothing. Thus, it can be a very effective treatment approach with clients who present with sexually addictive behaviours in the context of personality difficulties.

References

American Psychiatric Association (APA) (1997). *Diagnostic and Statistical Manual of Mental Disorders 4th Edition—Revised.* Washington DC: American Psychiatric Association.

Baer, R. A. (2003). Mindfulness training as a clinical intervention: a conceptual and empirical review. *Clinical Psychology: Science and Practice,* 10(2): 125–143.

Bion, W. (1962). *Learning from Experience.* London : Heinemann.

Bowlby, J. (1988). *A Secure Base: Clinical Applications of Attachment Theory.* London: Routledge.

Bryer, J. B., Nelson, B. A., Miller, J. B., & Kroll, P. A. (1987). Child sexual and physical abuse as factors in adult psychiatric illness. *American Journal of Psychiatry,* 144: 1426–1430.

Delmonico, D. (2001). Altering the bible: Changing the *Diagnostic and Statistical Manual. Sexual Addictions and Compulsivity,* 8(3–4): 185–186.

Fonagy, P., & Target, M. (2000). Attachment and borderline personality disorder: a theory and some evidence. *Psychiatric Clinics of North America,* 23(1): 103–122.

Herman, J. L., Perry, J. C., & van der Kolk, B. A. (1989). Childhood trauma in borderline personality disorder. *American Journal of Psychiatry,* 146: 490–495.

Jacobs, D. F. (1986). A general theory of addictions: a new theoretical model. *Journal of Gambling Behaviour,* 2, 150–131. Reprinted in D. L. Yalisone (Ed.) 1997, *Essential Papers on Addiction* (pp. 166–183). New York: New York University Press.

Khan, M. M. R (2003). Introduction. In: D. W. Winnicott, *Through Paediatrics to Psychoanalysis: Collected Papers* (pp. xi–l). London: Karnac.

Klein, M. (1946). *Notes on some schizoid mechanisms.* In: M. Klein (1975) *The Writings of Melanie Klein, Volume 3,* 1–25.

Krystal, H. (1978). Self-representation and the capacity for self care. *Annual of Psychoanalysis,* 6, 209–246. Reprinted in: D. L. Yalisone (Ed.) 1997, *Essential Papers on Addiction* (pp. 109–146). New York: New York University Press.

Laplanche, J., & Pontalis, J. B.(1973). *The Language of Psychoanalysis.* London: Hogarth [reprinted London: Karnac, 1988].

Linehan, M. M. (1993a). *Cognitive–Behavioural Treatment of Borderline Personality Disorder.* New York: Guilford Press.

Linehan, M. M. (1993b). *Skills Training Manual for Treating Borderline Personality Disorder*. New York: Guilford Press.

Rado, S. (1933). The psychoanalysis of pharmacothymia (drug addiction). *Psychoanalytic Quarterly*, 2, 1–23. Reprinted in: D. L. Yalisone (Ed.) 1997, *Essential Papers on Addiction* (pp. 52–68). New York: New York University Press.

Ronningstam, E. F. (2000). Narcissistic personality disorder and pathological narcissism : long-term stability and presence in Axis I disorders. In: E. F. Ronningstam (Ed.), *Disorders of Narcissism: Diagnostic, Clinical and Empirical Implications* (pp. 375–413). Northvale,NJ: Jason Aronson.

Rosenfeld, H.(1960). On drug addiction. In: H. Rosenfeld (1965), *Psychotic States: A Psychoanalytical Approach* (pp. 128–216). London: Maresfield Reprints.

Ryle, A. (1991). *Cognitive Analytic Therapy—Active Participation in Change: New Integration in Brief Therapy*. Chichester: Wiley

Ryle, A. (1997). *Cognitive Analytic Therapy and Borderline Personality Disorder: The Model and the Method*. Chichester: Wiley.

Ryle, A., & Golynkina, K. (2000). Effectiveness of time-limited cognitive analytic therapy for borderline personality disorder: factors associated with outcome. *British Journal of Medical Psychology*, 73: 197–210.

Ryle, A., & Kerr, I. B. (2002). *Introducing Cognitive Analytic Therapy*. Chichester: Wiley.

Sandler, J. (1976). Countertransference and role responsiveness. *International Review of Psycho-Analysis*, 3: 43–47.

Segal, Z. V., Williams, J. M. G., & Teasdale, J. D. (2003). *Mindfulness-Based Cognitive Therapy for Depression: A New Approach for Preventing Relapse*. New York: Guilford Press.

Westen, D. (1990). Towards a revised theory of borderline object relations: contributions of empirical research. *International Journal of Psycho-Analysis*, 71: 661–693.

Wurmser, L. (1974). Psychoanalytic considerations of the etiology of compulsive drug use. *Journal of the American Psychoanalytic Association*, 22(4): 820–843. Reprinted in D. L. Yalisone (Ed.) 1997, *Essential Papers on Addiction*, 87–108. New York: New York University Press.

CHAPTER ELEVEN

Psychoanalytically-informed CAT: a first treatment for problems of sexual relationships

Heather Wood

Introduction

Among the caseload of psychotherapy, psychological therapy or counselling services there will be a small proportion of patients whose principal difficulties are enacted within sexual relationships and often expressed through their sexual behaviours. They may be referred initially because of relationship difficulties or with a "ticket of entry" to the service such as depression or anxiety, but at assessment it may become clear that compulsive or destructive behaviours or fantasies in sexual relationships are central to their difficulties.

Psychotherapy can play a useful part in the treatment of patients with disorders of sexual arousal, desire, or response where the problem is psychogenic, but this is not the group that I will focus on here. The group of patients I am concerned with are those who present loosely with what *DSM IV* (American Psychiatric Association, 1997) refers to as "paraphilias" or *ICD 10* (World Health Organization, 1992) refers to as "disorders of sexual preference"— what psychoanalysts have traditionally thought of as perversions. I use the term "loosely" because *DSM IV* and *ICD 10* use strict diagnostic criteria to describe fixed, repetitive, often ritualized behaviours. Many patients seen in practice might not have problems that meet these criteria, yet they present with compulsive sexual behaviours or behaviours enacted within sexual relationships that assume a sexual charge or excitement (such as sadomasochistic modes of relating) that are a source of distress to them and often also to their partners.

It is no coincidence that clinicians treating people with problems in the sexual sphere often draw on psychoanalytic ideas. For Freud, sexuality, sexual energy, and sexual preoccupations were at the core of the personality. Psychoanalytic thinkers have contributed extensively to the debate about the origins and vicissitudes of our sexual preferences and functioning. Psychoanalytic ideas, and particularly psychoanalytic ideas about sexuality, have also provoked controversy, dissent, and criticism. Psychoanalysis as a treatment is often not available, affordable, or practical. Moreover, patients presenting with troubling or compulsive sexual behaviours who might seem like prime candidates for a psychoanalytic approach are often so anxious, guilty, and ashamed that they shun the idea of an intensive and prolonged contact with a therapist. Indeed, talk of long-term therapy or seeking specialist help may alarm them so that they retreat from seeking any help at all. At most, they might be persuaded to put a toe in the water of psychotherapy, and to agree to a time-limited treatment. Cognitive Analytic Therapy (CAT) offers a therapeutic approach that is engaging and acceptable to many anxious patients; furthermore, it lends itself to the incorporation of psychoanalytic insights within a brief, focused therapy. Most commonly used as a sixteen-session treatment, CAT offers an appealing combination of focus and depth.

This chapter focuses on the development of a CAT approach to the treatment of patients with problems of sexual relationships. The key features of CAT will be outlined before summarizing some psychoanalytic views on perversions and elaborating those aspects that have been particularly useful when developing a CAT approach to the treatment of sexual relationship problems. Case descriptions will be used to illustrate these concepts, which are composites of cases treated by myself and others, disguised in order to protect the anonymity of the particular patients whose treatment informed our thinking.

Key elements of CAT

CAT focuses on repeating patterns in relationships; "relationships" here includes the relationship to the self, to others, and to functions such as work. Developed by Anthony Ryle (1990, 1995, 1997; Ryle & Kerr, 2002), CAT draws on the cognitive tradition in using self-monitoring, the explicit statement of therapeutic aims, and insight as important instruments in achieving change. It draws on the psychoanalytic tradition in being concerned with internal templates of relating that shape subsequent perceptions of, and interactions with, others (see also Chapter Ten for a description of the key elements of a CAT approach).

In psychoanalytic terms these internal templates of relating may be thought of as internal objects; in CAT, it is thought that we internalize a knowledge of a relationship consisting of two roles, "reciprocal roles", which are complementary. Thus the person who has been abused, and has experienced concomitant fear, rage, and a sense of worthlessness, will also internalize a knowledge of how to abuse, and an awareness of accompanying cruelty and triumph. The reciprocal role may be represented as shown in Figure 1.

Often when people present for therapy they are primarily aware of only one of these roles within themselves, and present either as victim to others, or as perpetrator and unaware of their own vulnerability or hurt. Part of the work of the therapy will be to help them

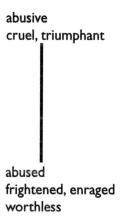

abusive
cruel, triumphant

abused
frightened, enraged
worthless

Figure 1.   The reciprocal role.

to become aware of the potential within themselves to enact both roles. For the person who presents only as victim, this may entail drawing their attention to the way they treat themselves or others (including the therapy) in abusive ways; for the person who presents only as "perpetrator", this may involve recognizing their own vulnerability and fear of others.

Like psychoanalytic therapy, CAT addresses the strategies used to manage and avoid experiencing the emotional pain and unmet needs associated with these reciprocal roles. Whereas in psychoanalytic terms these would be thought of as defences, in CAT they are construed as linked sequences of mental and behavioural processes, known as "procedures". When these procedures effectively compound the problem they are known as "problem procedures", and when they become a focus of therapy, they are known as "Target Problem Procedures" or TPPs. Thus, the person who cannot bear identifying with the position of one who is the victim of abuse, may seek to feel empowered and invulnerable by behaving in an abusive way towards others, which would be represented as shown in Figure 2.

What would be seen in psychoanalytic terms as the defence of identification with the aggressor, is here represented as the transition between the two poles of the reciprocal roles by means of a TPP: "Feeling at risk of being abused, I am determined never to let anyone treat me like that again and so I make sure that I am the one who is in control and on top, 'If you can't beat them, join them'".

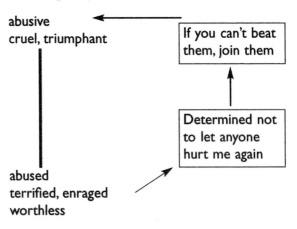

Figure 2.   An example of a target problem procedure.

In common with psychoanalytic therapies, CAT also emphasizes the importance of attending to re-enactments of these patterns in the relationship with the therapist (transference and countertransference).

Central to CAT is the notion of an active, collaborative relationship between therapist and patient. It is thought that the patient comes with their own formulation of their difficulties, but this is a formulation that does not serve them well. It may be very self-blaming, very blaming of others, or lack psychological coherence (e.g. "I had a perfect childhood, but now I'm unable to make relationships or sustain any kind of job"). The formulation that the patient comes with has not enabled them to surmount their difficulties, and may often compound feelings such as bitterness, low self-esteem, or powerlessness. The task of therapist and patient in the initial sessions is to arrive at an explicit "reformulation" of the patient's difficulties that provides a meaningful account of the issues with which the patient struggled as a child, the strategies they have developed to manage feelings or needs that seemed unacceptable or unbearable, and the ways in which they may now inadvertently perpetuate negative patterns. The aim is to construct a reformulation that encapsulates the possibility of change, through attributing responsibility more accurately, showing the patient where they have the potential to take control of their lives, and identifying emotional pain that needs to be addressed and worked through. In addition, the reformulation communicates that feelings and experiences that the patient may have been unable to acknowledge previously have been witnessed and understood.

There are three key elements to this reformulation. First, the therapist writes a letter that is read out to the patient in the session, summarizing key aspects of the patient's history, the impact these have had, characteristic ways that the patient coped with painful affects or situations, and the ways in which these habitual modes of thinking, feeling, and acting (the RRs and TPPs) may now perpetuate the patient's difficulties. Second, the therapist constructs, with the patient, a diagram that maps the principal templates of relating. The map, known as a Sequential Diagrammatic Formulation, or SDR, illustrates the main reciprocal roles and TPPs. The third component of a reformulation is the verbal description of approximately three or four problematic but habitual sequences (the TPPs).

When all components of the reformulation have been agreed with the patient, explicit "exits" from these patterns will be identified and recorded.

In a formal CAT therapy this reformulation will be developed during the first four or five sessions, leaving the remaining eleven or twelve sessions to focus on effecting change, and working through the feelings, thoughts, and memories associated with these target areas. When working with complex problems, arriving at a reformulation can be a more protracted process and the therapist may proceed more slowly, exploring which aspects of the reformulation connect with and seem meaningful to a particular patient.

The use of the term "perversion"

An appreciation of the historical context may be useful when considering those elements of the psychoanalytic theory of perversions that seem to have some enduring clinical value, and those that are more problematic. It is important to bear in mind that, since its inception, psychoanalysis has been identified with a focus on sexual behaviour; psychoanalysis and psychoanalytic therapy have therefore attracted patients who felt that their own sexual behaviours were extreme, compulsive, sometimes disabling or self-destructive, and often at odds with other aspects of their selves. Psychoanalytic theory did not develop to explain ego-syntonic variations and experimentation in sexual practice, but to address the distressing and often extreme behaviours for which patients sought help. Increasingly liberal attitudes to modes of sexual behaviour and sexual expression may have relieved the burden of guilt and shame about sexual practice for many people, but there continue to be people who seek help because their sexual fantasies or behaviour are ego-dystonic or threaten to harm themselves, their relationships, or others. It is this latter group with whom I am concerned.

Is it clinically useful to think of some of these behaviours as "perversions"? The term "perversion" is an unfortunate one, with powerful moral connotations. Definitions in the *Shorter Oxford English Dictionary* include "turning aside from truth or right; diversion to an improper use; corruption, distortion". There is no doubt that moral judgment is implied: there is a right way of doing things, and there is a perverted way of doing things. In the study of sexual behaviour many have therefore rejected this term in favour of the more neutral "paraphilia". However, the term "perversion" is still used and believed to have a clinical meaning within the psychoanalytic field, although its use has varied over the last century and between different schools of thought.

What is it that gets "perverted"? Writing a hundred years ago, Freud (1905d) proposed that it was the sexual instinct which became perverted from the "normal aim" of sexual intercourse, and the "normal object" of a heterosexual partner. He suggests that perversions are sexual activities which "extend, in an anatomical sense, beyond the regions of the body designed for sexual union" or "linger over the intermediate relations to the sexual object which should normally be traversed rapidly on the path towards the final sexual aim" (Freud, 1905d, p. 150).

Although his view of normal behaviour is very narrow, he considered deviations from this "normal" aim and object to be so common as to be virtually universal:

> No healthy person, it appears, can fail to make some addition that might be called perverse to the normal sexual aim; and the universality of this finding is in itself enough to show how inappropriate it is to use the word perversion as a term of reproach. [*ibid.*, p. 160]

Clinically these "perversions" were acceptable as long as they only represented foreplay. If the behaviours became the exclusive source of pleasure, or had the characteristics of a fixation, or they were extreme (requiring the individual to overcome normal reactions of shame, horror, disgust, or pain), then they were viewed not only as perversions but also as pathological.

Freud may have wanted to challenge the very narrow views of acceptable sexual behaviour which prevailed at the turn of the last century, but with the wisdom of hindsight we can see that he failed to recognize how immersed he was in that culture, and how culture-bound were his own definitions of normality and pathology. Many authors (e.g., Denman, 2004) have noted the unfortunate and repressive ways in which his views were subsequently applied.

Stoller (1977) recognized the potentially damaging consequences of confusing a moral position with clinical judgements of sexual behaviour, and suggested that we should look beyond behavioural descriptions to the underlying motive for the behaviour. For Stoller, what becomes perverted is not the aim of heterosexual intercourse, but the ideal of sex as a vehicle for the expression of love, or the establishment of constructive, intimate object relationships. Stoller used the term "aberration" to refer to all those erotic techniques or constellations of techniques that were used as a complete sexual act and differed from a specific culture's avowed definition of normality. He reserved the term "perversion" for those aberrations that were habitual, preferred, necessary for full satisfaction, and—here is his emphasis—primarily motivated by hostility.

> We no longer need to define a perversion according to the anatomy used, the object chosen, the society's stated morality, or the number of people who do it. All we need to know is what it means to the person doing it. [Stoller, 1977, p. 4]

In contrast to Freud's stated position, within Stoller's framework, heterosexual behaviour driven by hostility and the urge to triumph over and demean the other would be seen as pathological, whereas a loving homosexual relationship would not. However, it poses the question of how the motive for a piece of behaviour should be ascertained. Who decides whether and when a behaviour is driven by hostility?

Limentani (1989) emphasized that what is central to perversions is the perversion of truth. He proposed that the sexual behaviour represented a turning away from an intolerable "truth", citing as an example the turning away from the reality of gender difference in transvestism. In a similar vein, one might consider that there is a turning away from species difference in bestiality, and a turning away from generational difference in paedophilia. In Limentani's view, the perversion "attacks reality". In a more general way, the term "perverse" is still used to denote a failure to make a clear differentiation between that which is experienced as good, and that which is experienced as bad. Thus, idealization of destructiveness would be seen as "perverse", entailing a blurring of the "truth" of these basic categories of experience.

Even notions of "truth" are contentious, as demonstrated by recent discussions about the extent to which transsexuals have legal rights within their assumed gender. Transsexuals sometimes insist that "the truth" is that they were born with the wrong body. Some psychoanalytically-orientated therapists (e.g., Hakeem, 2002) who view transsexualism as a delusional belief, might argue that "the truth" is that transsexuals suffer a burning discomfort with their given body.

Thus, across the century, "perversion" has been taken to refer to the perversion of the sexual instinct, the perversion of the object relationship, or the perversion of psychological truths. Each of these conceptualizations is problematic, and might seem particularly problematic when applied to ego-syntonic variations in sexual practice. A more contemporary view, expressed by Harding (2001) is to consider, not whether sexuality is normal or perverse, but whether it is used expressively or defensively. Is sex used to enhance intimacy and the sense of self and other, or to protect the self or others from anxiety or to disguise or erotise aggression and hostility? This latter view blends more comfortably with a CAT perspective, in which sexuality could be seen as integral to adaptive and functional reciprocal roles concerned with expression, acceptance and affirmation of self and others represented as shown in Figure 3.

Alternatively, sexualization could be seen as one of a number of potential procedures that might be used to deal with intolerable affects associated with the reciprocal roles as in Figure 4. Within this approach, enactment in the sexual sphere of the unresolved feelings

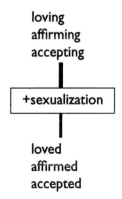

Figure 3.   Reciprocal role of expression, acceptance, and affirmation of self and others.

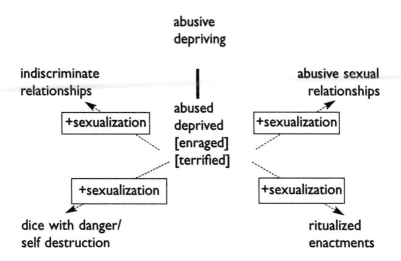

Figure 4.   Sexualization used to deal with intolerable affects associated with a reciprocal role.

or needs associated with the reciprocal roles would be analogous to enactment through the eating function in eating disorders, or through drug or alcohol abuse. The critical issue is not whether the function is utilized for pleasure as opposed to its biological aim, but whether it is used to avoid pain. The sexual function has specific characteristics, notably the association with excitement and associated feelings of power and triumph (sometimes also acquired through drug use), which render it a particularly useful channel when the feelings to be avoided are of vulnerability or humiliation, and the feeling-states sought are associated with triumph and control.

Psychoanalytic theories of perversion

The CAT therapy that was undertaken was largely informed by the views of Stoller and Glasser concerning the underlying dynamics of perversions, and these are elaborated below. This is prefaced by an outline of Freud's view of perversions, taking as an example his theory of fetishism, as some elements of his original formulation are evident in subsequent theorizing.

Freud (1905d, 1927e)

Freud wrote his classic paper on fetishism in 1927. In this he boldly states that the inanimate object which becomes a fetish represents the mother's penis. Freud argues that, for the young boy, the sight of his mother's genital confronts him with the possibility of castration. For some boys (and Freud admits that he does not know why this applies to some and not others), this castration anxiety is intolerable. The boy both knows that the woman lacks a penis, and cannot bear to know this. He can no longer sustain the belief that she has a penis exactly like his own, and so he invests in a substitute—an object that is invested with the power to thrill and excite, which is often something glimpsed in the moments before he became aware of his mother's "castration"—shoes, stockings, or underwear, for example, or fur or velvet standing for the pubic hair. Thus, intolerable anxiety is transformed into sexual excitement, and the fetish then becomes "a token of triumph over the threat of castration and a protection against it" (1927e, p. 154). This might be represented by a CAT diagram (Figure 5), where the initial relationship to an exciting object can become a threatening relationship to a potentially damaging object; through adoption of the fetish, Freud argues that the boy becomes the one in control, and the threat of castration is controlled or tamed:

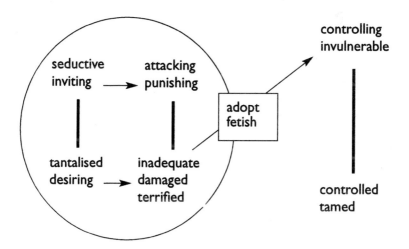

Figure 5.   Freud's view of fetishism as an SDR.

Freud holds that the fetish enables the boy/man to continue to relate to women as sexual objects by endowing the woman with a symbolic phallus and so she ceases to embody the threat of castration. Furthermore, the fetish can be controlled and accessed by the boy/man at will. "What other men have to woo and make exertions for can be had by the fetishist with no trouble at all" (Freud, 1927e, p. 154).

This account of the aetiology of a fetish now seems concrete and anachronistic; as an attempt at explanation, it leaves many questions unanswered. For example, can we assume that the boy first becomes aware of sexual difference at this pre-Oedipal stage, but had previously assumed that men and women were anatomically identical? If the boy seeks to regain control over the anxiety aroused in the relationship with the mother, why resort to sexualization of the mother's possessions and not retreat to a more narcissistic investment in the self and detachment from others? Despite such limitations, Freud's account is thought-provoking because, in his characteristic way, he offers a compelling clinical description and some of his ideas remain implicit in thinking about perversions or paraphilias today.

The first is the idea that the perversion, in this case the fetish, enables the individual to escape from an awareness of his own vulnerability (in Freud's words, the threat of castration). Instead of being at the mercy of another who has the power to excite but also to punish and arouse anxiety, the individual invests an inanimate object with the power to excite, but an inanimate object that is entirely within his own control. Thus, the individual escapes from anxiety and vulnerability and feels empowered, triumphant, and in control. This is resonant with Stoller's (1977) more contemporary ideas about perversion and is elaborated below.

The second is that the adoption of the fetish allows the preservation of the relationship to the object. Intimacy becomes possible because the terrors that that relationship might otherwise evoke have been negated. The woman, who might otherwise represent an unbearable threat, is made safe, since, in Freud's view, she still has a symbolic penis after all. There are parallels between this and Glasser's (1979) notion of the "core complex", which is discussed later.

The third is that two completely contradictory ideas can be held in the mind at the same time: the reality of the woman's "castration" is both acknowledged and completely denied. This has subsequently been seen as a seminal paper because it introduced for the first time the idea of a split in the ego. We can both know and not know something simultaneously. (This idea is explored in Chapter Five with respect to risk-taking in sexual behaviour.) Of more contemporary writers, Limentani (1989) is particularly concerned with the recognition and denial of psychic truths in states of mind characteristic of the paraphilias. People can "know" that paedophilia harms children (if only because they have been told so by others or the media), and yet believe they are expressing love to the child they abuse; others can "know" they are male yet derive pleasure from assuming the clothes and identity of a woman.

Stoller (1977)

Stoller's (1977) classic study of perversions primarily focuses on pornography, transsexualism, and transvestism. It is notable that, writing nearly thirty years ago, he fails to make the clear diagnostic distinctions that would now be made between transsexualism, dual role transvestism, and fetishistic transvestism (ICD 10). Nevertheless, as with Freud's descriptions, there are features of his formulation that seem clinically applicable and useful. Stoller argues that there is always a trauma in the history of those presenting with perversions, but this trauma is not simply, as Freud suggests, exposure to the reality of sexual difference. In Stoller's view the historical trauma is some attack on the sexuality or gender identity of the developing child. He describes children of unambiguous biological gender being dressed or reared as members of the opposite sex by parents or parent-substitutes, or being ridiculed and bullied in relation to their gender identity.

Stoller proposes that the perverse act is then an act of revenge. The man who cross-dresses in order to obtain sexual excitement may appear to want to imitate and become like a woman, but actually this imitation is a caricature in which femininity is often parodied. In the cross-dressing ritual, the secret of the man's masculinity is hidden, but at the end of the ritual he masturbates and ejaculates, reasserting his masculinity and mentally triumphing over those who have humiliated or denigrated him.

Thus, Stoller argues that the act serves as an apparent re-enactment of a traumatic past; the man repeats that which has been done to him, denies his masculinity, and assumes the identity of a woman. However, this is a re-enactment in which history is rewritten: this time the man is not left as the humiliated victim, but through sexualization this re-enactment of the trauma culminates in his pleasure and triumph.

In this way the victim becomes victor, trauma becomes triumph, and passive suffering is converted into active revenge, usually in fantasy but sometimes enacted. This resonates with Freud's idea that the fetish enables the individual to escape from intolerable castration anxieties to a position of control and triumph. Stoller's view might be represented by a CAT diagram (Figure 6).

Case illustration

Mr A presented for therapy because his compulsive use of prostitutes and denigrating sexual behaviour towards his partner threatened their relationship. He was so anxious and ashamed at the outset of therapy that he could barely speak. It became apparent that he imagined that the therapist would berate him and punish him for his thoughts and actions, and it later emerged in therapy that he would experience some gratification if the therapist could be drawn into behaving in this way.

In therapy it emerged that Mr A had felt repeatedly humiliated by his father, who alternately "seduced" him with the promise of affection and warmth, and then taunted him mercilessly and cruelly for any

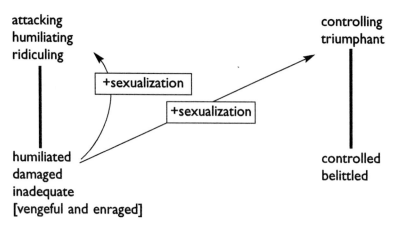

Figure 6.   Stoller's view of perversion as an SDR.

failings or imperfections. He felt that his mother stood by ineffectually, and although he was protective towards her, his anger about her passivity and complicity began to emerge. In the course of therapy, Mr A was able to recognize the gratification he derived from triumphing over others in order to escape the risk of being "triumphed over", and the "pleasurable suffering" he experienced when he presented himself to others as a failure and berated himself for his behaviours.

He appeared to derive great relief from the mapping of these behaviours (Figure 7), and at the end of this brief therapy was considerably less anxious and able to contemplate more intensive therapy.

Glasser's "core complex"

Glasser (1979) locates the historical trauma at an even earlier stage of development than Stoller. In his view, at the centre of the psychopathology of those presenting with perversions is a constellation of feelings, attitudes, and ideas that he calls the "core complex", rooted in early infantile experience. A key element of this is a profound longing for union, even fusion, with another, the fantasy of a blissful state of oneness, in which the individual is made absolutely secure and all destructive feelings are contained and made safe, a "back in the womb" type of experience. While such longings are found in many loving relationships, in some individuals this fantasy

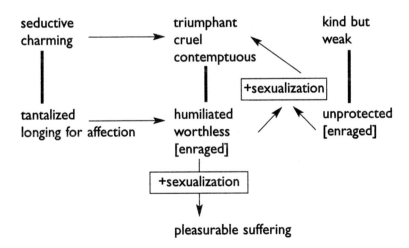

Figure 7.   Mapping of Mr A's behaviours.

evokes terror: a fear of permanent loss of self, annihilation, falling into a black hole. If the individual responds to this terror by retreat to a safe distance, he or she risks isolation and exposure.

In CAT, a similar dynamic is recognized as the "porcupine's dilemma": two porcupines on a cold hillside face a choice, either to huddle together for warmth (but then they stick their spines into each other and get hurt), or to withdraw (and then feel cold and exposed). In CAT this is summarized by the TPP: "Either I'm involved with someone and likely to get hurt, or I don't get involved and stay in charge but remain lonely". This may be seen as a classic claustrophobic–agoraphobic dilemma (see Rey, 1979). However, in Glasser's view, the anxieties aroused by this type of oscillation in core complex states are not just about being lonely or hurt, they are primitive, overwhelming terrors of annihilation and total abandonment.

Glasser was a contemporary Freudian and, like Freud, thought that the fundamental task of the ego was to guard psychic homeostasis, a steady state of well-being. Threats to this homeostasis evoke aggression, which aims to eliminate the source of the disturbance. In the core complex, the threat of annihilation evokes aggression, yet if the individual were to destroy the exciting stimulus he or she faces an even greater threat, that of total abandonment by the object. Glasser argues that, in perversions, the solution found to this dilemma is to sexualize the aggression. Aggression—the impulse to destroy the source of threat—is converted into sadism; the wish to destroy the object is converted into a desire to hurt and control the object. As in Freud's account of fetishism, a relationship to the object is preserved, by sexualization of the intolerable affects that would otherwise preclude an intimate relationship to the object.

Glasser observes that in the clinical histories of such patients there is often evidence of an early relationship with the primary caregiver, who both used the child to meet their own narcissistic needs (thereby intensifying annihilatory anxiety and aggression), and neglected the child's needs (thereby amplifying abandonment anxieties and consequent aggression). He also reports histories of overt and excessive sexual stimulation by the caregiver. Thus, environmental factors may have led to increased and intolerable aggression, acute fears of abandonment, or a predisposition to sexualize intolerable emotions.

Again, I think it is not necessary to adopt Freud and Glasser's rather biological model of instincts, organisms, and homeostasis to find the useful clinical insights in this view. In object relations terms, Glasser is highlighting the intense and primitive anxieties aroused for some people by the promise of longed-for intimacy. The intense consuming merger that is desired is also seen as deadly and terrifying. In self-protection, aggression may be evoked that in turn threatens to destroy the very relationship that is so desired. How can this be made safe? By sexualizing the aggression, and expressing it though ritualized enactments such as sado-masochistic sexual behaviours or "exciting" fights, for example. Glasser's formulation also raises unanswered questions: if this dynamic is thought to originate in the anxieties of early infancy, at what point in development is sexualization available as a defence, and when and how does this become organized into a habitual paraphilia? As an explanation it remains incomplete, but clinical experience confirms the prevalence of these "core conflict" anxieties in patients presenting with these types of sexual problems.

As an SDR, Glasser's model might be represented as shown in Figure 8.

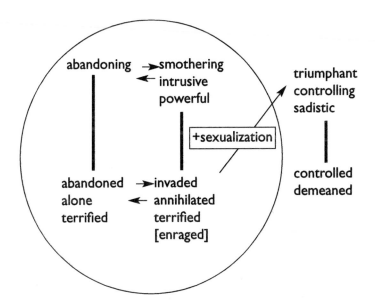

Figure 8. Glasser's "core complex" as an SDR.

Case illustration

Ms B sought therapy in a depressed and anxious state, apparently worried that she risked losing her job through baiting her colleagues. In the early stages of therapy it emerged that she was caught up in a couple relationship with her partner that had strong sado-masochistic elements. The couple would argue and snipe at each other, and would knowingly escalate conflicts until physical violence would erupt. The fight would expose both to the risk of serious physical injury. Ms B had a history of sexual relationships in which emotional cruelty, violence, and bondage were recurrent features.

In her background, her father was an exciting but violent man, who terrorized his wife and children. Ms B sought safety in her relationship with her mother, yet felt smothered by her. By mapping these issues in the diagram below (Figure 9), she was able to see how, in her adult life, she was recreating the violent relationship with her father, which she consciously abhorred. This awareness brought considerable sadness, but she was able to begin to see the fights and self-destructive sexual behaviours as less "exciting" and to begin to address her fears about closeness, based on fears of merger with an all-consuming mother.

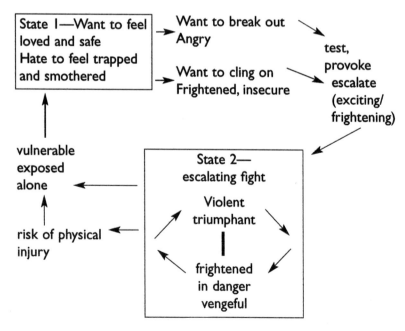

Figure 9.   Mapping of Ms B's procedures.

A common feature of clinical cases with these problems is the rapid oscillations between the "violated, humiliated, in danger" position, and the "violent, cruel, triumphant" position. In the course of a violent argument the individual may oscillate between these positions so rapidly that their position at any one time becomes blurred. In psychoanalytic terms this might be thought of as the alternating operation and failure of projective identification: the bad, attacking aggressor is temporarily projected into the other, then reowned, then again evacuated.

In one CAT therapy, when this was drawn (Figure 10), it was observed that this image resembled a washing machine. The therapist then began to talk with the patient concerned about the "spin cycle", and this image became a useful focus in the therapeutic dialogue.

"Knowing" and "not knowing"

The CAT diagram allows the therapist, in discussion with the patient, to map aspects of the self, or the self's relationship to others, which seem contradictory or incompatible. Thus, the mother may have been experienced as warm and seductive (and inviting feelings of excitement and longing), and cruel and belittling (evoking feelings of fear, humiliation, and a desire for revenge). Arrows

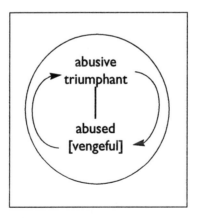

Figure 10. Oscillations between "abusive, triumphant" and "abused and vengeful" positions.

on the diagram can mark the shifts between starkly different modes of relating.

Reciprocal roles encompass the position of both "victim" and "perpetrator" where abuse is involved, and recognize that the patient has both elements within him or herself. Where a position or feeling is inferred but the patient has no conscious knowledge or awareness of it, this can be written on the diagram, initially in square brackets. Subjectively, a patient may only be aware of terror in response to bullying or humiliation, yet we might infer that somewhere there are feelings of rage, which in turn fuel observable self-punitive or abusive behaviours. Thus, "[rage]" may be included on the diagram, and the brackets removed if at some point the patient becomes more in touch with these feelings.

Other devices may be used to reflect splits or fractures between parts of the self on the diagram, so that roles and procedures "known" in one state of mind are distinguished between those "known" in other states of mind. Where narcissistic structures prevail, for example, an idealized–idealizing reciprocal role may be drawn on top of a pedestal, and a contemptuous–contemptible reciprocal role below, effectively "in the gutter", which the patient may believe to be the only alternative to being on the pedestal. In the context of narcissistic personality traits, sexual behaviours may be used to try to attain an idealised–idealizing relationship, yet expose the individual to the risk of crashing into self-hatred and contempt for self and other (see Chapter Ten).

Thus, CAT lends itself to the identification of apparently contradictory states of mind—masculine and feminine aspects, victim and perpetrator, longing coupled with fear and hatred of the object, superiority and triumph side by side with acute feelings of inadequacy. Once these have been named and drawn, they exist within consciousness and within the therapeutic dialogue, and the patient can be helped to acquire a more integrated "meta-perspective" on the seemingly incompatible aspects of themselves.

Clinical applications

In cases treated by a small group of clinicians over several years, these psychoanalytic ideas have informed the construction of SDRs.

The SDR can be used to map the way in which the patient uses sexualization to get from the painful vulnerability usually associated with the lower poles of the reciprocal roles to a position of dominance, control, triumph, and sometimes active abuse associated with the upper poles of the reciprocal roles.

Glasser's ideas have alerted us to the danger of assuming that intimacy will be seen as comfortable and potentially good; for some patients it is associated with claustrophobic terrors, and is seen as both alluring and dangerous. Verbal or physical fights and sometimes life-threatening violent and sexual behaviours may offer an apparent way of dealing with the terrors of intimacy, and these sequences can be traced diagrammatically. The "spin cycle" is a useful way of describing the oscillations between victim and perpetrator or abused and abuser, which can lead to dangerous and rapid escalation in some relationships. Fractures or splits between parts of the self can be mapped on the diagram and brought into awareness.

CAT lends itself to uncritical naming of the elements of the self. The experiences of this client group may sometimes seem extreme and the use of sexualization may be a source of shame and embarrassment. The construction of an SDR is then particularly valuable in establishing a shared language for discussing these experiences and for acknowledging that there will inevitably be aggressive and vulnerable elements to the self. The SDR enables the patient to see how sexual behaviours are often rooted in feelings of fear, vulnerability, or anger, and thus behaviours that might have seemed irrational, intense, and driven may be given meaning and the destructive sexual charge may thereby be lessened.

Outcomes

There is widespread recognition that problems of sexual behaviour are very difficult to treat. It has been suggested that the sexualization provides a degree of gratification that means that the individual is reluctant to relinquish the behaviour. Some psychoanalytic theorists hold that the behaviour serves as a defence against unbearable "truths" that will be very difficult to face in therapy. Most psychoanalytic therapists would insist that it is only when the disturbed dynamics have been re-experienced and understood within the transference, perhaps repeatedly, that change can occur. What, then, can we hope to achieve in sixteen or twenty-four sessions? Inevitably, I think, our aims must be modest, but not trivial.

With patients who are very frightened and ashamed, the first consideration may simply be that they have an experience of therapy that is containing, accepting, and does not deter them from seeking further help. A number of cases seen for CAT were able to move on to more intensive or long-term psychotherapeutic help.

In every such case treated with CAT that I have been involved with, some part of the process of naming, describing, and drawing what was going on has reached the patient and offered some insight and relief. Having acquired this meta-perspective, some patients are able to interrupt automatic sequences of destructive behaviours. For others, this process may take longer. As one patient said, "I've found the box but not found the key yet."

If an impulsive individual has more capacity to think instead of act then I think CAT therapists would concur with psychoanalytic therapists that there has been some progress. In Freud's language, "Where id was, there ego shall be". In CAT terms, the Target Problem Procedure has been recognized and revised, and alternative strategies are now available to the patient to deal with painful emotions.

References

American Psychiatric Association (1997). *Diagnostic and Statistical Manual of Mental Disorders—4th Edition*. Washington, DC: APA.

Denman, C. (2004). *Sexuality: A Biopsychosocial Approach*. Basingstoke: Palgrave Macmillan.

Freud, S. (1905d). Three essays on the theory of sexuality. *S.E.*, 7: 123–245

Freud, S. (1927e) Fetishism. *S.E.*, 21: 149–157.

Glasser, M. (1979). Some aspects of the role of aggression in the perversions. In: I. Rosen (Ed.), *Sexual Deviations* (pp. 278–305). Oxford: Oxford University Press.

Harding, C. (2001). *Sexuality. Psychoanalytic Perspectives*. Hove: Brunner Routledge.

Hakeem, A. (2002). Transsexualism: A case of the emperor's new clothes? *FRAME, The Newsletter for the International Association of Forensic Psychotherapy*, 6: 34–40.

Limentani, A. (1989). *Between Freud and Klein*. London: Free Association Books.

Rey, H. (1979). Schizoid phenomena in the borderline. In: J. LeBoit & A. Capponi (Eds.), *Advances in the Psychotherapy of the Borderline Patient*. Reprinted in E.Bott Spillius (1988), *Melanie Klein Today. Vol 1: Mainly Theory*. London: Routledge.

Ryle, A. (1990). *Cognitive Analytic Therapy: Active Participation in Change*. Chichester: Wiley

Ryle, A. (Ed.) (1995). *Cognitive Analytic Therapy: Developments in Theory and Practice*. Chichester: Wiley

Ryle, A. (1997). *Cognitive Analytic Therapy and Borderline Personality Disorder*. Chichester: Wiley.

Ryle, A., & Kerr, I. B. (2002). *Introducing Cognitive Analytic Therapy*. Chichester: Wiley.

Stoller, R. J. (1977). *Perversion: The Erotic Form of Hatred*. London: Quartet.

World Health Organization (1992). *The International Classification of Mental and Behavioural Disorders (ICD 10)*. Geneva: World Health Organization.

CHAPTER TWELVE

Loss of sexual interest and negative states of mind

Janice Hiller

Introduction

Sexual activity between people creates an emotional and physical bond that provides a foundation for connectedness in intimate couple relationships. Most loving adult partnerships contain an element of attraction and pleasure from physical contact, although the extent and the importance of these will vary greatly. Within a normal range it is, of course, possible for a couple to be non-sexual if this is their choice; similarly, an individual may have no sexual needs for the whole life course, with no harmful consequences. What does concern people is when sexual needs change, either in a way that alters the sense of self as a sexual being, or when couple dynamics are impinged upon such that harmony is impaired.

The feeling that a valued part of the self, or a relationship, has been lost and cannot be recovered by conscious choice, can be most distressing. Some people who experience an absence of sexual interest construe the change to mean that something is wrong, emotionally or even physically, within themselves. Alternatively there may be doubt about the validity of the relationship as a whole, with fears that it is no longer tenable. In a clinical setting, patients may express concern about letting a partner down, or causing pain, which is often accompanied by guilt at not living up to expectations. While some people feel a sense of loss, others say that given a choice they would prefer not to have sex again, and a request for help is to avoid damage to the relationship.

Research into referral patterns at sexual problem clinics has shown that far more women than men request help for decreased or absent desire for sex with a partner in a committed relationship. In the most recent London survey, 40% of the female referrals were for low desire, compared to 6% of the male referrals (Hems & Crowe, 1999). There are signs that this well-established gender difference may be changing though, at least in the USA. Pridal and LoPiccolo (2000) found an equal number of men and women with low sexual desire referred to their clinic in Missouri in the 1990s, compared to previous decades. They consider this change in the ratio to stem from women becoming sufficiently empowered to ask male partners to seek therapy with them, rather than living with dissatisfaction. Sociocultural changes that encourage women to be more assertive, and enable men to admit to sexual needs that are less than a partner's, could lead to similar patterns in the UK too.

The concept of "disorders of sexual desire" was added by Kaplan (1979, 1995) to Masters and Johnson's (1970) original classification of sexual problems, which addressed difficulties in the arousal and orgasmic phases of the sexual response cycle. Kaplan (1995) also introduced the notion of a dysfunctional regulation of sexual motivation, which she described as ranging from phobic avoidance to hypersexuality. Despite the high prevalence of a lack of motivation for sex, this form of psychosexual problem is recognized as one of the most difficult to treat. What accounts for this inability or unwillingness to be sexual with a partner, when linked to absence of desire, in a relationship where people want to stay together? Rather than emphasizing individual dysregulation, Crowe and Ridley (2000) have employed a behavioural-systems framework to describe the phenomenon as an incompatibility of sexual interest, usually in the form of female reluctance and male demands. They advocate a negotiated timetable of sexual activity that removes the pressure from one person, thereby freeing space for dealing with other, conflictual features of the relationship. A formulation that recognizes incompatibility, rather than a dysfunction within one person, offers a helpful theoretical and therapeutic approach. Crowe and Ridley's (2000) perspective views female reluctance as a response that balances an otherwise male-dominated relationship, and creates the demand for a forum where partners can work on troubling thoughts and feelings about the partnership.

My aim in the present chapter is to elaborate on this concept by describing the negative emotional states that are associated with an absence of sexual motivation. These negative emotions, experienced by both women and men, include resentment, hostility, disappointment, and fear. They may be conscious or unconscious and are often, but not always, based on misunderstandings and assumptions in the current partnership. Even when negative emotions are consciously experienced, people rarely make the causal connection between negative thoughts and feelings and absence of desire. The purpose of therapy, then, is to enable individuals to link involuntary sexual withdrawal with painful emotions that have threatened the sense of connectedness with a partner. Finding alternative ways to express thoughts and feelings can foster emotional closeness, and set the scene for re-establishing mutually rewarding sexual contact.

Although there are significant gender differences in the links between feelings, emotions, and sexual expression, this is not the focus of the present chapter. Previous discussions have recognized the need to address resentment in couple therapy using a behavioural or systemic model (e.g., Crowe and Ridley, 2000; Hawton, 1985), but my aim here is to explore in more detail the meaning of potentially destructive emotions within an object relations framework and to link these states with absence of sexual interest for a specific partner. Recognizing the significance of hostility, resentment, or fear is not necessarily for the purpose of encouraging their open expression in couple communication, as this could elevate tension and cause further disruption. Instead, I wish to show, first, that negative states of mind can arise from processes either within, or external to, the partnership; second, their nature and source needs careful assessment and formulation to guide therapeutic strategies. A further distinguishing feature of this approach is that the constellation of absent desire and negative emotions, whatever the source, is not viewed as a punitive attack to avenge real or imagined painful experiences. Instead, it is seen as representing an involuntary, self-protective retreat from an emotional and physical bond that has become a perceived threat to emotional homeostasis.

Clinical work indicates that both sexes tend to be equally unaware of the cause of their sexual disinterest, but there are gender differences in how this impacts on a sense of self and other. Women, from my experience, tend to hold themselves responsible, to believe they need treatment, and to be fearful of damaging, or losing, the relationship. Men, by contrast, are less likely to be distressed about a partner's needs, her state of mind, or the possible harm for the relationship as a whole. Women's tendency to guilt and self-blame is not helped by a culture that seems to consider regular sexual activity to be the norm, and female avoidance as being "unfair" to men, who will understandably seek sexual outlets elsewhere. The successful introduction of oral medication for the most common male problem, erectile difficulty, has only served to increase female fears of inadequacy or dysfunction. Despite the efforts of pharmaceutical companies, an equivalent preparation or "Viagra for women" has not been found. Attempts to increase female desire through increased physiological responsiveness have been based on the mistaken assumption that there is automatic feedback from physical/genital to emotional arousal in women, similar to that of most men. In fact, studies have shown that female genital changes, including lubrication and expansion, are not in themselves sufficient for subjective feelings of desire (Everaerd, Laan, Both, & van der Velde, 2000). Bancroft (2002) has commented on the danger of medicalizing sexuality by defining what might be an adaptive response to relationship issues (loss of desire in the context of painful emotions) as a disease entity that can be treated by a tablet. Psychological rather than pharmacological approaches are required for this sensitive area of couple interaction.

The following examples are compilations of psychosexual therapy cases I have seen in an NHS clinic, selected to illustrate the relevance of exploring negative states of mind as part of an approach with either individuals or couples. As with all psychological treatments, this approach is based on formulation of the presenting issues; it incorporates object relations, psycho-educational and directive models where appropriate, for people who present with unwanted withdrawal of sexual interest.

Clinical examples

Frequently, with absence of sexual desire, a couple's shared life events have been insufficiently discussed, and negative feelings have built up that impinge on couple dynamics. Although one partner may be able to describe her emotional state in the consulting-room (men, in my experience are less likely to do this), the topic has been avoided with the other person and has not been consciously linked with changes in sexual activity.

Negative emotions arising from desired changes in the relationship

A, a married woman in her twenties with an eighteen-month-old son, was referred by her GP following a request for antidepressants, which he did not prescribe. She attended on her own because her partner B, "blamed" her for the absence of sex since the baby was born, and refused couple therapy. In the first session A expressed her resentment at how her life had changed radically since the birth, while B's had not. He continued to work, met his friends, and pursued his sporting interests. A had given up her job and was unable to meet friends or have any time to herself, as B was unwilling to be left alone with the child. Despite recognizing the divergence in their lifestyles, A felt she was "wrong" to find motherhood frustrating at times, and sex a chore that she avoided. She had previously enjoyed sex and had wanted the baby, so could not understand the change in her feelings. There were regular rows about sex, which exacerbated A's inability to imagine that her feelings would return.

A was helped by a formulation that viewed her withdrawal from sex as stemming from her understandable disappointment and resentment at the lack of support from her partner (shared by other women in similar situations), rather than a personal failing. Sessions were focused initially on thinking about how she could explain to B that she wanted affectionate hugs and kisses that did not automatically lead to sex, and that she needed some time for herself. From discussions about child-care she realized that B lacked the confidence to manage the child on his own for long, and needed advice. He was also resistant to the concept of making an effort with his partner, rather than having spontaneous sex the way they used to. B's refusal to attend for therapy with A meant that I needed to maintain a focus on couple interactions to avoid bias for the partner in the room, and encourage sensitivity to B as the absent other (see Hiller, 1999). Giving B a presence in the therapy enabled A to become more aware of the meaning of his behaviour, and therefore less resentful, as she developed a greater understanding of her own emotional responses. Changes were made in their daily lives and, as A regained a sense of her individuality, her sexual feelings returned. Without two people in therapy, misunderstandings are likely to occur, however, as when A suddenly approached B for sex after a fun night out with her friends; caught off-guard, he accused her of feeling sexual because she had flirted with someone else. Through exploring this and other events, the couple developed a better understanding of each other's needs and responses and sexual activity was resumed.

In the example above, negative emotions arising from a change in the couple's shared life that they both wanted had nevertheless created a barrier to sexual activity. Individual work that retained a focus on the couple's current functioning, without more in-depth exploration, was sufficient to lift the barrier. For couples with more complex difficulties, joint psychosexual therapy is required to explore the dynamics and provide an integrated treatment approach.

Negative emotions arising from unsolicited changes in the relationship

C and D attended together following a referral for marital tension due to avoidance of sex by C, the female partner. They had been married for fourteen years and had three children. D was impatient and angry about C's withdrawal, while she was confused and also guilty about the bad atmosphere in the home, which impacted on the children. Neither partner could offer an explanation beyond mutual accusations, but it became apparent that their family circumstances had changed significantly in the previous two years. D's elderly parents had started to spend six months of the year with them and the other six months with his sister's family. Since then C had found it very hard to manage the intrusion and extra work on top of her job. She admitted to hating the period when her in-laws stayed, and dreaded their return after they left, but accepted that it was her duty. D was shocked to hear the extent of her feelings about his parents, although C explained it was the increased domestic burden rather than his parents as people. At first hostility grew as D accused C of wanting his parents dead, and refusing sex to punish him. He also felt rejected and could not see why having sex at the end of a stressful day was not a form of relaxation for C, as it would be for him. D would have liked just closeness and physical affection at first, but C interpreted his approaches as sexual in nature and could not comply.

The couple's difficulties were formulated as arising from changes in their home life that had not been properly discussed, resulting in resentment and tension for both partners, but especially for C. Her withdrawal from sex was viewed as enabling her to regain some personal space to counteract the intense demands on her time; D's responses had exacerbated the situation by maintaining the distance between them. We agreed to work initially on removing the atmosphere of mutual blame, and untangling the misconceptions, with the overall aim of re-establishing harmony and sexual contact. Early sessions required containment of the hostility, which was projected on to the therapeutic space (when D denigrated the treatment) as well as the relationship. Exploring their current situation, progress was made when D was able to admit to his own ambivalence at his parents' arrangements, as he thought his sister, who did not work and had one child, should have them full-time. This enabled C and D to share their feelings, rather than be torn apart by perceived differences. It was also helpful to normalize the impact on their sexual relationship by clarifying that women commonly lose desire with negative emotions while men are more able to feel sexual, despite their presence.

At the stage when C gained some insight into D's dilemma, and D accepted that C's withdrawal was not an outright rejection, it was possible to introduce home-based assignments to address their sexual relationship directly. Starting with gentle caressing at a mutually agreed time, the couple moved on to sensual pleasuring exercises (initially without a sexual aim), to remove barriers to physical contact. Sessions during this phase involved a combination of addressing conflictual family issues, with discussions of their responses to the gradual approach to shared sexual intimacy. Ongoing intrusions and misunderstandings were overcome more readily as emotional and physical trust, and eventually sexual activity, was regained.

For C and D, hostilities stemming from current family dynamics were the focus of a therapeutic approach that also addressed their sexual relationship through joint directive work.

Another common pattern is when unresolved family-of-origin issues become re-enacted in the current partnership and impair sexual interest. The emphasis is then on exploring how painful aspects of development are re-experienced in an intimate relationship, and become maintained by couple dynamics, as the next example will illustrate.

Negative emotions arising from unresolved family-of-origin issues

TREATED AS A COUPLE

E and F were referred to the psychological therapies department by a psychiatrist after E's hospital admission following an overdose attempt. She was in her mid-forties and felt desperate about not having children. Her despair was connected with her partner's avoidance of sex and apparent inability to offer emotional support. F was twelve years older, expressed some concern for his partner, but explained her erratic behaviour and mood swings of the last five years as due to premenstrual tension and work stress. They both described a relationship characterized by constant bickering, with no real discussion of important issues. F admitted retreating from "conflict" by hiding behind a newspaper, while E wanted to discuss a future without children, but had been unable to find the courage. Their sex life had been good for the first two years but almost non-existent for the last ten years, due to F's reluctance. During the assessment it became apparent that there were numerous aspects of their daily interactions that created mutual disappointment and retreat. In the first few sessions it was a struggle to move beyond their descriptions of a recurrent scenario in which E would come home from work in a rage, describe her frustrations with colleagues in an aggressive way, and refuse advice from F. She expected support but felt uncared for, and he wanted to help but felt denigrated.

The family backgrounds of both partners were explored, but of particular significance for understanding F's state of mind were certain factors of his childhood that seemed to be projected on to the relationship with E. F was the only child of an alcoholic father who he described as "useless" and a "disgrace" as a parent. As a teenager he had urged his long-suffering mother to get away from his aggressive father. F was unaware of negative feelings in the context of his interactions with E, just the need to get away from her outbursts.

In the formulation, F's emotional and physical withdrawal was seen as representing an unconscious sense of being both "useless" like his father, and fearful of E's aggressive manner, as he and his mother had been of his father's temper. His retreat from emotional and sexual contact was conceptualized as a form of self-protection from recognizing E's distress that he felt powerless to influence. F's pattern of getting away from high emotion had left him safe, but created distance and led to the communication difficulties becoming more entrenched.

A central theme of the couple work was to connect these issues with the way they related, and also to enable E to accept her own projections as these were impairing positive communications. For example, E's reluctance to make a direct request was linked to her strong sense of guilt at the sacrifices she thought her parents made for her education. At the same time attention was given to the manner in which E and F discussed ongoing experiences so that each could listen and be supportive to the other rather than feeling attacked. As the disharmony lessened it was possible to introduce a negotiated timetable for sensual pleasuring exercises, similar to the previous case. This time the pace was set by the needs of the male partner, whose anxiety about being an effective and wanted sexual man, unlike his father, had previously disrupted his motivation for sex. As E became more able to express herself calmly and feel supported by F, she accepted they would not have children, and decided to retrain for a job she had always wanted. F became more confident of his value as a partner, and sexual activity was gradually resumed.

When a range of negative emotions are re-evoked in a current partnership, and maintained by misunderstandings, therapeutic work with both people is essential to disentangle the issues and facilitate new ways of relating. Sometimes, as in the next case, there appear to be no maintaining factors, and individual therapy is indicated. The task is then to explore unconscious processes that are projected on to the intimate relationship.

TREATED IN INDIVIDUAL THERAPY

G was a woman in her late twenties who had been married for three years, but six months after the wedding she had felt unwilling to have sex with her partner H. He was her first serious boyfriend after a series of casual encounters, and she had felt comfortable and enjoyed sex with him while they were dating. There was no tension between them concerning the lack of sex, but G was anxious that H might be drawn to other women at work. It was important for G that her partner accepted her as a non-sexual person, but she also felt he could not be expected to tolerate the absence of sex indefinitely, and as well as missing the sexual part of herself she felt panicky at the prospect of losing him.

In the assessment sessions, an unusual family background emerged. G and her sister had grown up with a father who insisted on an open marriage and had constant affairs with local women. The father was a charismatic and forceful man whom she admired, while being constantly aware that her mother disliked the arrangement, but was too unassertive and dependent to challenge it. G's mother did not discuss sex with her, and as far as G knew she did not have any other sexual partners, despite encouragement from her husband. From the age of fourteen, G started having sex with boys, and became pregnant at fifteen. She had a termination but felt traumatized by the callous attitude of the doctors and nurses who examined her when she was naïve and self-conscious. G continued to feel exploited by boys until she met H, when she felt safe. In the past five years, G's father had suffered a stroke, becoming dependent on his wife for support, so that G now felt very sorry for her parents' predicament.

G's early move into sexual activity was viewed as an attempt to be the kind of sexual woman her mother was refusing to be, in order to gain acceptance. However, the termination had led G to identify with her mother's predicament. G's unwillingness to be sexual was formulated as stemming predominantly from an unconscious identification with a mother who resented the pressure to be sexual, and experienced shame about her partner's overt sexual behaviour outside the marriage. Additionally, there seemed to be denial of sexuality as a part of healthy relationships, linked to anger with her father and other males who exploited women for their own needs.

In individual work, G gradually saw the unresolved issues that were being projected on to her relationship with H, thereby blocking her ability to feel sexual in the present. She felt unable to plan any form of sensual or sexual contact with H, which felt like another pressure to be a sexual person before she was emotionally ready. H supported her therapy, but she was unwilling to discuss her progress with him, which seemed to represent an attempt to keep sex out of the family. Eventually she initiated sex with H unexpectedly; he was caught by surprise and felt they should stop, much to her distress. The importance of talking openly to H about her sexual feelings was highlighted, as part of overcoming the prohibitions she had grown up with. G grew in confidence as she understood the source of her negative emotions. She learnt to talk more openly with H and to listen to his frustrations too. When she was next able to initiate sexual contact, H was ready to respond positively, and eventually there was a return to spontaneous sexual activity.

In the next example of male reluctance for sex, the female partner's distress had brought them both to therapy. Treatment involved individual work to explore unresolved issues of fear and anger stemming from childhood, and subsequent couple therapy to reintroduce sexuality into their relationship.

COMBINED COUPLE AND INDIVIDUAL THERAPY

K and L were a couple in their thirties who had been together for seven years, with no sex in the past two years despite an active sex life at the beginning. K was a successful man who was embarrassed at both his lack of sexual desire and his inability to explain it. He found L very attractive and their daily life was harmonious, except when she wanted to discuss plans for the future (moving house or having a baby), at which time he would become silent. He dreaded L starting a conversation about where their lives were going, which was confusing, as shared goals and interests had brought them together originally. L had insisted on therapy as she felt unattractive and unloved, and feared their relationship would not last.

Discussing their respective family backgrounds in joint assessment sessions was illuminating for both partners. L's mother had been a demanding woman, whom L was determined not to be like, while experiencing mounting anxiety at K's lack of communication. It soon became clear that K's parents had a very troubled marriage that he had been unable to think clearly about, and now seemed to be repeating in the growing distance with L. K was the youngest child, with three older siblings, and the only child at home from the age of ten. His parents had separate bedrooms for as long as he could remember, very little conversation, and no affection. There was a particularly difficult phase of arguments in K's teens, that he thought was about how his father's family treated his mother. He recalled his mother's despair that nothing could be done, and her growing isolation and unhappiness. K's father was a respected, benign man whom K could not get close to. K's mother impressed on him that no one else could know about their problems and disliked him talking to his older brothers. He felt helpless and in a "black hole" until he left home.

It seemed that L's wish for changes and plans had re-evoked feelings in K of weakness, despair, and isolation that had pervaded his life. Unable to engage with L's requests, he had identified with both his unresponsive father and his angry, rejected mother; fearful of disappointing her, he had retreated to a separate non-sexual room in his mind. K was relieved at a formulation that linked his absence of sexual interest with conflictual aspects of his parents' relationship projected on to his interactions with L, rather than a depressive condition within himself, which he feared. It was agreed that K would continue with individual therapy to address developmental intrusions that impaired his sexual expression, prior to resuming couple work to focus on their sexual contact.

K worked hard on his early experiences, bringing letters, dreams, and memories to individual sessions. He finally felt able to discuss his parents' relationship with his siblings, which he found very supportive. K remained fearful of disappointing L, as he thought he had disappointed his mother, and couple psychosexual therapy was slow. Over time, K was able to feel less like a useless son, and more like a self-assured man who could relate both emotionally and sexually with his partner.

Discussion

These cases have been described to show an approach to some of the inter- and intra-personal difficulties that can impair the desire for sex with a specific partner. Understanding the developmental history of negative emotions is often integral to this approach, which integrates different models, but is based on the restructuring of the meaning of sexual withdrawal in the context of negative states of mind.

From the perspective outlined here, loss of sexual interest is a psychologically understandable phenomenon, and is therefore not a dysfunction in the medical sense. In men who present with loss of sexual interest, I have observed a common pattern of developmental intrusions. The recurrent theme is the lack of a sufficiently empowered father figure for identification and the boy's sense of helplessness when faced with a mother's need for connectedness and emotional responsiveness. Whereas the ability for sexual arousal may not be impaired, an intimate relationship with a female partner who becomes distressed can re-evoke a disempowered male object and lead to sexual withdrawal. My impression is that women are equally susceptible to the effects of developmental intrusion, but are far more likely than men to lose the motivation to be sexual when there are negative emotions arising from current issues with a partner. Research into gender differences in terms of psychophysiological mechanisms for sexual excitation and inhibition has indicated that women show a significantly higher level of inhibition than found in men (Bancroft, 2002). This suggests that disturbing aspects of a relationship or situation are likely to intrude on women's emotional responses, inhibit arousal, and undermine sexual feelings. Such a tendency may offer a partial explanation for the greater number of women struggling with lack of motivation for sex. Variation in the propensity for inhibition of the sexual response will, of course, interact with the many sociocultural constraints that have been particularly relevant for female sexual expression.

Sexual interest can sometimes return spontaneously with therapy. In most instances, though, a gradual non-threatening and negotiated approach to physical intimacy, the cornerstone of psychosexual therapy, is a helpful adjunct to the exploration of meanings and history and to the re-establishment of sexual contact. Although the partner with low sexual desire may become the person who exerts control over the couple's sexual contact, the principal function of withdrawal does not seem to be aimed at consciously controlling the other in a punitive way. Rather, it seems to represent a need to protect the self from feelings or interactions that are imagined to be aversive or unbearable. Clinical experience indicates that negative emotions such as disappointment, resentment, and hostility are present, but frequently unrecognized and therefore disruptive to sexual expression. Once they can be verbalized and explored, the pressure to enact such feelings through sexual withdrawal is frequently diminished.

References

Bancroft, J. (2002). The medicalization of female sexual dysfunction: the need for caution. *Archives of Sexual Behaviour, 31*(5): 451–455

Crowe, M., & Ridley, J. (2000). *Therapy with Couples: A Behavioral-Systems Approach to Marital and Sexual Problems.* Oxford: Blackwell Scientific Publications.

Everaerd, W., Laan, E. T. M., Both, S., & van der Velde, J. (2000). Female sexuality. In: L. T. Szuchman & F. Muscarella (Eds.), *Psychological Perspectives on Human Sexuality* (pp. 101–146). New York: Wiley.

Hawton, K. (1985). *Sex Therapy: A Practical Guide.* Oxford: Oxford Medical Publications.

Hems, S. A., & Crowe, M. (1999). The Psychosexual Dysfunction Clinic at The Maudsley Hospital, London: a survey of referrals between January and December 1996. *Sexual and Relationship Therapy, 14*(1): 15–25.

Hiller, J. (1999). The presence of the absent other: ethical issues in individual work for relationship problems. *Sexual and Relationship Therapy, 14*(3): 237–253.

Kaplan, H. S. (1979). *Disorders of Sexual Desire.* London: Bailliere Tindal.

Kaplan, H. S. (1995). *The Sexual Desire Disorders.* New York: Brunner/ Mazel.

Masters, W. H., & Johnson, V. E. (1970). *Human Sexual Inadequacy.* London: Churchill.

Pridal, C. G., & LoPiccolo, J. (2000). Multielement treatment of desire disorders: integration of cognitive, behavioural, and systemic therapy. In: S. R. Leiblum & R. C. Rosen (Eds.), *Principles and Practice of Sex Therapy* (pp. 57–81). New York: Guilford Press.

INDEX